# The Art of LITHUANIAN KNITTING

## 25 TRADITIONAL PATTERNS
### and the People, Places, and History That Inspire Them

by Donna Druchunas & June L. Hall

TRAFALGAR SQUARE
North Pomfret, Vermont

First published in 2015 by Double Vision Press
Published in paperback in 2017 by
Trafalgar Square Books
North Pomfret, Vermont 05053

ISBN: 978-1-57076-848-4
Library of Congress Control Number: 2017943868

Technical Photographs © 2015 Donna Druchunas
All photos in Chapters 7 and 8 © Dominic Cotignola

All other photos © as listed in captions:
BB: Balys Buračas
DC: Dominic Cotignola
DD: Donna Druchunas
JLH: June L. Hall

Technical Editor: Kate Atherly
Copy Editors: Kim Werker and William Thomas Berk
Lithuanian Editor: Audronė Tamulienė
Art Director: Marius Žalneravičius
Interior Design: Sarah Jaworowicz
Index: William Thomas Berk
Knitting Charts: Susan Santos
Technical Illustrations: Oren Lundgren
Cover Design: RM Didier

Printed in China

10 9 8 7 6 5 4 3 2 1

# Acknowledgments

This book is dedicated to all Lithuanian knitters past, present, and future. Thank you for your inspiration!

## Donna Druchunas

Thank you to everyone who helped to make our dream of creating this book come true.

**Our team:** Dominic Cotignola, Kate Atherly, Audronė Tamulienė, Marius Žalneravičius, William Thomas Berk, Oren Lundgren, especially Susan Santos and Sarah Jaworowicz, who went the extra mile.

**Test and sample knitters:** Susan Barnhart, Christina Bieloh, Joanne Conklin, Jillian Hastings, Katrina King, Denise Layman, Helen Marshall, Lise Pellerin, Amanda Quintanilla, Janine Robertson, Ruth Roland, Rohn Strong, Jennifer Unger Kroc, Mira Whiting, and Marge Yee-Norrander. Special thanks to Terri Shea for help with knitting gloves.

**Yarn support:** A Verb for Keeping Warm, Brown Sheep, Cascade, Colinette, Crystal Palace, Dream in Color, Nordic Fiber Arts, Holiday Yarns, Kauni, Knitpicks, Koigu, Litwool, Madelinetosh, Shibui Knits, Teksrena, and Meg Swansen at Schoolhouse Press.

**Special thanks to** Deborah Robson and Anne Berk for believing in our project and supporting us in our work. And to everyone I met in Lithuania, I can't thank you enough for being so friendly and helpful, especially Sonata Eidikienė at Mezgimo Zona.

## June L. Hall

So many people and organisations have given freely of their help and advice, shared their lives and work, and provided hospitality and friendship, that it is an impossible task to list them all with due credit. Here is my best effort. I hope that anyone accidentally omitted will forgive me.

Sheep and wool.

**Žilvinas Augustinavičius**, head of the *Lithuanian Sheep Breeders Association*

**Dr. Birutė Zapasnikienė and colleagues**. Institute of Animal Science LUHS, Baisogala

**Arūnas Svitojus**, Director, Baltic Heifer Foundation.

*Anatolijus Morozovas*, "Siūlas" Woollen Mill, Lygumai.

**Gediminas Pupsys**, JSC Litwool, Vilnius.

**Kęstutis and Inga Samušiai**, Molėtai, Skuddes Sheep and felt making.

**Dr Juozapas Mikutis**, Šeduva state (since 2010–JSC) sheep breeding enterprise.

**Lolita Griškevičienė**, Gelvonai, sheep farmer.

**Museums and Cultural Organisations**, for research and access to reserve collections and for providing exhibition venues.

M. K. Čiurlionis National Museum of Art, Director **Osvaldas Daugelis** and staff, particularly **Inga Nėnienė** and **Janina Savickienė** (textiles)

Vytautas the Great War Museum, for permission to use photographs.

Marijampolė Local Lore Museum.

Vilkaviškis Area Museum.

Open Air Museum of Lithuania, Director **Violeta Reipaitė**.

Mažeikai Museum.

Biržai Region Museum "Sėla".

Panevėžys Local Lore Museum, **Daina Snicoriūtė**

Ukmergė Local Lore Museum.

Alanta Manor Museum-Gallery.

Šiauliai Aušros Museum.

Vilkija, Antanas and Jonas Juškos Ethnic Culture Museum,

Lithuanian Art Museum and **Daina Ragauskienė** of the Conservation Department.

Vilnius Teachers House.

Lithuanian Folk Culture Centre,
**Teresė Jurkuvienė.**

## Vilnius University

Department of Lithuanian Studies, for the language course, which has been indispensable.

**Žilvytis Šaknys, Auksuolė Čepaitienė, Vytautas Tumėnas,** for photographs and information, Lithuanian Institute of History.

**Zina Gineitienė,** Economics Department, for encouragement.

## Knitters in many communities.

Pociūnėliai, Baisogala, Vilnius, Biržai, Marijampolė, Anykščiai, Mažeikiai, Palanga and Žagarė.

Individual knitters—

**Nijolė Šopienė,** Šiauliai, knitter, farmer and cheese maker.

**Aušra Kaveckienė,** Kuršėnai, who provided a splendid collection of original fashion garments for a show in England.

**Inga Nėnienė,** Šiauliai, for historical examples of knitted mittens.

**Marijona Mališauskienė,** Šiauliai, for the beautiful clothes she had knitted.

**Irena Juškienė,** Vilnius, for the loan of *riešinės*, (wrist cuffs), for exhibition in England.

**Zita Niemantienė,** Kaunas, and Kraitė Magazine.

## Felt makers and textile artists.

**Eglė Ganda Bogdanienė,** Principal of Vilnius Academy of Arts, formerly Head of Textiles, and many of her students. These include the members of **Baltos Kandys** (White Moths) group, listed in the text. Also, **Jūratė Daukšytė,** who exhibited textile art at Woolfest in England, and introduced me to her family in Druskininkai.

**Viktoras Liutkus,** now Head of Painting at Vilnius Academy of Arts, who was my first contact in Lithuania and who provided introductions, when I knew no one.

## Vilnius Academy of Arts, Kaunas Faculty

**D. ir Z. Kalesinskų liaudies amatų mokykla,** (Folk Art College in Vilkija, now closed), Director **Zigmas Kalesinskas** and staff, particularly, **Asta Vandytė** and **Rasma Noreikytė,** and students, for involvement in numerous courses, exhibitions and workshops, and bringing Lithuanian textile traditions and regional costume to England.

**Česlovas Koreiva,** manager of Litenterp Bed and Breakfast Apartments, in Vilnius, and cheerful staff, who have provided extremely convenient accommodation for many years.

## Individuals.

**Zigmas Kalesinskas,** now Director of Kaunas District Museum, Raudondvaris , for many years of friendship, hospitality, inspiration and joint enterprises.

**Audronė Tamulienė** for hospitality, friendship, translation, research, and immeasurable help. Her husband **Jonas Tamulis** for professional photographs and personal recollections.

**Audra and Kęstas Damanauskas** and their family, **Tomas and Modesta,** in Baisogala, who have provided a second home for me in Lithuania, and have become my "adopted family".

**Roma Rimkuvienė,** *seniūnė* (head) of Skėmiai, and the headteacher, staff, children and cooks at Pociūnėliai Basic School, who have been a constant support, wonderful company and a delight to know.

**Guido Wolf, and Indrė,** in Vilnius.

**Marius Žalneravičius,** our graphic designer, and **Julija Vosyliūtė,** for their professional help, warm friendship and their children's company.

**Professor Antanas Buračas,** for providing historic photographs and encouragement.

## Friends in Cumbria, England.

**Joy Hall,** founder and chairman of Lithuania Link, a charity formed to promote contact between Cumbria and Lithuania, especially the community of Žagarė. Without Joy and the first grant-aided visit to Lithuania the whole project would never have happened.

**Alex Gibb,** Lithuania Link's project director, in both England and Lithuania, where he now lives. Alex has never failed to offer help at all times.

Other members of Lithuania Link—**Bill Dufton, Bill Hogg, Annette Gibbons, Anne and Sally Chambers, Michelle Armstrong, and Sarah Rabagliati.**

Last but not least, my sister **Vivien Wilson** and her husband **Peter,** who have accompanied me on many visits, met and taken me to airports at unearthly hours, provided beds for Lithuanian visitors and raised money for Pociūnėliai school.

# Table of Contents

# Preface

It's been a decade since I first visited Lithuania and met June Hall, co-author of this book. A lot has changed in Lithuania during those years. Yarn shops have opened and closed. Museum exhibits have changed. The Soviet-era statues on the Green Bridge, pictured on page 126, have been taken down. Some of our friends have passed away. And more and more people are knitting. It's impossible to go through this book page by page and make changes, but I'd like to introduce you to two new knitting friends who are also creative designers:

Folk artist Sigita Damanskienė, like me, has been knitting and crocheting since she was a child. She is fascinated by folk art and traditional fiber arts, and teaches traditional Lithuanian crafts to pass on her passion and folk traditions to the next generation. Today she does most of her knitting near rivers and lakes while her husband is fishing, and they often come home from a fishing trip not only with a fresh catch, but also with a brand new finished project. Sigita makes all of her own clothes, and her designs combine the spirit and motifs of long-held traditions with the styles and ease of modern clothing. Over the past five years, she's been a member of the Lithuanian Folk Artists' Association and her work has been featured in many exhibits and won many awards. My favorite example is the knit-and-crochet ensemble that won first place in the 2015 contest "Costume for Milda, Lithuania's goddess of love", which included a crocheted dress and apron topped off with a stunning wool jacket made with entrelac, with traditional colorwork motifs.

*Sigita (right) and model wearing "Milda" ensemble.*

*Raimundas at the Sock Knitting Championship.*

Expert knitter "Mezgejas" Raimundas Mikuševičius caught the "knitting bug" when he was a boy and spent most of his childhood and youth knitting. During Soviet times, he was able to make a living by knitting and often earned 300 rubles a month, over twice the average salary of an engineer at the time. Like many knitters, he stopped knitting for a while and worked full-time in another career, but eventually found that he regretted leaving his passion behind. Today he knits almost constantly and sells custom hand-made mittens and socks with traditional and modern motifs, both online and at events all around Lithuania.

Both Sigita and Raimundas participate in the annual Sock Knitting Championship, which is now in its eighth year. The contest lasts for five hours and participants compete to demonstrate knitting skill, creativity, and traditional inspiration. Each entrant also brings several pairs of socks made with their own original designs to exhibit. Those who aren't already expert sock knitters can watch, take knitting workshops, and shop for yarn and finished items in the market.

I'll be attending the Annual Sock Knitting Championship this summer with a group of knitters as we tour Lithuania to learn about historical knitting traditions and current trends. As you read through these pages and pick up your own yarn and needles to cast on for a project, you'll be traveling with us in spirit!

—Donna Druchunas

**Barton, Vermont**

**May 2017**

*Children watching sheep, playing a pipe, and knitting. 1935, Šiauliai region. (Balys Buračas, vaikai, page 21).*
*Facing page from left to right: Knitting sample; June; Donna.*

# Chapter 1: An Introduction

## A Book in Two Voices

We hope you enjoy hearing from two different authors as we explore Lithuania, a country that means so much to us. We come from different backgrounds, and though we have complementary interests, our perspectives vary greatly. The delight we find individually in the treasures of Lithuanian textiles has been enhanced by these differences, as well as by our friendship and collaboration. Part of what we would like to convey throughout the book is a sense of mutual discovery.

Lithuania has a historically complex culture. The accounts we offer you here are written from personal experience. They are, therefore, partial and subjective, based on our personal understanding of the country, its people, its history, and the fundamental changes that have been occurring there throughout the recent period of transition from Soviet times to independence, along with accession to the European Union. We've written sections of the book in our individual voices and with our own words (and even with our own English and American spellings). Come, let us show you around Lithuania, and introduce you to its knitting traditions.

—**June & Donna**

**Note:** Where first names only are given, it is either to preserve the privacy of individuals or because they are friends of the authors and their family names have been introduced elsewhere in the book.

# Finding My Roots in Knitting

**Donna's Journey of Discovery**

## Where on Earth is Lithuania?

"I'm going to Vilnius this summer," I say.

"Where's that?"

"It's the capital of Lithuania." No response. Blank stares. As if my friends want to ask, "Where on Earth is Lithuania?" but are afraid to admit they don't know.

"Oh. Interesting," they may say, if I'm not fast enough to respond.

"It's in Eastern Europe, near Poland."

To many Americans, Lithuania is an exotic place, an unknown world, a fictional land like Middle Earth or Narnia. To me, Lithuania is Grandma's kitchen.

My family would discuss news from this faraway place behind the Iron Curtain as we sat around Grandma Druchunas's grey Formica dinner table eating homemade potato pancakes with sour cream, kielbasa and sauerkraut, and pickled beets. "Ke-BAH-see," we said, using the New York-Polish name for the fresh Lithuanian dešra (sausage) that Grandma made from scratch, stuffing her own mixture of meat and seasonings into sausage casings using a ram's horn that her mother had probably brought over from the old country. Lithuania is where my father's grandparents were born. A mystical place, as far away from New York as could be. A land of dreams and memories, cut off from us by Communism even though our family (and the U.S. government) never recognized that Lithuania was part of the U.S.S.R.

When she wasn't making sausage or having a cigarette, my grandmother crocheted hats, hats, and more hats. I don't remember if she ever made anything else. Grandma wasn't a big crafter, but she crocheted while watching afternoon soap operas, her "stories," on TV. It was my mother's mother who taught me to knit, but Grandma Druchunas, on my father's side, infused in me a desire to know more about the Lithuanian nation and people.

## Growing Up with Crafts

Every year as I was growing up, I learned a new craft and left the others behind. Knitting came first, then crochet, embroidery, needlepoint, weaving, beading, decoupage, and candle making. When I was in third grade, I learned how to sew, and I spent the next ten years making all of my own clothes. In high school, because I already knew how to sew, I took metal shop and wood shop instead of home economics. Finally, when I was in my twenties and early thirties, I stopped doing crafts altogether, because I'd started working in a department store and it was just as cheap to buy my clothes as it had been to make them. As we all know, knitting today is no bargain when you compare the cost of yarn to the price of inexpensive imported clothing at Walmart or Sears—at least when costs are measured only in currency.

Our craft is not about frugality—or even about the need to keep warm—but about creativity, charity, and meditation. We pick up our needles and seek out exotic yarns from around the world to experience the joy of making something from scratch. We snap up every opportunity to experiment with the colors and textures of new yarns. We make tiny caps for preemies; we stitch soft comfort shawls for women who have suffered violence or loss or illness; and we knit millions of scarves, mittens, and socks to warm the homeless every winter.

*Donna with Grandma Druchunas, Druchunas family photos*     *Current day Lithuania*

We escape from the hectic schedule of daily life and breathe deeply to the soft rhythm of needles clicking as luxurious yarns slip through our fingers. For all these reasons, if not for parsimony, we find ourselves knitting.

Recently, I've found another reason to knit: to find my roots.

# Lithuanian-American

My grandparents were all born in the United States, but their parents came from Russia and Lithuania. As a third-generation American, I didn't hear Lithuanian, Russian, or Yiddish spoken around the house when I was growing up. I never met the relatives who came to the United States on ships at the turn of the century; they all died before I was born. I barely remember the bedtime stories about life in a Pennsylvania coal-mine town that my grandmother told me when she came to visit. Now my grandparents are gone, too, and my parents don't like to talk about the past.

I started knitting and crocheting again when I was thirty-five, a year or so after both of my grandmothers passed away in the same year. I don't know why I suddenly became interested in these crafts, when I hadn't picked up a hook or needles in twenty-five years. Maybe I needed a way to stay connected to my grandmothers after they were gone. Soon after I made my first sweater, I discovered books about knitting. I encountered pattern collections, new and familiar techniques, and stories about knitting and yarn. At first, I promised myself that I would knit at least three projects from any book before allowing myself to buy another, but soon my voracious reading habit took over and I started spending as much on books as I did on yarn. As I read through the books I purchased, I discovered that historical and ethnic knitting techniques grabbed my attention most. I came across a few tidbits about my own heritage, too: gloves from Lithuania in *Mary Thomas's Knitting Book*; featherweight lace shawls from Russia in *Gossamer Webs,* by Carol R. Noble and Galina Khmeleva; a pair of Lithuanian socks in *Folk Socks,* by Nancy Bush.

One day I did a Google search for "Lithuanian knitting." Only a few hits showed up, but one of them was for a whole book on Lithuanian gloves, with text in both Lithuanian and English. I wanted to buy a copy, but it took a year before I found one for sale on a website in a language I could read. I snapped it up. What a find! In addition to the gorgeous photos of mittens, *Lietuvininkų Pirštinės: Kultūrų Kryžkelėje* (Gloves of Lithuania Minor at the Cross-Roads of Cultures), by Irena Regina Merkienė and Marija Pautieniūtė-Banionienė, includes a huge number of color knitting charts and fascinating information about the history and culture of the Lithuanian people.

I hadn't thought much about the cultures or histories of my family before. I'm American, after all. My great-grandparents from both sides of my family came to America in the first years of the twentieth century. They first settled in Canada and Pennsylvania, and later moved into the big melting pot. They became New Yorkers before I was born. But knitting found a way to draw me toward my roots and to awaken a passion for my family's stories. It may be too late to collect the details that passed away with my ancestors, but I believe that just like genes are passed down through generations of biology, the soul of a culture can be passed down through its art and craft. We, as knitters, can be the guardians of these traditions, practicing them for our own fulfillment, and preserving them for future generations.

# Visiting the Old Country

With my newfound passion firmly established, I started buying up Lithuanian craft books on eBay, reading about Baltic folk art in travel guides, and ultimately booking a ticket to visit Vilnius, the capital city of Lithuania. I have since visited Lithuania almost every year, a habit I plan to continue.

I remember that first trip like it was yesterday. As soon as the plane's wheels touched the runway, its passengers erupted in applause. We'd arrived in Lithuania; we'd landed safely! Walking across the tarmac to the terminal, then standing in line to go through passport control, I was nervous about visiting a new country and not speaking the language. The young man stamping passports had a wrinkled brow and pursed lips. In his green uniform, he looked like a soldier. My husband Dominic and I stepped up to the window together, and I handed our passports through the small opening in the glass. The man raised his eyebrows when he saw the dark blue color of our passports: we were obviously from the U.S. He glanced at our photos, then scanned the details. Suddenly his entire demeanor changed. I think he may have noticed my Lithuanian surname. I can't otherwise explain what happened next. He looked me right in the eye and his face broke into a genuine smile. "Welcome to Lithuania!" he shouted.

The rest of that first trip was a whirlwind. We had only five days to explore the nation's capital, yet in those few days we stumbled onto knitting and crochet time and again: in Old Town at the tourist market, in fiber-arts galleries hidden in small alleys spidering out from the town center, in museums, at a national folk-singing festival with thousands of performers dressed in historical costume, and in demonstrations of traditional crafts at Cathedral Square. There were also yarn shops hiding in nooks and crannies around the city.

# Finding My Roots

In Lithuania I found the roots I was looking for. I found my family name in the phone book, and I learned in which parts of the country Druchunas (Dručiūnas) had been a common surname during the first half of the twentieth century.

That short trip didn't satisfy me, and almost before it was over I planned my next one. I returned in the summer of 2008, this time for seven weeks. After spending four weeks on my own, I was joined by Dominic and by our friend, June Hall, and we traveled around the rest of the country, visiting knitters and crocheters, spinners and weavers, museums, folk-art schools, woolen mills, and sheep farms. Our research had officially begun! As we traveled to big cities, small towns, and even tiny villages, I discovered that museums around Lithuania are filled with exhibits about textiles, for those who have the dedication to look for them. Knitting and crochet often take a back seat to spinning and weaving, but all of these crafts are present throughout Lithuania as part of textile and folk-art collections.

# Knitting in Lithuania

Contemporary Lithuania is a hub of European textile production and a haven for fiber artists. Visitors to the capital city of Vilnius find the narrow cobblestone streets flanked by hidden yarn shops, fiber artists' studios, fabric shops, and stores selling clothes and home decor items made of linen. The tourist market in Old Town overflows with hand-knitted mittens, socks, and caps, as well as an assortment of manufactured linen and woolen garments. Museums in the capital and around the country maintain rich textile exhibits and collections, and traditional handcrafts are demonstrated at street festivals and open-air museums throughout the short weeks of summer. As soon as autumn's cool breezes kick up, the streets become a veritable knitwear fashion show. Although Lithuania doesn't have a reputation as a major tourist destination, the country is a knitter's paradise.

Knitting arrived in Lithuania in the eighteenth century, several centuries later than in many other European countries. It followed a long path from the Middle East into Egypt, Spain, and then north, around the top of the Baltic Sea, and down through Estonia and Latvia. Lithuanians quickly adapted traditional weaving designs to this new craft, using them to create colorful mittens and gloves, socks, and sashes with motifs that have been common in the Baltics for thousands of years.

Fiber arts, particularly spinning and weaving, are honored as part of the Lithuanian national heritage. Displays of woven garments and knitted accessories provide glimpses into the home-lives of Lithuanians before the twentieth century brought modern tools and mass-produced clothing. Ancient spindles and antique spinning wheels, linen hackles, and weaving looms, along with bright, colorful collections of handwoven clothing and hand-knitted mittens and gloves, are reminders of the central role textile production has long held in the life of rural Lithuanian women.

Today, knitting in Lithuania is not only a trendy hobby like it is in the United States, it also remains common craft, known and practiced by women of all ages. Yarn shops' shelves are filled with yarns imported from Italy, Turkey, and Russia, with a smattering of locally produced threads and yarns. I've found a few yarns that were labeled with a shop's logo and address, as well as Lithuanian, Latvian, and Estonian yarns that are not available in the United States. The yarn shops didn't carry many books written in Lithuanian but I did find some in local bookstores. I also found vintage Lithuanian knitting books at craft fairs. The contemporary hand-knitted pieces at fiber artists' galleries and the traditional-style items in the tourist market and museums more than made up for any shortage of Lithuanian-language books in the yarn shops.

Here's what I discovered during my several trips: whether it's traditional or trendy, kitschy or couture, comfy or chic, historical or contemporary, if it's made of wool or linen, it can be found in Lithuania.

*Knitting in Vilnius. All photos: DC.*

*June's Soay sheep. JLH.*

*June at Palanga (cactus house).*

# The Unbroken Thread

**June's Personal Adventure**

*Sheep, Wool, and Knitting,*
*Past, Present, and Future.*
*A Project in Lithuania.*

In August 2001, I spent one week in Lithuania. That was the start of something which has come to play a large part in my life, both here in England and in the Baltic States. How did this come about?

## Searching for My Roots

There is a story in our family that my sister Vivien and I have an ancestor who was born in Lithuania when it was part of Tsarist Russia, and who came to live in England. The facts are lost, but in 2001, after the death of our mother, the two of us were curious to visit Lithuania to see if we felt an affinity with the place and its people. As it turned out, we were fascinated by everything we saw and we wanted to return.

The opportunity to do so came rather unexpectedly. In 2002 I moved house from the Yorkshire Dales to Cumbria, on the edge of England's Lake District. My husband had died, I was retired, and my little flock of rare Soay sheep had been killed during the outbreak of foot-and-mouth disease the previous year, when the government ordered the slaughter of farm livestock in affected areas. My healthy sheep became victims. I decided to make a move.

Having had a lifelong wish to live in an old house, I bought a small farmhouse dating from around 1700. The farmland and outbuildings had been sold off, and only two small paddocks remained—just enough to keep a few sheep. I bought Soays again. These are the smallest sheep native to Britain, a primitive breed that was isolated on St. Kilda, the remotest islands in the British Isles, a far-flung part of Scotland forty-five miles west of the Outer Hebrides. Related to the southeast-European mouflon, they were the earliest type of sheep to move to the extreme western edge of Europe during the Bronze Age, over 3,000 years ago.

Having moved to a community new to me, I joined a few local organisations, including the Cumbrian Organic Gardeners' Society. At the end of one of the newsletters published by this group was a short article with the headline, "Interested in Lithuania?" A member of the gardening club wrote that there were bursaries, obtained by a small charity she belonged to, to support projects in Lithuania. Volunteers were invited to a meeting to offer suggestions for projects. Those proposals that were accepted would receive financial support to spend thirteen weeks in Lithuania performing social or environmental work. Vivien and I went along and were introduced to a charity called Lithuania Link.

## Lithuania Link

Since 2003, Lithuania Link has provided me with moral support, as well as small grants from time to time. I eventually became a trustee of the organisation, and meetings at the founder's home were always happy gatherings of friends.

My proposal to investigate Lithuanian hand-knitting traditions and their place in the cultural life of rural communities was accepted. On the first visit that Vivien and I made to the country, we had seen beautiful gloves and socks for sale, so that seemed like a good place to start. It would combine many aspects of my life and work in our second visit—sheep, wool, knitting, rural life, folk art, and historical research.

From childhood, I have knitted. My grandparents kept a grocery shop in which I spent a lot of my time, and next door was a wool shop full of colour—a magnet for me. Each week I spent my small amount of pocket money there on wool, which I would knit into small items such as dolls' clothes, purses, and scarves. As I grew older, I made clothes for myself and my family.

Throughout my career as a teacher and education adviser in rural areas of England, the local environment, both natural and cultural, has played a prominent role. Encouraging teachers and pupils to take an interest in their surroundings, with a strong emphasis on enquiry, provided a vehicle for learning across the curriculum. Any quest to discover the unique qualities of an area led to fieldwork, libraries, archives, museums, and community memories. I felt I could put this approach to use in exploring Lithuania.

I formulated a plan to find out the extent to which hand knitting had contributed to rural life and economy in the past, the part it was playing in contemporary life, and how it might contribute to women's lives in the future.

This plan has far outlasted my original thirteen-week trip and has been a useful guide to many years of work.

## Visiting Lithuania

I set out on my first one-week working visit to Lithuania in November 2003, to find my way round and to make contacts. The only person I knew in Lithuania was Alex Gibb, the man whose mother had put the notice in the gardening newsletter. Alex, from Cumbria, had been involved with Lithuania Link from its beginning.

Žagarė is a small town in northern Lithuania, on the border with Latvia. There, Lithuania Link was helping to improve residents' quality of life through social and environmental projects. Alex was soon to become director of the charity, a role he would fulfill through his years at university and beyond. He now lives with his family in Vilnius.

Alex developed projects in Žagarė in cooperation with the local youth club, the national park and other organisations. He introduced me to the first knitters I met in Lithuania. On this first visit, I was also invited to Pociūnėliai, a village between Šiauliai and Kaunas. The municipal leader had heard that I was interested in knitting and had arranged an exhibition of craft work by local women. I have since made many friends in the village and have returned often.

## Making New Friends

Gradually, over many visits, my circle of friends, acquaintances, and contacts widened. While the main focus of Lithuania Link's interest in Lithuania has been in Žagarė, I soon found that I needed to look further afield for information on knitting traditions. Lithuania's folk art varies across geographic regions and over time. The wool itself and the sheep which provided it became significant elements in my search.

Wherever I went in Lithuania, I bought hand-knitted gloves, mittens, and socks from local women. Having studied the history of the hand-knitting industry in the Yorkshire Dales, I found interesting comparisons, and this led me to organise an exhibition that in turn created connections between artisans in Lithuania and England.

# Hand in Glove: An Exhibition

I designed an exhibition to present two traditions, spanning three centuries, at opposite extremes of Europe. The Dales Countryside Museum, located in the Yorkshire Dales National Park in northern England, has an excellent collection of knitting artefacts. In 2005, this museum supported an exhibition called *Hand in Glove*. Five large information panels formed the basis for the display, in which I presented my examples of Lithuanian knitting alongside items from the museum's collection. I gave an opening lecture and local women came to knit and interact with museum visitors.

Later, I took the exhibition to Lithuania for a tour of regional museums. At each venue, the participating museum added to the basic display from their own historic examples and invited local knitters to show their work. This project helped to raise the profile of knitting as a branch of folk art and to celebrate the skill of women in their communities. (Details of the venues are given in Chapter 6: Knitters and Folk Art.)

# From My Notebook

## June

*I arrived at Riga Airport, in the capital city of Latvia, in the evening. The first setback occurred when I couldn't find the flat box containing the exhibition panels. Being oversized, it would not fit on the carousel. Where was it? Enquiries proved fruitless. After considerable time and much searching on my own (no one else seemed very interested), I found the box in a corner of a large hall. Asta, the teacher at the Folk Art School of Vilkija, was waiting for me. The drive south into Lithuania and on to our destination of Vilkija would take about five hours. The next problem was that the box would not fit into Asta's small car. We pushed and pulled without success. Finally, we took out a shelf in the back of the car and the box went in with less than an inch to spare. At the border, a uniformed guard inspected our passports and noticed the box. He asked about it in Lithuanian, and Asta told him what it was. "I want to see what is in that box," he said in a very severe tone. I used my little bit of Lithuanian to say it was an exhibition of old knitting, which seemed to further raise his suspicions. "Open that box!" As it was firmly sealed with tape and staples, I asked if he had a knife. He didn't. We stood for a moment, fearing confiscation, but the guard lost patience and dismissed us with a wave of the hand and we drove on, relieved to finally be in Lithuania.*

Visiting the Vilkija Folk Art School. JLH.

June has written a series of guides to Yorkshire villages. This guide to Pociūnėliai was written with people from Pociūnėliai, in Lithuanian and in English. JLH.

Giedrė, Dalia and Roma from Pociūnėliai, at June's home in Cumbria. JLH.

# A Cultural Exchange

My research has always been a two-way process, involving activities in both Lithuania and England. Every year since 2004, Lithuanian guests have come to stay in my home. I have found work for Lithuanian students on local farms, in shops, and in restaurants, so they can earn money to fund their university courses. Textile artists have come to exhibit, demonstrate, and teach at Woolfest, an annual fibre festival of which I have been a co-organiser since it began in 2005.

Among my early visitors were three women from Pociūnėliai, a village in the lovely countryside where there was very little paid work. They travelled to Cumbria to experience rural tourism so they could help to develop tourist facilities in their village as a way of improving the economy.

Another guest, Aušra, from Kuršėnai, near Šiauliai, showed me the beautiful clothes she had designed and knitted and asked if I could help her to sell them in England. A young married woman with small children, Aušra has knitted and crocheted since childhood. When she was twelve years old, she won first prize in a competition in Moscow, the Soviet capital. I decided to bring the clothes to Cumbria and arrange a fashion show. Most of the garments sold that evening. Since then, Aušra has visited Cumbria and has exhibited her work at Woolfest, held annually in June.

For most of my guests, it was their first visit to western Europe. Indeed, most of them had not been outside Lithuania.

Their reactions are interesting. Most of Lithuania is below 200 feet above sea level, whereas my house is situated at about 750 feet and the mountains rise to 3,000. Visitors have been intrigued by the narrow lanes and the dry-stone walls which divide the fields, and of course the traffic, which is driven on the left side of the road and not the right, is disconcerting until they get used to it.

One question they often pose initially surprised me: Why did I live in an old house, when I could buy a new one? This goes deep into cultural roots and brings up different attitudes to the past. While many English people value their family history and belongings, and enjoy the ambience of earlier periods, most Lithuanians, especially the young, want to leave their troubled past behind and modernise their homes. While understandable, I find this attitude dangerous with regard to cultural heritage during a period when rapid change is taking place in Lithuanian society. As Lithuanians adopt Western standards and values, any accompanying tendency to despise "old-fashioned" customs could lead to the loss of skills, knowledge, and experience that would break the thread of traditional culture. Fortunately, there are organisations dedicated to conserving the traditional culture of Lithuania. I have been very fortunate to meet many skilled specialists in museums, archives, conservation centres, and colleges, who are working to ensure that the thread from the past into the future remains unbroken. There are many women who continue to knit and pass on their skills in their own homes, and who have shared their work with me. I hope that by appreciating the traditions and the work being done to preserve them, I have helped in a small way to encourage those involved to feel that their work is valued and worthwhile.

*June's house, "Chapel Farm," in Cumbria. JLH.*

# Speaking the Language

On Vivien's and my first visit to Lithuania in 2001, the language was totally new to us. We had arranged the trip through a small company in England, but had to manage on our own upon arrival. Our flight landed at Vilnius airport late at night and we collected the hire car which Peter, my brother-in-law, offered to drive. We set out for Kaunas in the dark. When we phoned for directions to the bed and breakfast address, the woman who answered spoke no English; fortunately, her twelve-year-old grandson, who learned English at school, came to our rescue. The boy and his grandmother came out onto the street and waited for us to appear. We picked up a few Lithuanian words during the several nights we stayed in their flat.

I soon realized that in order to do any serious work in the country, I would have to learn the language. I am no linguist. The French I learnt at school, decades ago, is barely functional. But I had to try. Fortunately, Vilnius University organises a Lithuanian language course every January and July. I opted for a two-week winter course, starting at the introductory level, and have since participated twice more. Classes are small—ten students at the most, including people from Japan, the United States, and all parts of Europe.

Although I know that I shall never be fluent in Lithuanian or have a convincing accent, I can now find my way around, use public transport and taxis, order food in cafés, handle money, book tickets, and engage in simple conversation. Most people seem to appreciate my effort to speak their language, although it is a little disconcerting to enter a restaurant and be offered an English version of the menu before a word is spoken. I sometimes think that I have the word "English" written across my forehead.

*June Hall and Vivien Wilson in Lithuania, 2005. Photo by Peter Wilson.*

In some of the villages I have visited, I was the only English speaker. Sometimes a teacher or pupil from the local school would help me, but if not, I am on my own. Few older people speak English, so I try my best to communicate with them in Lithuanian. The language is very attractive, and I love to listen to people speaking it. Every written letter is pronounced distinctly and the sounds are consistent, unlike English, with its silent letters and varying pronunciation.

# Join Me on My Journey

I have found it a great privilege to be involved with the people of Lithuania, to have access to special places I would never have known about without their guidance, and to experience their culture during a period of transition. I hope you will enjoy reading about my personal journey and learning about knitting, sheep, and wool in Lithuania.

*Knitter with Charts. DC. Facing page from left to right: Knitting sample; Laisvės Alėja (Freedom Alley) in Kaunas. DC; Farming near Žagarė. DC.*

# Chapter 2: The Land and the People

## The Stories Behind the Stitches

**Donna**

Knitting is fascinating not only because it is beautiful and functional, but also because each stitch infuses a hand-knit project with the story of its maker and details about the time and place in which it was made. The materials and stitches chosen tell us about what yarns and patterns were available to the knitter, the gauge and evenness of the stitching tells us about her skill level, and the wear (or lack thereof) on the knitting gives us clues about whether it was made for everyday use or just for special occasions. Ultimately, I believe that what makes the knitting of Lithuania—or any place—special is the spirit of the people and the soul of the place. To fully understand what is unique about Lithuanian knitting, I wanted to meet Lithuanian knitters, their families, and friends, and get to know the country. When I met June in person for the first time, in England in 2007, I was so excited to find out that she had already made several trips to Lithuania specifically to meet knitters and learn about knitting. We'd been emailing back and forth for several months, but it's always so much fun to meet online friends face to face.

The second time I saw June, we met in Lithuania in the summer of 2008 and traveled around the country together. June introduced me to many people and places I may never have discovered on my own, and her love for all things Lithuanian influenced my own experiences as I began to explore the country on my own on later trips.

In the following pages, June and I will show you what we love about the land and the people of Lithuania. This chapter is almost like a summary of what you will find in the rest of the book. We will return to many of the subjects in later chapters, in more detail.

As you knit some of the projects included in later pages, we hope that you will be reminded of the knitters who made similar projects in a different place and time.

# Town and Country: Two Worlds Side by Side

**June**

## Glimpses of Rural Lithuania

Lithuania is a land of forest, rivers, lakes, and gently undulating, open farmland. There are few dramatic features to cause a sudden surprise. The seasons are clearly marked by nature and by the people, who, despite rapid modernisation of all aspects of their lives, are still close to their traditional roots. Motifs representing forest trees, garden flowers, rivers, and animals appear on knitted mittens and gloves, reflecting an enduring closeness to nature.

## The Forest

The forest (miškas) burrows deep in the psyche of all Lithuanians. They seem to be aware of its presence wherever they are, and whatever the season.

I remember driving through the forest one day in early April with Roma, the mayor of the area of Skėmiai and Pociūnėliai. Traces of winter snow lingered on the ground. She was on her way to a meeting, elegantly dressed, high heels and all. Yet she suddenly pulled to a halt, leapt out of the car, and disappeared among the trees. Moments later, she emerged, beaming and holding a bunch of bright blue flowers (žibutės)—the first blooms of spring.

The forest provides food, a strong connection to the wild and natural world, practical materials for heating and construction, and the inspiration behind many art forms and creative visions. The hunt for forest mushrooms (grybai) begins in summer, and by autumn becomes feverish. Wolves and wild boar still live in the forest.

In the fourteenth century, Lithuania became the last European country to convert to Christianity. Pagan influences continue to mingle with both Christian and secular imagery in motifs found in wood carving and knitting, and folk traditions remain a part of daily life.

The forest is one of the most frequent sources of inspiration for Lithuanian art and music. The symphonic poem Miške (In the Forest), a sweeping evocation of Lithuania's forests, is a well-known work by the country's most famous artist and composer, Mikalojus Konstantinas Čiurlionis (1875–1911). In 2007, a Vilnius-based group of young textile artists called Baltos Kandys (White Moths) created a collaborative felt installation called Forest Floor. Both fine art and folk art in other media, including knitting, also involve strong forest imagery.

*Photos clockwise from top right: Forest animal on knitted mitten; man picking mushrooms in the forest; floral mittens.*

The connection to the natural world is also deeply embedded in the Lithuanian language. For example, the months of the year are named after natural events, plants or creatures: March is kovas, the rook; April is balandis, the dove; July is liepa, the lime tree; August is rugpjūtis, the rye harvest; and November is lapkritis, leaf fall. The seasons provide natural medicines such as birch sap, drunk in early summer, to clear the system. Lime flowers are eagerly gathered in July, and dried to make tea to treat winter colds.

## Kaime: In the Village

As you travel by car or bus on the long, straight roads that connect Lithuanian towns and cities, you pass through a succession of open farmland, forest, and lakes (there are said to be 40,000, but in reality the number is closer to 6,000). You see a land of nucleated villages, each consisting of painted wooden houses built less than a century ago, though many are falling out of use. Other houses, built of brick to the standard Soviet plans, stand near square blocks of flats, erected for workers on collective farms, for teachers, and for builders.

In recent years, as many Lithuanians have become more prosperous, new and large houses have come to dominate the villages. Completing the picture are the church, the school, a community centre (or "culture house"), a shop or two, and maybe an agricultural-machinery depot

or a filling station. A stork's nest sitting atop a pole or a disused chimney is a familiar sight. Everywhere, there are gardens filled with flowers and fruit trees, vegetables and potatoes, chickens and geese, and hives of bees.

## Local Produce

Lithuanians are accustomed to providing good, healthy produce for themselves. In gardens round the houses and in larger plots grouped together, families turn out to dig, plant, weed, and harvest their crops. A few working horses are still kept, to pull a plough or a traditional cart. In late summer, surplus apples, plums, vegetable marrows, and flowers are offered for sale at the roadsides. In good years, lorries stacked with apples are driven to juice factories, and fallen fruit rolls about in the roads.

City dwellers who board buses after weekend visits to family in the countryside are laden with bags of tomatoes, beetroot, and cucumbers. The town food markets abound with colour. At the same time, supermarkets have begun to challenge this way of life, as many people prefer the convenience of shopping in these large stores rather than in smaller, local shops and markets.

Honey is found everywhere in Lithuania, and a honeycomb-texture knitting stitch is very popular on everyday mittens and gloves. On my first visit to Pociūnéliai, I developed a sore throat and asked for help with the language so I could buy honey in the village shop. "No, no, no, you go to Elena to buy honey," said Ona, our English-teacher friend, so off we went.

Beehives stood in an orchard, between still-bare fruit trees, and Elena, with her guard dog, met us in her yard. She invited us into the house, where we were soon tasting samples of honey from large spoons arranged on a plate, followed by fruit tea and biscuits. When Elena asked how much honey I wanted, I indicated the size of jar I would normally buy in a shop at home, about five inches tall. This caused great amusement in Ona and Elena, after which Elena brought out her smallest jar, which contained one litre of golden honey. Somehow I managed to transport it around Lithuania for the rest of my stay, and yes, it soothed my sore throat.

## Farming and Agriculture

Every so often when travelling around the country, you pass the remains of a collective farm: the large, low buildings recall the centralised farming that operated on a system regulated by the Soviet state. Many small farms outside the village centres were abandoned during the Soviet era. If you see a few trees in the middle of a huge area of ploughed land, they may be the last vestige of such a farm. Some former collective farm buildings have been put to use as barns or warehouses, and others have simply been deserted.

Land was restored to former owners or their heirs after the collapse of the Soviet Union in 1991. Little by little, as the older generation gives up their land and young people follow careers in cities or abroad, their holdings are bought up by larger farms. The countryside is being modernised, and agriculture in Lithuania is once again moving toward fewer, larger farms. Some change is being influenced by agricultural policies of the European Union (EU), which Lithuania joined in 2004.

*Photos clockwise from top: Blossom in the park, Pociūnéliai. JLH; Geese in a household garden. DD; Beehives. JLH; Gloves with honeycomb pattern; Cottage in Pociūnéliai. JLH; Mitten with geese on cuff.*

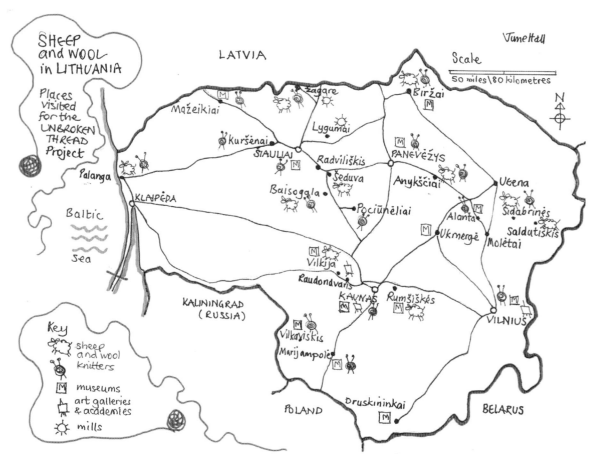

SHEEP and WOOL in LITHUANIA

Places visited for the UNBROKEN THREAD Project

LATVIA

June Hall

Scale
50 miles \ 80 kilometres

N

Palanga

Baltic

Sea

KLAIPĖDA

KALININGRAD (RUSSIA)

Mažeikiai

Kuršėnai

ŠIAULIAI

Žagare

Lygumai

Radviliškis

Baisogala

Šeduva

Pociūnėliai

Biržai

PANEVĖŽYS

Anykščiai

Alanta

Utena

Sidabrinės

Saldutiškis

Ukmergė

Molėtai

Vilkija

Raudondvaris

KAUNAS

Rumšiškės

VILNIUS

Vilkaviškis

Marijampolė

POLAND

Druskininkai

BELARUS

Key

sheep and wool knitters

M museums

art galleries & academies

mills

Top: Traditional fences. JLH. Bottom: Places visited in Lithuania. Drawing by JLH.

# Urban Lithuania

Vilnius, Lithuania's capital, is the most northerly Baroque city in Europe. Built around the unforgettable Old Town, it offers exquisite architecture at every turn. Education runs deep in the history of Vilnius, and the city remains famous for its university, founded by the Jesuits in 1579. Also a centre of Jewish scholarship, the city was once known as the Jerusalem of the North.

Vilnius today abounds in contrasts—ancient and modern, rich and poor sit side by side. Local residents, foreign visitors, and students enjoy a wealth of art, music, dance, theatre, opera, and museums, as well as shops, fine restaurants, and the brash youth culture brought in by the free society. Modern trends in knitting, felting, and other fibre arts are seen alongside traditional folk-art designs, and some knitters work traditional patterns with modern yarns and colour combinations.

Much of the glory of Vilnius is revealed by its buildings, many of which have been carefully restored, painted, and gilded. Some, such as the Palace of the Grand Dukes of Lithuania, located near the Vilnius Cathedral, have been totally reconstructed, while other areas await conservation. The older, unrevised structures are often, to my eyes, the most picturesque, but I fear that many, if not most, will eventually be modernised or developed to suit today's standards, rather than restored to their past glory. That said, in 2009, Vilnius was one of two cities selected as a European Capital of Culture under a programme of the European Union (the other was Linz, Austria) and underwent a good deal of restoration.

Outside the Old Town, Vilnius seems to have spread further every time I visit. Wide roads lead in every direction, lined with modern businesses and high-rise housing developments.

When I travel around Lithuania, I use public transport, usually buses. Once my luggage is stored away, I settle into my pre-booked seat and, armed with a bottle of orange juice and a bar of chocolate, I happily watch passengers come and go. Occasionally someone will ask me a question or make a remark in Lithuanian, which makes me feel all the more at home.

The biggest cities in Lithuania are Vilnius, with a population of about 557,000, and Kaunas, with about 343,000, followed by Klaipėda, Šiauliai, and Panevėžys, each with a population of under 200,000. Since the fall of the Soviet Union and Lithuania's entrance into the European Union, all have been undergoing modernisation and development. In the country's ten counties, each region has a main administrative town, which serves the local villages. Some of these towns have an old centre, often located on the banks of a river, with a castle, a prominently sited church, and a museum.

*Sketch from June's Notebook*

# Vilnius Old Town

Knitting can be found throughout the Old Town of Vilnius, hidden in small shops on side alleys, and displayed in souvenir shops, art galleries, and bookstores.

From the Gates of Dawn, situated in the old city wall, down to the cathedral, the road leads past churches, monastic precincts, the National Philharmonic Hall, and the Lithuanian Academy of Music and Theatre, to Town Hall Square, resplendent with new paving, trees, and street furniture. In the Aušros Vartų meno galerija (Gates of Dawn Art Gallery), finely knitted wrist warmers, mittens, and socks, as well as lace shawls and crocheted doilies, are among the traditional Lithuanian gifts made by local artisans and students of the Vilniaus dailės akademija (Vilnius Academy of Arts).

To the left is the old Jewish quarter. The synagogue and several houses retain Hebrew inscriptions. In this area, the Jewish population was decimated during the Second World War, during which women are known to have knitted in the ghetto in the months before it was liquidated (see Jewish Lithuania, page 46).

The road narrows and passes more churches and former palaces, arriving next at the street market where tourist souvenirs are on sale. Further along the cobbled street are restaurants, along with shops selling amber, linen, and books. Every bookstore has a crafts section with knitting books by local authors, as well as several translated to Lithuanian from English. In the linen shops, as well as in craft shops on side alleys and in stalls in the tourist market, knitted items abound.

At this point, on the left are the old university buildings, and beyond them lies the Presidential Palace. Then comes the cathedral, a classical building on ancient foundations. The campanile, a freestanding bell tower, is an unmistakeable landmark. Above, forming the backdrop, stands the medieval Vilnius Castle Complex, including Gediminas Tower, and the Hill of Three Crosses.

From the portico of the cathedral, the view encompasses the wide, straight, modern thoroughfare of Gedimino Prospektas (Gediminas Avenue) the city's main street. Past the National Drama Theatre and the Lithuanian National Opera and Ballet Theatre, the broad pavement leads to the parliament buildings.

This main street is filled with booths during several annual fairs, including Sostinės dienos (Capital Days) and Kaziuko mugė (St. Casimir's Feast), where traditional foods and crafts, including knitted mittens, gloves, socks, and beaded wrist warmers, are sold in large booths and by individual knitters staking out a small space along the kerb.

In contrast, narrow streets lead from Pilies Gatvė (Pilies, or Castle, Street; the lower part of the main street) to the Vilnia River. Here are Saint Anne's Church (a complex medieval structure made of brick in Gothic style) with the Bernardine Monastery just behind it (Gothic style, with Baroque and Renaissance additions). The Vilnius Academy of Art is here, too, occupying both modern and older premises. Nearby stand Artifex, the art academy's new gallery, and the Folk Life Centre, located in the park. Across a bridge is the area called Užupis (from už, over, and upė, river), being revitalised as the artistic quarter of the city.

Photo opposite: Katedros aikštė (Cathedral Square). This page: Pilies gatvė (Castle Street). DC.

*Photos clockwise from top right: Gedimino pilies bokštas (Gediminas Castle Tower), Statue of Grand Duke Gediminas, knight and castle motifs on knitted gloves and mittens. DC.*

# The People

**June**

The people of Lithuania are descended from the many tribes that inhabited the Baltic area from prehistoric times. The country itself has grown and diminished in area, as geopolitical power struggles have played out over the centuries. It has been taken over by various regimes; influenced by foreign systems that have affected the language, settlement patterns, and culture; seen the destruction of wars; and suffered long periods of occupation. Its time of greatest power was during the medieval era of the Grand Duchy of Lithuania. All of this is reflected in the range of knitting motifs and patterns found on accessories in museum collections around the country.

Against a political background of repeated redefinition and occupation (see The History, page 38), Lithuania has emerged as an independent nation with a highly developed awareness of its own ethnic identity. Its people continue to live according to traditions which have endured for centuries, while adapting to life in the western world and the Eurpoean Union. Lithuanians have learned to adapt while retaining their cultural identity through language (even during periods of proscription), dress, and song.

Without exception, the Lithuanians I have encountered from all walks of life have been proud of their heritage and appreciative of the interest shown in their lives by people from elsewhere, including myself. I am impressed with the strength of their sense of Lithuanian culture, while at the same time I feel concerned that the pace of modernisation and the adoption of Western attitudes may lead, over time, to a rejection of their own values. The modern Western world entices young people, rather than forcing them to change, as was the case during past occupations. Many Lithuanians have taken the opportunities open to them, as members of the European Union, to work in Western Europe and earn wages far higher than they could at home. In this period of rapid change and "globalisation," this is a worldwide tendency, and of course people everywhere want a higher standard of living. I see it as a sad mistake if Lithuanians, belonging to a nation which has survived for so many centuries under continually changing circumstances, should turn their backs on their past, rejecting that which seems "old-fashioned," and losing skills which they may value in the future.

## Past, Present, and Future

The struggles between maintaining a traditional lifestyle and culture while embracing the advantages of modernisation are reflected in knitting, as well. In the past, many rural families kept one or two sheep, but today, few Lithuanians raise sheep. Spinning mills often import merino wool from New Zealand, and yarn stores sell imports from Turkey and Italy, while wool from local sheep is most often used for insulation or is left to rot in barns (see Lithuanian Sheep, page 48 and The Wool, page 60).

The same contrasts between past and present, tradition and modernisation, country and city life, can be seen in the types of projects knitters make. Some enjoy working traditional folk-art designs for themselves or to sell in the tourist markets and at craft fairs, while others prefer to knit designs from contemporary books, or download patterns from the internet.

Maybe it will be possible for today's and tomorrow's Lithuanians to have the best of both worlds: richer lives with wider horizons and opportunities, together with the strength of families, communities, education, and traditions to take with them into the future.

*Dancers in regional costume, taking part in celebrations on 1 May, 2004, when Lithuania joined the European Union. The future for these young people will offer greater possibilities than their parents and grandparents had. JLH.*

*Older women in Vilnius, selling home products, 2003. Left: JLH. Right: DC.*

*Man and horse, heading home after work in the fields, Pociūnéliai, 2004. JLH.*

# Coming Home?

**Donna**

Outside the borders of its few cities, Lithuania is a rural place, a wild place, a place of wolves and storks and rivers and forests. Nature is very important to Lithuanians. Even most who live in the few large cities yearn for the countryside and dream of picking mushrooms in the forest, spending summer vacations at the lake, taking a dip in the Baltic Sea, getting out of town for long weekends. In August, the cities empty out and highways fill with traffic as people head to the sea, the lake, and the forest to lose themselves in nature, and to rural villages to visit relatives.

Awareness of the land is deeply ingrained in the Lithuanian culture and psyche, and many Lithuanian folk-art motifs come from the landscape and nature. Woven and knitted fabrics are decorated with suns and stars, flowers and leaves, birds and rivers. Ancient symbols and pagan designs were first represented in small geometric patterns in weaving and knitting, and later in more detailed pictorial motifs in weaving, embroidery, and knitting. Until recently, the colors of the textiles also came from nature, with hues produced by dyes derived from mountain ash bark, mushrooms, berries, and wildflowers from the forests and meadows contrasting with the neutral shades of undyed wool and linen.

I was the first of my American family to set foot in Lithuania in over a century. The past is present everywhere in Lithuania; so is the future. In small towns, kids with iPods and earbuds walk down unpaved streets alongside their chubby babushka-clad grandmothers; in Vilnius, women wear traditional beaded riešinės (wrist warmers) while they send text messages on their cell phones.

Almost as soon I arrived, I realized that Lithuania didn't feel foreign to me. Even on my first trip, when I was taking the bus from Kaunas to Vilnius, the scenery felt familiar. It reminded me of the eastern United States, most like Pennsylvania, but reminiscent of parts of New York. I began to see why my family felt at home in those places after they came to America, and why, traveling around Lithuania, I also felt at home across the ocean from where I was born. The land seemed to be calling out to me, welcoming me, telling me, "Come home to stay."

As I traveled around Lithuania, I couldn't even imagine what my relatives must have thought when they arrived at Ellis Island at the beginning of the twentieth century. Even if they'd seen Lithuanian and European cities, there would have been nothing to compare to the first sight of the New York skyscrapers rising out of the sea. But my ancestors didn't find cities paved with gold, as they and so many others had expected; instead they found caves and tunnels filled with coal in the Pennsylvania coal mines, and dingy apartments in New York tenements. And they died there, leaving their children as orphans who needed to steal food to survive. No, it was not at all what they'd expected, and I found myself wondering if they had ever wished they'd stayed in Lithuania.

When I see how much the Lithuanian people love the countryside, I feel sad for my grandmother, who spent most of her life in New York City, living in a small apartment that was supposed to be a temporary stop when she first got married. When I was little, my grandparents went to the lake in the country every summer. When I was in the Lithuanian countryside in 2009, and I felt the spirit of wild Lithuania calling to me for the first time, I realized that my grandmother never visited that lake in the country again after Grandpa died in 1976.

Seeing the Lithuanian countryside for myself continually reminded me of my grandmother, and it saddened me that she would never be able to visit the homeland of her family with me.

*Woman spinning, painting by Jonas Buračas, 1953, oil. Jonas Buračas was one of Lithuania's leading artists in the twentieth century. Painting owned by the artist's family. Facing page from ledt to right: Trakai Castle Turret; Vilnius Cathedral; house near Vilnius. DC.*

# Chapter 3: The History

**Donna**

Every time I visit Lithuania, I feel like I'm on a journey through time. With the largest Old Town in Europe, the capital city provides a window onto the nation's past. Once, when I rode the Vilnius trolley bus for just one stop, I was transported from the Middle Ages at the Mindaugo Tiltas (Mindaugas Bridge)—named for the nearby statue of Lithuania's only king, who was crowned by the Pope in 1253—to the 1950s at Žaliasis Tiltas (the Green Bridge)—flanked by statues of Soviet workers.

From the top of Gediminas Castle in the center of Old Town, I saw Medieval, Renaissance, Gothic, Baroque, and Romanesque churches peppering the neighborhoods of Vilnius. Then I turned around to look across the river and saw the glass skyscrapers of the late twentieth century. Even shopping was an adventure, as I visited both old-fashioned Soviet-style stores—where merchandise is securely guarded behind counters and stern shop clerks gather items for you—and modern, capitalist, help-yourself shops.

As June and I rode around the countryside (with my husband driving) on our 2008 research trip, we saw old women wearing babushkas milking cows by hand not far from noisy highway traffic, and geese in front-yard kitchen gardens scuttling around the feet of blue-jean clad teenagers texting each other on cell phones. Concrete Soviet apartment blocks are present in all but the smallest rural villages, neighboring houses have bright gold paint chipping off the clapboards, and new modern houses pop up wherever people have the money to upgrade. Elaborate wooden crosses decorate the landscape, and the roadsides are crowded with people selling forest berries and mushrooms from their parked cars. All these things may make Lithuania seem unusual to visitors, but to locals they feel like home.

Seeing this vast overview of history on my visits to Lithuania led me to seek out information in bookstores in Vilnius, and then in the library and on Amazon.com after I returned home. Over the past few years, I have read dozens of books and hundreds of articles about the history of Lithuania and its neighboring states.

In the West, we tend to view history as a straight line moving from past to future as people transform from savage to civilized and cultures evolve from primitive to sophisticated. The history of Lithuania is much messier. No arrow of Manifest Destiny gives shape to its story. The thread of Lithuania's history lies in a tangled mess on the floor of time. It doesn't easily straighten out into a plumb line if you try to pull one end of the string up toward the ceiling or the sky.

Although the topic intrigues me to no end, it seemed like almost none of the facts I was learning pertained to knitting. Yet the history of a country and its people is directly related to the development and evolution of folk art, including home production of textiles and the use of traditional motifs in weaving, embroidery, and—my strongest interest—knitting.

## Medieval Era

Lithuania rose out of the mist of pre-history in 1009 when the nation was mentioned in the Annals of Quedlinburg. The story was of Roman Catholic missionaries, led by Bruno of Querfurt, traveling to the Russian border with Lithuania to baptize a tribal leader, Netimer. The Lithuanian people did not welcome the influence of this new religion, and Netimer's brother, Zebeden, beheaded Bruno and his followers.

In this early period, before knitting came to Lithuania, its precursor for making socks and mittens was naalbinding, a technique for making fabric using an eyed needle to create stitches that resemble knitting and crochet. This technique is still demonstrated at craft fairs around Lithuania today.

## Lithuania's Golden Age

Lithuania's Golden Age—or its Age of Empire, depending on your viewpoint—took place during the Middle Ages when it rivaled the Roman Empire at the height of its power in size and influence, encompassing lands inside the borders of modern-day Poland, Belarus, Ukraine, and Russia, its borders reaching from the Baltic to the Black Seas.

The Grand Duchy of Lithuania was formed in the thirteenth century when smaller pagan duchies in the Northern Crusades joined forces to fight the continuing encroachment of the Roman Catholic Church under the banner of the Teutonic Knights. Many of Lithuania's contemporary tourist destinations are the locations of medieval fortresses, and popular names for baby boys and streets in cities and towns are the names of the most famous of Lithuania's Grand Dukes: Vytautas and Gediminas; as well as the country's only monarch, Mindaugas who reigned from 1251 to 1263, first as Grand Duke, then as king.

The Golden Age continued when Lithuania joined forces with its closest neighbor, Poland, and Grand Duke Jogaila married Polish princess Jadwiga and became King of Poland. This finally converted pagan Lithuania to Roman Catholicism in a way that did not require surrender to a foreign power or a loss of sovereignty for Lithuania. The combined Lithuanian-Polish army, with the support of the Pope behind them, finally defeated the Teutonic Knights at the Battle of Grunwald (Žalgiris) in 1410.

*Views of Vilnius Old Town and the new city from Gediminas Castle Tower. DC.*

*Trakai Castle. DC.*

During the early years of this union, Lithuania expanded its borders to their furthest reaches and its population was more diverse than it had ever been before or ever would be again, including ethnic Lithuanians, Roman Catholic Poles, Orthodox Slavs, and Jews. Over time, the balance of power shifted and Poland became the dominant partner in the union as Polish language and culture was adopted by the upper classes, leaving the Lithuanian language, long-held customs, and even some remnants of pagan beliefs and traditions in the domain of peasants. While the upper classes adopted Polish and Western European fashions, the peasants—or serfs, who were not liberated until 1861—continued to spin and weave their own fabrics to make traditional clothing. These peasant styles would become very important to ethnic Lithuanians of all classes in the following centuries, and many of the traditional patterns and motifs would be adapted for use in knitted accessories.

The marriage of people, politics, and religion known as the "Union of Two Nations" would last until the end of the eighteenth century, when political power shifted and Austria, Prussia, and Russia each annexed parts of the Polish-Lithuanian Commonwealth into three "Partitions of Poland," the third and last of which occurred in 1795.

5 Litas note, c. 1993.

Lietuvos Mokykla (Lithuanian Schooling) 1864–1904 by Petras Rimša. Photos by René & Peter van der Krogt, www.vanderkrogt.net.

# Czarist Russia

After the Third Partition of Poland in 1795, Lithuania ceased to exist as a sovereign nation and was absorbed by Czarist Russia.

In the name of "Russification," publishing, printing, or importing materials in the Lithuanian language using the Latin alphabet was banned from 1864 to 1904. Under Russian rule, in no small part due to the suppression of markers of Lithuanian identity, a new Lithuanian nationalist movement was born. Books were printed in East Prussia and smuggled into the other parts of Lithuania, and children were homeschooled in their own language. The statue pictured (opposite page), *Lithuanian Schooling*, illustrates the strong ties of textile production and clothing to the Lithuanian identity, as the sculptor's mother is shown spinning while teaching him to read. A drawing of the sculpture was printed on the 1993 five-Litas banknote.

It was while Lithuania was part of the Russian Empire that knitting came to these lands, and motifs from weaving were adapted for use on hand-knit accessories.

# Early Twentieth Century

The Lithuanian nation would not exist as a separate political entity again until the end of the First World War. It gained independence after its capital city, Vilnius, was ceded to Poland, and its Baltic coastline was ceded to East Prussia. The government was moved to Kaunas, 60 miles (100 kilometers) to the west of Vilnius.

This brief ray of sunshine was quickly blotted out by the storms of World War II, during which Lithuania was occupied by the Soviets, then by the Nazis, and again by the Soviets.

In 1939, Hitler and Stalin signed the Molotov-Ribbentrop Pact, placing Lithuania under the Soviet "sphere of influence." In June 1941, Hitler broke this pact by invading the Soviet Union and occupying Lithuania. The murder of Lithuanian Jews began almost immediately, with Nazi Einsatzgruppen (mobile killing units) shooting almost 3,000 Jews at the Seventh Fort in Kaunas (see Jewish Lithuania on page 46) on July 6. In 1944, the Soviet army defeated the Germans and the Lithuanian Soviet Socialist Republic was established, with its capital in Vilnius.

# Soviet Times

During the first eight years of the second Soviet occupation, under Stalin's rule, over 100,000 Lithuanians were deported to Siberia and other locations, and many were held as political prisoners. In the KGB Prison, now the Museum of Genocide Victims, in Vilnius, at least 1,000 people were executed in the basement between the end of the war and 1960.

During the Soviet occupation, commercial fabric, thread, and yarn were often in scarce supply and hand-spinning became prominent once again as older women provided materials to their neighbors, and sold yarn and thread on the black market. Wool was spun for knitting yarn and linen thread was spun for use with sewing machines. Knitting books from the middle of the twentieth century don't seem very different from those available in the West from the same time. The raglan sweaters, gored skirts, lacy cardigans, and gloves featured would look right at home in 1950s America, as would the style of illustration.

After Stalin's death in 1953, life became easier in the Soviet Union, but it wasn't until *Perestroika*, under Mikhail Gorbachov in the 1980s, that it became permissible to protest in public. Music became one avenue for groups of people to do just that, by singing national anthems and regional folk songs.

In the late '80s, many women began weaving to reproduce traditional clothing of Lithuanian peasants as costumes for these singing groups.

Ethnographic studies such as this were not discouraged by the USSR government, and were even encouraged or performed by Soviet academic organizations. Visits to local museums became popular as women went to see vintage clothing and study the colors and weaving techniques that would be appropriate for reproducing the fabrics authentically. Women who knew how to sew used these woven fabrics and nineteenth century sewing techniques to make blouses, aprons, skirts, and other women's accessories for singers and dancers to wear during performances.

Museum collections also included knitted accessories—mittens, gloves, wrist warmers, and socks. Because most women knew how to knit, having learned in school as girls, it was easy to add these knitted accessories to the costume ensembles.

Across Lithuania, Estonia, and Latvia, music festivals began turning into peaceful protests, with many performers wearing traditional clothing. Folk songs, banned national anthems, and rock 'n' roll music all served to unite the people against the communist government.

On August 23, 1989—the 50th anniversary of the Molotov-Ribbentrop Pact—over two million people held hands to form a human chain that stretched from Tallinn, in the north of Estonia, to Vilnius, in the east of Lithuania. This "singing revolution" would help lead to independence for all three Baltic nations: Lithuania, Estonia, and Latvia.

Lithuania declared independence on March 11, 1990, a year after the Berlin Wall fell and a year before the Soviet Union dissolved. After maintaining power for half a century, the Soviets didn't let go without a struggle. In January of 1991, Soviet troops entered Vilnius. Once again, protestors gathered to sing in defiance of Russian tanks. Fourteen people were killed and about 700 injured in the protest. Today, the site of that protest, the Vilnius Television Tower, stands as a monument to the independent spirit of the Lithuanian people.

My Grandma Druchunas was in poor health at that time, at her home in New York, and though she lived until 1998, I don't know if she ever learned of Lithuania's independence.

## Today

Since achieving independence, the transition from a communist economy to capitalism and democratic rule hasn't always been easy, but today Lithuania is a member of both NATO and the European Union, and is embracing both its roots as an independent nation and its new place in the heart of Europe.

# Lithuanian National Costume

Walking down the streets in Vilnius, I always notice what people are wearing: college students in jeans and miniskirts, business people in suits and dresses, construction workers with boots and helmets, and a few old women wearing 1950s-style house dresses and babushkas. But it is only since the end of the nineteenth century that mass-produced garments have been prevalent in Lithuania. Before that, and even into the early decades of the twentieth century, the majority of people wore homemade clothing.

By the time factory-produced textiles became available and desirable throughout the country, a folk-art movement was spreading through Europe. Collectors, many of whom were Lithuanian-Americans, gathered examples of the holiday and festival clothing worn by peasants and displayed them in exhibits in Paris and other cities around the Continent. Today, many museums in Lithuania have collections of antique clothing, as well as reconstructions of clothing items that have been found, usually in advanced states of decay, in archaeological sites around the country.

The concept of a "Lithuanian national costume" was developed in the late nineteenth century and established in the early part of the twentieth century, as a way to promote Lithuanian nationality and ethnicity. This costume was based on what could be learned about the holiday clothing of peasants; everyday clothes were largely ignored. In 1938, Antanas and Anastazija Tamošaitis's published an extensive study of Lithuanian national costume. (It was similar to their 1979 English-language book, *Lithuanian National Costume*). For their collection, Antanas Tamošaitis gathered a select group of items that had been made by hand from homespun yarns and fabrics, and included only garments and accessories that he considered to be uniquely Lithuanian. His definition of "authentic" did not include any mass-produced reproductions.

Because Lithuania was occupied by several different nations over the course of the twentieth century, the traditional costume became a strong and important part of the national identity. When the Lithuanian language was suppressed by the Soviet Union and speaking out against the Communist Party was dangerous, wearing a pair of hand-knitted gloves might have been the only way a person could safely display a quiet resistance. Now that Lithuania is once again an independent nation, people dressed in reproductions of traditional garments cheerfully fill the streets and shops on national holidays and during summer music and crafts festivals.

# Knitting in the National Costume

In Lithuania, knitting was traditionally not considered a very important craft. Every woman knew how to knit, some with more finesse than others, but spinning and weaving—especially of linen—were the skills that gave a woman prestige in the community. Much more weaving than knitting needed to be done, because knitting was used only to make small accessories that would warm hands and feet: socks, mittens, gloves, and wrist warmers. Only rarely did women knit sashes, hats, or sweaters. Instead, Lithuanians turned to looms to churn out yards of cloth from which they sewed clothing and made myriad household fabrics. Even so, they knitted for special occasions, including holidays and weddings, making small accessories that displayed elaborate patterning and meticulous workmanship. They also knitted some everyday accessories, less elaborate but no less finely crafted—unless the knitted cloth was intended to be fulled. Fulling wool by agitating it in warm water creates a densely, and permanently, interlocked fabric especially well suited for cold-weather socks and mittens.

Most gloves and mittens were elaborately patterned, although only two, or at most three, motifs would be used on a single object. Sometimes the fingers and thumbs were solid-colored. The hand of a mitten or glove might be covered with many individual motifs arranged in horizontal, vertical, or diagonal bands, or might be decorated with an all-over, interlocking pattern. Individual motifs might also be surrounded by an interlocking lattice pattern.

Socks were sometimes worked with all-over patterning, but just as often had patterned cuffs above plain legs and feet. For summer wear, socks were knit in lace or stockinette stitch out of undyed linen yarn, or with undyed and dyed linen in stripe patterns.

Wrist warmers for holiday wear were worked on fine yarn, usually purchased especially for this project, with small glass beads stranded on and knitted into the fabric in elaborate patterns. For everyday wear, wrist warmers were made with a variety of stitches and colors, probably using yarn scraps left over from other projects.

Today, women in Lithuania knit from contemporary books and patterns, and they make sweaters, shawls, afghans, toys, and a huge variety of fashionable and kitschy projects, just like knitters everywhere else. Because traditional Lithuanian knitting produced accessories worn as part of the national costume, knitters around the country also pick up their needles to make reproductions of these items that are then worn by performers in singing groups and at holiday festivals and craft markets.

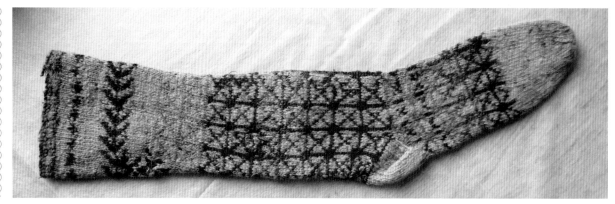

*Men's colorwork socks, Šiauliai Aušros Museum. DC.*

# Jewish Lithuania

*Lite*, Yiddish for Lithuania, refers to an area of Eastern Europe that extends beyond the borders of current day Lithuania and includes parts of Poland, Belarus, and Russia, where Jewish culture flourished for centuries, and where my mother's grandparents lived before emigrating to the United States.

In 2007, when I started studying Lithuania to learn about its knitting tradition, I kept finding references to Jewish knitters. I discovered that in many villages, as well as in some larger cities, Jews—often comprising half or more of the pre-World War II Lithuanian population—knitted for pleasure and for pay. But as I traveled around the country during my first two trips, I found little or no mention of Jewish history or culture.

The mass killings of Jews during the Holocaust began in Kaunas just four days after the German invasion of the USSR in Operation Barbarossa on June 22, 1941. By the end of the war, over 90 percent of Lithuanian Jews had been murdered by the Nazis and local collaborators—a higher percentage than in any other country.

I expected to see remnants of the rich Jewish cultural contribution to Lithuania in museums, but I was surprised to find only a few mentions of Jews in Holocaust memorials and at mass-grave sites. Virtually no Jewish material culture has been preserved in Lithuanian ethnographic collections. The only way to find out what people were knitting in Jewish communities is to talk to Holocaust survivors, look at old photographs, and read statistics about trades practiced in each village and city. This is beginning to change, albeit slowly, and I hope that we will see more and more appreciation of Lithuania's Jewish history in museums in the future.

This dearth of information led me to plan a third trip to the region, specifically to study Jewish history and culture, and of course to learn about knitting.

Jewish women around Lite knit, just as their Lithuanian, Polish, and Russian neighbors did. They made socks, mittens, and gloves to keep warm during the cold winter months. Some women knit for themselves and their families, while others had nannies and servants who did their knitting for them. But what their hand-knits looked like, with very few exceptions, will remain a mystery to us. In all of my research so far, I have only been able to see photographs of one pair of mittens in the Artifacts Retrieval Department of Yad Vashem, the Holocaust memorial in Israel, and one pair of socks knit by a Jewish woman in Belarus before the First World War. The socks are in the State Ethnographic Museum in St. Petersburg, Russia, along with two other pairs I have not been able to see yet.

After the Nazi invasion, Jewish women and girls continued to knit in ghettos, in concentration camps, in hiding, and in the forest while fighting with partisans. Some knitters made items for themselves and their loved ones, others worked on commission, making garments and accessories for Jews and for German soldiers, still others worked in knitting "workshops" and factories. It is well known that amongst groups targeted by Nazis, anyone who had a skill—even something as seemingly commonplace as knitting—had a survival advantage, because they could be put to work by the Nazis and were therefore more likely to be kept alive for a longer period of time. Maintaining traditions and participating in cultural activities such as knitting, theater, or even reading library books, gave people a sense of normality, purpose, and dignity, as well as sometimes serving as a subtle form of rebellion.

By the end of the Second World War, Eastern European Jewish society had been virtually wiped out. Today, it is difficult to find remnants of the material culture of communities that had previously survived in this part of the word for hundreds of years. The loss of knitted artifacts and other textiles, as sad as it is, is nothing compared with the terror endured by the Jews during World War II and the tragedy of lost lives that ensued.

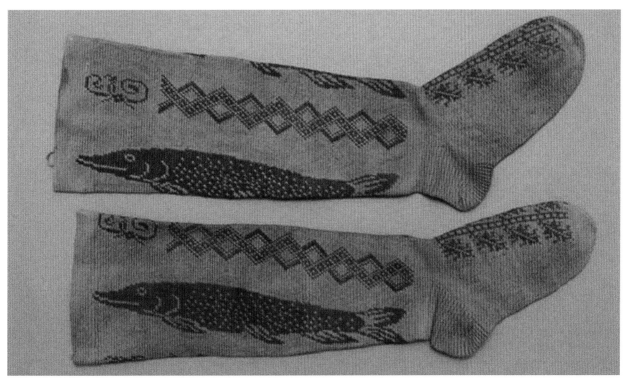

*Fish socks. Credit: The Russian Ethnography Museum in St. Petersburg, Russia.*

*Sheep shearing. 1934. Puponys village, Panevėžys county. BB Facing page from left to right: Knitting sample; June spinning. DD; Blackface Sheep. DC.*

# Chapter 4: Lithuanian Sheep

### Donna

Knitting with breed-specific wool has been getting more and more popular over the last few years, due in no small part to the work of people like June. Her experience raising sheep, being a member the Wool Clip fiber-artist co-operative in Cumbria, organizing WoolFest—one of the largest sheep and wool events in Great Britain—and serving on the board of the Rare Breeds Survival Trust in the UK make her uniquely qualified to offer us a glimpse into the world of Lithuanian sheep breeds and their wool.

Not long ago, few knitters knew the names of any sheep breeds besides Merino. Today, as knitters are becoming more interested in learning about where their yarns come from and are increasingly aware of the need to preserve the genetic diversity of sheep, Blue Faced Leicester, Shetland, Wensleydale, Romney, and Coopworth are becoming household names (in knitters' households, at least).

We hope you will be as entranced by the information in this chapter as we are.

## June

Domesticated sheep have inhabited the lands of Lithuania since at least 2000 BCE. Throughout the country's history and under its shifting political regimes, sheep have been valued providers of meat, wool, and skins.

Despite their historical persistence, I rarely saw sheep in Lithuania when I began my project in 2003, especially in the winter. Sheep meat barely appeared on restaurant menus, and when it did, it came as a Georgian dish called saslikas, a kind of kebab, somewhat grimly translated on one menu as "sheep strings."

I wanted to learn about breeds and their history; about the "sheep year" and how it differed from the annual farming cycle in our Lake District hills in England; about how many sheep were kept in Lithuania; about their wool, its qualities and how it was used; and about how the old customs of husbandry and textile processes were changing.

A family I stayed with in Baisogala introduced me to the Institute of Animal Sciences of the Lithuanian Veterinary Academy (LVA Gyvulininkystės institutas). Founded in 1952, this government organisation occupies the former manor house in the village, one of Lithuania's grandest houses. Its setting is a beautiful park with winding paths among handsome trees, beside a lake. The dairy, a well-house, stables, farm buildings and a now ruined windmill remain from the days of the lordly estate. In this splendid setting, I met with Dr. Birutė Zapasnikienė, Head of Animal Breeding and Genetics, who through an interpreter explained to me the policy of the organisation regarding sheep breeding. I also consulted with another organisation that works hard to provide rural communities with livestock, and therefore with a livelihood: the Heifer International Baltic Foundation (see page 59 for more). I also visited several remote farms and cottages where families keep one or two sheep each.

The following is some of what I learned from these sources.

# Background

The sheep indigenous to this region is the Lithuanian Coarse Wool (šiurkščiavilnė, abbreviated SV), which in the 1920s was crossed with imported breeds from Britain (mainly Shropshire and Suffolk) and from Germany, to produce the Lithuanian Blackface (juodagalvė, abbreviated JG). Unrecorded crosses confuse the picture of sheep in the past, and further recent introductions and crosses have led to greater variety, but the Coarse Wool and the Blackface are now being conserved in national flocks.

During the Soviet era, Lithuania's livestock farming was concentrated on rearing pigs and cattle to supply pork and dairy products, and sheep-keeping declined.

Sheep numbers were at their height in 1926, with 1.5 million countrywide, and fell to a low of 11,500 in 2001. Since Lithuania joined the European Union in 2004, sheep are regaining importance in agriculture, and numbers have been increasing year by year.

The situation is changing rapidly, as farmers are being encouraged to cross their Lithuanian breeds with heavier sheep from the United Kingdom, Germany, and the Netherlands to produce more meat. By 2006, meat from Lithuanian sheep was being exported to Germany.

*Photos facing page from left to right: Lithuanian Coarse Wool Sheep. JLH; Right: Lithuanian Blackface Sheep. DC.*

There were 462 recorded flocks of sheep in Lithuania in 2010, ranging in size from a single sheep to over a thousand.

About 45,000 sheep were kept for meat and wool, while over 9,000 produced meat and sheepskins. Just over 300 were milk sheep, and 89 individual animals were described as "decorative exotics." In 2009, farms varied in size from small holdings of two or three hectares (five to 7.5 acres) to around 600 hectares (1500 acres).

It can be seen from the following table that almost half of Lithuania's sheep in 2010 were in flocks of under 50, while only ten flocks contained more than one thousand animals.

| Largest Flocks of Sheep in Lithuania, 2010 | |
|---|---|
| **Flock Size** | **Breed** |
| 1680 | Lithuanian Coarse Wool |
| 1659 | Suffolk |
| 1632 | Lithuanian Coarse Wool |
| 1588 | Lithuanian Blackface |
| 1519 | Lithuanian Blackface |
| 1268 | Lithuanian Coarse Wool |
| 1214 | Romaov |
| 1211 | Lithuanian Blackface |
| 1064 | Lithuanian Coarse Wool |
| 1011 | Lithuanian Blackface |

| Flock Size, 2010 | |
|---|---|
| **Sheep** | **Number of Flocks** |
| 0–9 | 194 |
| 10–49 | 108 |
| 50–99 | 33 |
| 100–199 | 48 |
| 200–499 | 47 |
| 500–1,000 | 22 |
| 1,000+ | 10 |
| **Approximate Totals** | |
| 55,000 | 462 |

# Lithuanian Coarse Wool Sheep

The preservation of genetic diversity of farm livestock has been required by law in Lithuania since 1922. Scientists realised that old breeds faced extinction, if they had not already been lost. They searched the country for survivors—not on large modern farms, but on remote, rural small holdings, where "lonely old women" kept a few animals. The Lithuanian Coarse Wool was saved through these efforts.

To increase productivity, many Lithuanian Coarse Wool sheep had been crossed, but cross-breeding with Coarse Wool rams became illegal in 1949. Around 1990, when pure Coarse Wool sheep were located, they were sold to Germany. In 1995, a flock was founded at the Baisogala Institute, and was declared pedigree in 1999.

Originally, there were two types of native coarse-wool sheep: in the north, they had short-tails and dark wool; in the south, they had long tails and white wool. Over time, unrecorded cross breeding lessened the differences, and the conserved sheep are larger than their native predecessors and they produce more wool. They are being closely studied for biological characteristics and farming potential.

*Coarse Wool (SV) sheep at Baisogala, 2009. JLH.*

| The Old and New Lithuanian Coarse Wool Sheep | | |
|---|---|---|
| | **Baisogala Flock (New)** | **Old-Style Sheep** |
| **Rams** | 45–55 kg (100–120 lbs) <br> 80% horned | |
| **Ewes** | 41–49 kg (90–108 lbs) <br> 20% horned | 30–40 kg (65–90 lbs) |
| **Tail Length** | Medium | **In the north:** short <br> **In the south:** long |
| **Fleece Length** | 14–32 cm (5.5–12.5") | 6–11 cm (2.5–4.5") |
| **Fibre Diameter** | 31–41 microns | Fleeces are double-coated |
| **Fleece Weight** | 2.5–3 kg (5.5–6.5 lbs) | 1–1.5 kg (2.25–3.25 lbs) |
| **Fleece Colours** | Black, white, greys, brown | **In the north:** dark <br> **In the south:** white |

# Lithuanian Blackface Sheep

The Lithuanian Blackface breed was created in the mid-twentieth century by crossing the local Lithuanian Coarse Wool sheep with English Shropshire sheep, to shift their wool quality to a softer, more readily marketable type, and with German Blackheaded sheep, to increase the income from their meat. They have therefore become multipurpose, productive animals, and they have been bred to be without horns (that is, to be what is called polled).

To maintain a flock of purebred Lithuanian Blackface sheep as a nucleus for breeding, farms at Pasvalys and Telšiai were established in the 1950s. In 1963, breeders began a flock book to keep track of breeding programmes, along with a system of sheep identification and marking.

| Characteristics of the Juodgalvės, or Lithuanian Blackface Sheep | |
|---|---|
| Rams | 80–90 kg (175–200 lbs) polled |
| Ewes | 50–60 kg (110–130 lbs) polled |
| Fleece Length | 8–10 cm (3.5–4") |
| Fibre Diameter | 30–40 microns; fleece is described as "semi-fine" |
| Fleece Weight | 3–4 kg (6.5–9 lbs) |
| Fleece Colours | White, with black hair on face, ears, and legs |

*Lithuanian Blackface Sheep. DC.*

# Skudde Sheep: Homecoming of an Ancient Breed

Skudde, or heath, sheep were a primitive breed of the North European short-tailed group indigenous to the Baltic States and Prussia. During the time of agricultural modernisation in the mid-twentieth century, these small, native sheep were considered "old fashioned". Larger, foreign meat breeds from Germany, Holland, and Britain were brought into Lithuania to cross with native sheep to increase their meat output. During the Second World War, when Lithuania was occupied by German forces, Skudde sheep were shipped to German zoos in Munich and Berlin, to be used as food for the animals. These sheep are thrifty feeders and breed easily—it was because they were kept to feed the lions that they survived!

There is renewed interest in native livestock, throughout the world. Eventually, the Lietuvos škudžių avių augintojų asociacija (Lithuanian Skudde Sheep Breeders' Association) was formed to preserve the breed and to gain heritage status for it.

In Lithuania, Kęstas Samušis and his wife Inga Taminskaitė-Samušienė keep a flock of Skudde sheep on their organic farm deep in the forest in Molėtai region. Inga uses the wool to make felt slippers, shoes, and boots which she sends all over the world. Her designs are decorative and original, embellished with felt flowers and beads. Some slippers have clusters of amber, not only as ornament on the outside, but embedded inside the sole to massage the feet.

The sheep provide meat as well as wool for this family. The local farmers host shearing parties together with other farmers and their flocks, to raise awareness of the breed and encourage more farmers to keep them. Numbers are gradually increasing, but the breed is still classed as endangered and the Heifer Foundation is supporting their breeding programmes. These lively, hardy little animals are once again to be found in their native land, providing a living for Lithuanian families.

| Skudde Sheep | |
|---|---|
| **Ram** | 35–50 kg (77–110 lbs), horned |
| **Ewe** | 20–40 kg (44–88 lbs), hornless |
| **Lambs** | Mainly singles, but many twins, some triplets |
| **Wool** | Staple Length: 12–18 cm (5–7"); double-coated; short, fine undercoat, longer outer coat of coarser guard hairs |
| **Fleece Weight** | 1–2 kg (2–4 lbs) |
| **Colours** | Black, grey, and white |

*Skudde ram from the Samušis flock, showing large, curled horns. JLH.*

*Kęstas Samušis with Skudde sheep on his organic farm near Molėtai. JLH.*

In May of 2013, I was invited to a weekend festival at Saldutiškis, an estate in Utena region, organised by the Skudde Sheep Breeders Association. Arūnas Svitojus, Head of Heifer International Baltic Foundation, had purchased the Saldutiškis manor a few years earlier and is restoring it to provide a venue where skills concerned with sustainable rural life can be taught and practised.

Kęstas Samušis is secretary of the Skudde Sheep Breeders Association. Thirty farms in Lithuania now keep Skudde sheep. Flocks are located across the country, from Mažeikiai in the north to Alytus in the south, and from Klaipėda in the west to Utena in the east. Events are organised to popularise the sheep and to educate people in the possibilities of adding value to Skudde sheep and their wool. Members of the association and their

families gathered at Saldutiškis on a weekend of beautiful summer weather. There was a programme of talks, followed by activities outdoors, including watching Skudde sheep being sheared and their wool being spun, dyed or made into felt. Traditional Lithuanian food was cooked and served, including a stew of Skudde meat. Local singers and musicians entertained everyone there.

Arūnas Svitojus also keeps other rare livestock, including a breed of horse from lowland Žemaitija. It was once numerous and used for "everything", from riding to fighting, when Lithuania stretched from Estonia to the Black Sea. These light, manoeuvrable horses (žemaitukai) proved invaluable against the heavily armed Teutonic knights and their large horses, easily navigating the secret paths through the marshlands in the Middle Ages.

*Skudde sheep belonging to the Samušis family, near Molėtai. JLH.*

*Arūnas Svitojus, shearing a Skudde sheep, Saldutiškis. JLH.*

*Horse of old breed from Žemaitija at Saldutiškis festival, 2013. JLH.*

# Husbandry

Since time immemorial, Lithuanians have kept sheep on small farms in remote villages or in the forest. The people of this land have been accustomed to providing for themselves, and sheep have been a vital resource in the domestic economy. Some families still keep one or two sheep—ewes for wool and lambs, and rams for breeding and meat.

Winter can be long and cold in Lithuania, with snow covering the ground from November to April, and temperatures down to -30°C (-22°F). During the cold seasons, sheep are housed in farm buildings along with other livestock. In summer, they are tethered outdoors in the unfenced landscape.

Bells were necessary for locating sheep and other livestock on open pasture. The well-known Lithuanian photographer Balys Buračas (1897–1972), who realised the importance of recording everyday life, took pictures in 1936 that show boys tending sheep and playing music on pipes—a tradition stretching back to biblical times. His beautifully composed photographs convey his deep appreciation of the land and its people between two world wars, when Lithuania was independent.

Jonas Tamulas, of Šiauliai, recalls that when he was a boy in the 1950s, every family in his home village of Kentriai, in the Kelmė region, kept two or three sheep. Each little farm had a sheep house, built of strong logs, as wolves were an ever-present threat. Wolves would attack guard dogs by the throat and kill them, so many people kept geese to raise an alarm. Wolves could dig underneath the sheep-house walls, so people laid stones on the earth floors to deter them. Lambs could be born in the winter, and were easy prey for wolves.

In northern Lithuania, near Žagarė, Romas Simaitas and family have two sheep in their barn in the village of Gražaičiai, one a Lithuanian Blackface and the other a white-faced sheep. The family exchanges the fleece for knitting yarn, from which they make socks and gloves for their three growing boys.

We were warmly welcomed into their house, for coffee, sage tea, Easter eggs, gooseberry jam, and cake.

Lienė Dacaitė, nearby, also has two sheep: a ewe and a ram that she keeps in a barn. Her yard, which contains a well and a woodpile, is alive with turkeys, guinea fowl, ducks, hens, dogs, and a cat. Lienė's parents used to have around five hundred sheep on the local collective farm. She found an old Latvian book in the attic: published in the 1930s, it covered sheep husbandry and breeds, along with wool and spinning. Now Lienė breeds bulls for her living, and keeps the sheep for her personal use.

*Sheep bells photographed by Jonas Tamulis, in Šiauliai Aušros Museum. They are carved out of blocks of wood and engraved with dates, initials, and decoration.*

*Liené's two sheep, housed for winter, near Žagarė. JLH.*

*Liené Dacaité. JLH.*

*Janina Dagienė. JLH.*

*Four lumzdelis (pipe) players and a fiddler. Young shepherds are herding and playing music. Even the youngest shepherd brought an instrument to the pasture. In Vidiškis township, all children play lumzdelis, even those have just started walking. The children make their pipes themselves. 1936. Vidiškis village, Ukmergė county. BB*

# Sheep-Cheese Enterprise

In 2011, the only farm producing cheese from sheep milk in Lithuania was in the far north-east, in the Biržai region. The large farm has, in addition to the milk sheep, a flock of over a thousand Lithuanian Blackface sheep.

The sheep-milk enterprise began because one of Kristina's daughters is allergic to cow's milk. To provide her with an alternative, the family bought three East Friesian sheep from Germany. East Friesians are good dairy sheep, so soon they were producing a surplus of milk, and cheese-making seemed the best way to use it. The delicious cheese, some flavoured with garlic and some with fruit, quickly became popular among friends and neighbours, and the family now sells it at markets and fairs.

*Kristina making sheep-milk cheese. JLH.*

*A feast of sheep cheese awaiting my arrival, in October 2010. JLH.*

*East Friesian sheep. These are large sheep, with ewes weighing 80–100 kg (176–220 lbs). Fleece, 3–4 kg (6.5–9 lbs) of white wool, 20–25 cm (8–10") long. (There are black sheep of this breed, but they are not common.) Produces one or two lambs a year, and 1–3 litres (1–3 quarts) of milk per day for 8–10 months a year. JLH.*

## Organisations

The Institute of Animal Science of the Lithuanian Veterinary Academy (Lietuvos Veterinarijos Akademijos Gyvulininkystės Institutas) in Baisogala, located in the Radviliškis region, is the national centre for farm livestock education and research. Founded in 1952, it conducts studies concerned with animal genetics, biology, breeding, nutrition, production, welfare, conservation, and environmental issues.

The office of the director, Dr. Violeta Juškienė, is located in the former "palace" of Baisogala. The handsome nineteenth-century mansion has found a new use, unlike many other dvarai, or country manors, which have either fallen into ruin or been dismantled. The park, with mature trees, a lake, paths, and benches, provides the community with a beautiful location for leisure, in addition to accommodating the research facility.

Dr. Birutė Zapasnikienė is head of animal breeding and genetics. Her work includes the conservation of the state flocks of Lithuanian Coarse Wool and Lithuanian Blackface sheep.

In 1994, the Lithuanian Sheep Breeders Association (Lietuvos avių augintojų asociacija) was founded with the goals of preserving the Lithuanian Coarse Wool and Lithuanian Blackface breeds, improving meat production, helping farmers with breeding programmes and feeding and housing strategies, organising seminars and shows, and making links with similar organisations within Lithuania and internationally.

The organisation works closely with the Baisogala Institute and the Ministry of Agriculture. Dr. Žilvinas Augustinavičius, veterinary and farmer, is a leading official and has introduced me to his own and other farms.

The seeds of the Heifer International Baltic Foundation were planted in 1944, when Dan West, an American farmer and humanitarian, set out to end world hunger. Believing that it is more sustainable to provide livestock which produce milk than to send milk itself, he began to supply young cows, known as heifers, to undernourished communities. By raising livestock, a village could develop a sense of community and build confidence. Heifer International reached the Baltic states in 1999.

In support of rural society, Heifer International provides livestock to groups of ten participants, who then send the first offspring of their animals to another community, becoming benefactors as well as recipients. With technical assistance and training, Heifer International encourages cooperation, supports food security, encourages women's equality, and advocates for care of the environment. Heifer International has donated hundreds of sheep to communities around Lithuania. When I visited her in 2010, Lolita Griškevičienė, from Gelvonai village, in the Širvintos region in eastern Lithuania, was awaiting the arrival of sheep for her community.

*Palace, now housing the Baisogala Institute. JLH.*

*Lolita with her flock of Lithuanian Coarse Wool sheep. JLH.*

*Žilvinas Augustinavičius. JLH.*

*Spinner: Gurkšnys-Viščius. He spun hemp threads for weaving bags and knitting fishing nets. He used a drop spindle, not a spinning wheel. In Eastern Aukštaitija, many men used to spin hemp for bags and nets. 1935, Gaidžiai village, Zarasai county. BB*
*Facing page from left to right: Wool yarn from Lygumai mill. DC; Girl using hand spindles at Šiauliai Aušros Museum, "Days of Ancient Crafts," 2004. JLH; Family shearing sheep, 1938. Lithuanian Institute of History.*

# Chapter 5: The Wool

# Have You Any Wool?

**Donna**

Sheep are wonderful, but as a knitter, it is what we do with their fleece that interests me most. Every time I go to Lithuania, I look for yarn made from the wool of local sheep. Let me tell you, it hasn't been easy to find! I have stumbled onto a few skeins during my travels with June, and used the yarns I've purchased at markets and shops to make several of the projects in this book. It's only recently that one Lithuanian yarn company has started selling online (see Where to Buy Lithuanian Wool Yarn and Fibre, page 68).

In this chapter, we follow wool from Lithuanian sheep to discover the ways it has traditionally been spun into yarn for use by local weavers and knitters, and how yarn is processed both for personal and commercial uses today.

# From Sheep to Yarn

### June

Wool has been used for clothing and other domestic purposes for as long as people have kept sheep. In fact, I doubt if humans could have survived in northern Europe over the millennia without sheep, and vice-versa. Sheepskins provide warmth and comfort, but wool from living animals is a renewable resource.

Within living memory, Lithuanian knitting wool was produced by families in the countryside from the fleeces of their own sheep. Shearing, washing, carding, dyeing, winding, and spinning were regular chores for which wooden equipment, often homemade, can still be found in homes and in museums.

Jonas Tamulis remembers life in the 1950s and '60s, when he and his younger brother were growing up in the village of Kentriai, in the Kelmė region. This was during the Soviet regime, when farming was based on the collective system which had been introduced in 1947. Families were allowed to keep a few animals of their own, and Jonas's family had two cows. His aunt, who lived alone, had one. A specified amount of produce had to go to the collective— eggs, wool, geese—to feed town dwellers.

The Tamulis family also kept three sheep, each a different colour. The breeds were unknown and unimportant; the colour and quality of wool were their main concerns. Blackfaced sheep had thicker wool and quieter temperaments than other types. Jonas's mother taught the boys to spin and knit. He remembers knitting socks in his free time between school lessons, when pupils could walk round indoors during the cold winters. He used five needles made from bicycle wheel spokes—which he describes as "good metal."

Hand carders were used to comb wool for spinning, and some ingenious devices were invented to improve efficiency, including a carding "horse" (see photo at bottom left). Most communities had a hand-operated carding mill, and a few hand-operated carding machines still survive.

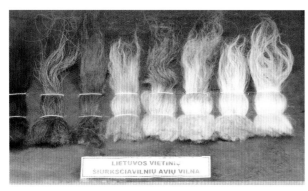

*Colors of wool from Lithuanian Coarse Wool sheep. DD.*

*Carding "horse" with one fixed set of wires, demonstrated by Jūratė, conservator. Mažeikiai Museum. JLH.*

*Eugenija's carders, Žagarė. JLH.*

*Julija Bunevičiūtė-Mocevičienė, Alytus region. This is a rare photograph of spinning wool, taken around 1960–'65. Julija was the grandmother of Audronė Tamulienė, of Šiauliai. Photo compliments of Audronė Tamulienė.*

In Jonas's village, the privately owned carder was nationalised in Soviet times. However, the former owner remained in charge of it, as he knew how it worked and was able to maintain it in working order. People took their fleece along and operated the machine themselves. Turning the large handles, one on either side, was "strong man's work," not considered for women. The wool came out as batts—flat layers of wool with the fibres combed in one direction—ready for spinning or felting. The batts were rolled and folded, then taken home in linen bags, which allowed the wool to "breathe."

Each collective farm in Žemaitija had flocks of sheep, tended by sheep watchers. The chief shepherd collected a salary and rode a horse, but every family had to help. If anyone could not take a turn, that person had to find someone to take their place. Watchers came to know the character of every sheep in their "brigada," or flock, which consistedof seventy or eighty animals.

In 2008, Donna, Dominic and I were able to see a hand-operated carding machine in a village near Vilkaviškis, in Suvalkija. Our host, Salomėja, and her late husband owned it, but it had not been used for several decades. During the years it was in operation, the machine in its tiny building helped many families to produce warm clothes.

Another such machine has been saved and restored by Gediminas Pupsys for use in his wool-processing business. His wife is a felt-maker and her father ran a woollen mill, using substantial machinery bought secondhand in the 1950s. When the Russian border was closed in 1991, trade dwindled because former customers were no longer able to buy from him. At the same time, cheap secondhand clothes from Poland and Western Europe became available. This took away the necessity for people to knit for their families. The machinery was switched off in 1996.

Gediminas's father-in-law now keeps a dairy herd in a former collective farm. Gediminas has moved the machinery into an empty building there, to process Lithuanian wool into felt and yarn. Large as they are, the machines for shaking, carding, felting, and spinning wool occupy only a small part of the building. Gediminas now markets his wool internationally, while his wife has opened a shop in Vilnius Old Town, where the hand-operated carding machine takes pride of place as a historic feature. Their wool is marketed online as Litwool (www.wool.lt).

Another enterprise, near Palanga on the Baltic coast, also involves making felt on a large scale. Antanas Poška is making yurts.

*Salomėja and her carding machine. DC.*

*Salomėja`s carding machine. DC.*

*Gediminas Pupsys with carding machine before it was moved to the new site. JLH.*

*Antanas Poška's yurt, Palanga. JLH.*

# Industrial Woollen Mills

Regional mills processed wool with machinery that was initially powered by water. Some were later converted to steam power or electricity. One of the last operating mills was in Žagarė, beside the Švėtė River, which originally powered the mill. The machinery was manufactured in Russia and Germany. It was already established by 1880, was later converted to a more modern power source, and continued running until around 1996. The mill building, with its chimney still in place, is now what is called a Technical Monument. While its machinery remains, it has been partly converted into flats. The wool room stands empty.

Anatolijus Gailiūnas of Pociūnėliai told me that his father was an engineer who travelled round the countryside to keep mills in working order. The last mill he worked on was the one at Žagarė.

At Lygumai, in the Šiauliai region, Anatolijus Morozovas has a working woollen mill called Siūlas (Yarn), producing knitting yarn and carded wool to fill what he refers to as blankets but I think of as quilts, or duvets. These are promoted for their health-giving properties, because the wool used to make them can "breathe," wick away moisture, and insulate well, and is also fire-retardant and natural. Although he uses Merino wool from the Southern Hemisphere, some local wool from Lithuanian sheep is also processed here, in its natural colours. The women who keep one or two sheep near Žagarė send their wool to this mill. Anatolijus collects it at the Žagarė market and sends knitting yarn in return. The three carding machines, made in Germany, are around a hundred years old. The spinning machinery is Russian.

Each time I have visited, this generous man has presented me with hanks of beautiful Lithuanian yarn.

As we write this chapter in 2013, the wool industry worldwide is in a period of change. As of 2011, when we reviewed the statistics, China was buying a large percentage of the Australian Merino which previously went to other industrialised countries. Meanwhile, in the European Union, legislation for the handling, transport, and scouring (washing) of raw wool has served to restrict production while new arrangements are being worked out. In 2008, no use had been found for this pile of wool shown in the photo on page 69, but in 2010, wool is in demand again.

Lithuanian industrial mills—some of which are located in Šiauliai, Kelmė, and Marijampolė—produce yarn and other wool products on a much bigger scale. For example, the mill at Marijampolė processes around a hundred tonnes of wool a year and exports its products.

*Lygumai Mill, exterior, 2008. DC.*

*Anatolijus Morozovas, of Lygumai, in his mill, 2008. DC.*

*Lygumai Mill, interior when working (unknown date, but before 1996). Photo compliments of Lygumai Mill.*

*Carding machine at Lygumai mill, 2008. DC.*

# Where to Buy Lithuanian Wool Yarn and Fibre

*From market traders in Vilnius, Donna and I have bought pure Lithuanian wool yarn, creamy in colour and still smelling of machine oil, but we could not find out which mill had produced it. After washing, it is beautifully soft.*

*Lithuanian wool yarn can be purchased at various markets and shops around the country, if you are lucky enough to be able to visit Lithuania. Litwool has a shop called Vilnos Namai (The Wool House) in Vilnius near the University at Universiteto g. 10. If you can't make the trip, you can order online directly at www.wool.lt or from their Etsy store at www.etsy.com/uk/shop/litwool.*

*Wool seller, Vilnius Market. JLH.*

*81 year-old woman from Marijampolė region, spinning in 1931. BB.*

# Hand Spinning

An old spinning wheel stands in almost every home I have visited, from remote rural farms to modern city apartments. The conversation that happens when I see this tool nearly always goes as follows:

"Do you spin?"

"No, but my grandmother did."

Hand spinning largely died out in the second half of the twentieth century. Wheels were put aside, and if sheep were kept, their fleeces were sent to a mill to be turned into yarn. Old photographs of people spinning wool are hard to come by. The museums have plenty of redundant hand-spinning equipment, and wheels are kept at home as ornamental reminders of a former way of life. That said, spinning wheels are still a potent symbol in the popular mindset. In a café in the new shopping mall in Šiauliai, a spinning wheel is part of the décor.

In April 2005, I was taken six kilometres down a forest track that led away from the main road to Druskininkai. In a clearing at the end of the track was an old farmstead, home of my friend Juratė's grandparents, Vincas and Ona, then in their seventies. They no longer kept livestock, except for some chickens, although they also had cats and a dog. In old wooden barns, their machines and implements stood quiet—a horse-powered mill for grinding grain that had later been driven by a generator, a turnip chopper, and many hand tools. A little way beyond the farm, the wide River Nemunas divides Lithuania from Belarus. In this traditional setting, the couple lived as they had always done, where they had brought up six children. Four of those members of the next generation, with their wives and children, assembled for a family gathering and I was privileged to be included.

We spent the day relaxing—walking in the forest, sitting in the sauna, then splashing in the stream beside the house—and then enjoyed a delicious feast of barbecued pork. When Ona heard that I was interested in spinning, she brought out her wheel and was delighted to demonstrate.

*Ona, spinning. Note the distaff, fixed to the wheel. She has a basket in the local style. A besom, an old-style broom made of twigs, stands near the house. JLH.*

*Pile of wool awaiting processing, Anykščiai region, 2008. DC.*

# Before Spinning Wheels

There is hardly an ancient site in Europe, from the Neolithic Period to the end of the Middle Ages, where spindle whorls have not been found. A spindle whorl is a fly wheel, usually made of stone or some other heavy material, which is fixed to a wooden shaft to make a spinning tool, called a spindle. Most of the shafts of ancient spindles have decayed, leaving only the whorls as evidence of their existence.

All-wooden Lithuanian hand spindles, one-piece designs from later dates that have not succumbed to the destructive forces of time, show up frequently in the country's museums. These have been shaped so that the lower half is wider, therefore heavier, to give the tool good turning momentum. A photograph taken in 1935 shows a man in bare feet, outdoors, using a spindle of this type to spin hemp yarn for bags and netting. He is drawing down the fibre from a distaff which is fixed to the stool he is sitting on (see photograph on page 60).

*One-piece spindles. DD.*

*Spindle whorl, replica in the Aušros Museum, Šiauliai. JLH.*

*Girl spinning at Kernavė "Days of Living Archaeology," 2008. DD.*

# Spinning Revival: Spinning School at Vilkija, 2006

As spinning seemed to be the missing link in the chain of turning wool from local fleeces into yarn, and because that is a skill I would be delighted to share, it was opportune for me to organise a spinning school during one of my trips to Lithuania. The idea was welcomed by Zigmas Kalesinskas, director of a unique independent college, the D. ir Z. Kalesinskų Liaudies Amatų Mokykla (the D. and Z. Kalesinskai College of Folk Crafts), located in Vilkija, about 14 km (8.5 miles) northwest of the city of Kaunas. Zigmas and his wife Dalia, an art and craft teacher, opened the school in the early 1990s. The elegant wooden house had been returned to Dalia's family after 1991, when Lithuania achieved independence from the U.S.S.R., and here she and Zigmas established courses in Lithuanian folk art—mainly weaving and ceramics—and traditional culture. Sadly, Dalia died in 1996, but she left a wonderful legacy in the school.

In March 2006, with deep snow and ice as far as the eye could see, I arrived at Vilkija with three other English women—Veronica, Rose, and Jean—each carrying a spinning wheel. At home, we had appealed for modern wheels in good working order, and our tools had been kindly donated by the Devon Guild of Weavers, Spinners and Dyers (in England) and the equipment suppliers Ashford and Haldane. At the airport, the wheels looked ghostly, swathed in bubble-wrap and parcel tape, but they survived the flight in good order and were soon put to work.

Students from the school and members of the public were invited to the ten-day course. Some of them brought old wheels from home. We spent a happy day pouring linseed oil over the dried-out wood and loose joints, fixing broken parts, and installing new drive bands. It was a joy to restore life to the neglected old wheels.

Soon, people were spinning with drop spindles and on wheels. They carded and spun Lithuanian wool in various natural colours, then plied the yarn and wound it into hanks. The students, already skilled in weaving, soon became proficient, and some experienced spinners helped to teach beginners. At the end of the course, we displayed the results publicly, and the media—both press and television—came to record the event.

*Restored Lithuanian spinning wheels. JLH.*

# Wool as Art

Almost until the end of the twentieth century, textiles in Lithuania were treated as essentially utilitarian. The exception were woven tapestries, which usually depicted religious themes. Weaving reached a high level of skill and regional variety in folk costume.

Wool and linen are the natural fibres used for textiles from prehistoric times. They continue as the basis for much of the artwork produced today, with the addition of (and in combination with) many other natural and synthetic materials.

The art academies in Vilnius and Kaunas have played a major part in pioneering the notion of textiles as fine art. In the last two decades, there has been a surge of creativity in many areas of art in Lithuania, in the context of which textiles have come to the fore.

The teaching of textile art began in Kaunas, which had been a centre of the textile industry, in 1940. It continued throughout the communist era, during which artistic self-expression was restricted, but decorative and folk art were encouraged as applied art with a practical purpose. Students made high-quality, aesthetically pleasing textiles, especially through the craft of weaving, for home furnishing and costume.

Because individual social, emotional, and political ideas were repressed, little stylistic development was possible until political freedom came in 1991.

Following independence, the technical skills which Lithuanians had developed under such constraints could be put to use in new ways. More recent textile art is outstanding in the ideas and techniques displayed. The new freedom, like the bursting of a dam, gave textile-art students the opportunity to produce works full of intellectual idealism and self-expression, and to convey their concepts in highly original forms.

The accomplishments of contemporary Lithuanian fibre artists have been recognised around the world. Eglė Bogdanienė, a textile artist who teaches at the Vilnius Academy of Art, has exhibited work not only in Lithuania, but internationally. Lina Jonikė, a student of Bogdanienė, has had work included in a number of major international textile exhibitions, including the famous international textile biennales, and has won frequent awards. Lina combines photography, printed onto woven fabric, with intricate embroidery in her works related to the human body. Her work invites viewers to reconsider their own attitudes to the subjects she represents.

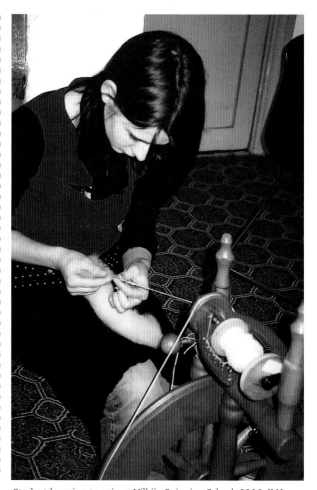

*Student learning to spin at Vilkija Spinning School, 2006. JLH.*

The first International Kaunas Textile Biennale took place in 1997 and attracted international acclaim from the start. In 2000, the Lithuanian Textile Artists' Guild was formed and a gallery opened, the only one in Lithuania until 2008, when Artifex, Vilnius Art Academy's textile art gallery, was established. Regular changing exhibitions are held in both galleries. In 2010, Artifex held an exhibition of felt art and included many works by the Baltos Kandys group and by Eglė Bogdanienė.

Weaving, dyeing, printing, knitting, felt-making, and some less orthodox techniques are used in contemporary textile art, in innovative ways. Among the materials employed are wool and other animal and vegetable fibres, along with metals, foods, or plastics. Pieces operate in two and three dimensions, often on a large scale. The subject matter ranges from abstract to highly figurative. Many works explore aspects of the human body, of the self or the other; consider self-examination; study the contrasts between the public and the private; reflect on the individual's place in the world; or assess attitudes to privacy, gender, age, death, and inequality. All of these difficult issues are interpreted with subtlety, sensitivity, humour, and frankness.

Nothing is excluded from the choices of subject or materials available to contemporary Lithuanian textile artists. For instance, Severija Inčirauskaitė-Kriaunevičienė used the extremely traditional embroidery technique of cross stitch on rescued metal objects to make memorable and startling work: roses on a car door (providing echoes of the funeral after a car crash), flowers on a spade, and fruit on pewter plates.

I met Eglė Bogdanienė on my first visit to the Vilnius Academy of Art in 2004, in her lively textile department. On the walls of the corridors, an exhibition by first-year students was entitled Fish. The place was bursting with ideas.

Every time I have been to the art academy since then, I have been caught in the same bustle of activity, warm welcome, and innovation. Eglė's presence and creativity pervade the department. She and her work are a single entity. In her own art, she becomes part of the work. And her influence on achieving the status of fine art for textiles in Lithuania is beyond doubt.

More recently, Laura Pavilonyte, one of the Baltos Kandys group has become head of the textile art department.

*Five of the Baltos Kandys group of felt artists, at our first meeting in 2004. JLH.*

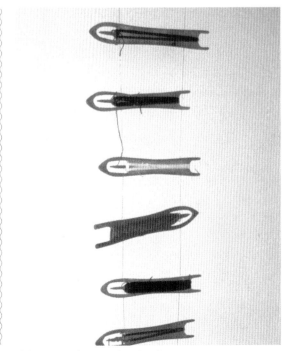

*Fish, 2004, using weaving shuttles. JLH.*

*Eglė Bogdanienė at work. JLH.*

*Knitter: Vaičiūnienė. She knitted and crocheted gloves and mittens, socks, shawls, and sweaters with rich combinations of colors and patterns. She learned from her mother and made items for sale. Circa 1940, Kutiškiai village, Šiauliai county. BB*

# Chapter 6: Knitters and Folk Art

**June**

One of my aims when I began my Lithuanian adventure was to get a feel for the role hand knitting plays in the domestic life and economy of families and individuals. I also wanted to explore how skill levels might vary between people who live in urban and rural communities. Because I have encountered people on a serendipitous basis, my results come in the form of impressions, not hard statistics.

## Earliest Knitting in Lithuania

On my first visit to Lithuania, I met Viktoras Liutkus, then director of an art gallery in Vilnius and now head of the painting department at the Vilnius Academy of Art. Regarding hand knitting, he said that the craft came relatively late to Lithuania and Latvia, which are predominantly Catholic and were most heavily influenced by their neighbours to the south. Knitting became established earlier in Estonia, where Protestantism and a northern Scandinavian influence prevailed. Although this does not go so far as to say that knitting is a Protestant activity, I found this perspective interesting. It does seem that knitting arrived in Lithuania by way of the Baltic Sea, and that it first became known in the coastal areas and then moved inland.

*Photos this page from left to right: Doll in Lithuanian national costume holding a traditional string instrument called a kanklės. JLH; a pair of mittens from June's collection. JLH; a mitten from June's collection. JLH.*

The journey hand knitting has taken, from its origins in North Africa and Spain (as an aside related to Viktoras's observation: a Catholic country), forms a fascinating story, with plenty of literature dedicated to it. Suffice it to say that when knitting finally did arrive in Lithuania, it was absorbed into the folk tradition and developed characteristics which make Lithuanian knitting distinct from the craft as practiced in neighbouring areas.

Knitting in Lithuania before about 1900 has left little tangible trace, either in documentation or in examples of actual work. As an everyday activity which made use of time when hands were not engaged in other household, family, or farming tasks, knitting was not considered important enough to record.

# Early Knitting Books

The first Lithuanians to value hand knitting as a form of folk art worthy of documentation were Antanas Tamošaitis, a teacher, artist, writer, and, later, political activist; and his wife Anastazija, an artist, weaver, and teacher. In 1935, Antanas and Anastazija noted the variations in knitted gloves and mittens across the five cultural

regions of Lithuania, and collected samples from each region to exhibit in Kaunas. They published many books about folk art, including *Mezgimas* (Knitting; 1935) and *Namie austi drabužiai* (Homemade Woven Clothing; 1937), by Anastazija, and *Sodžiaus menas, kn. 5: Mezgimo-nėrimo raštai* (Village Arts, no. 5: Charted Knitting and Crochet Patterns; 1933), by Antanas. The publication of the designs in these books "liberated" them from their places of origin (or adoption). Instead of being passed around only amongst family and neighbours, they became more widely available. This process has spread like ripples on a pond, from village to global horizons. Now anyone, anywhere, can knit patterns which evolved in remote Lithuanian farmsteads.

# Knitting Traditions

The popularity of knitting in Lithuania over time has followed economic trends. In the financially lean late nineteenth and early twentieth centuries, knitting was a necessary and practical means of providing families with warm accessories. People on small village holdings kept one or two sheep, and sheared, washed, and spun the wool by hand, then the women knitted gloves, mittens, and socks to keep themselves, their menfolk, and their children warm in the cold winter weather.

As seen in the development of folk art and crafts in all regions, tradition played its part

*Nijolė Šopienė's "India rubber" mittens. This resembles the pattern of a tyre's tread; it is very similar to the woven sashes worn at celebrations and by dignitaries. JLH.*

in the history and development of Lithuanian knitting. Gloves acquired a ritual or sacred significance, being made for the hand by the hand. From medieval times, gifts of gloves were highly prized status items in Europe. Gloves surviving from the medieval era include elaborate silk gloves that were given to kings and bishops. Throughout society, gloves were presented at weddings and funerals. In Lithuania, a young woman's suitability as a potential bride or daughter-in-law was in part judged by the skill she displayed in the quality and quantity of her hand-knitted offerings. If a prospective bride could knit splendid gloves, she would (the thinking went) make a hard-working, conscientious, and caring wife and mother, capable of maintaining a well-managed family home.

Fashion has been, and continues to be, a big influence on what is knitted. With the industrialisation of textile production, affecting both yarn and cloth, the absolute need to spin and weave in the home diminished. People with money could buy first the materials for their clothes, including exotic imports, and later could acquire ready-to-wear garments. Thus grew the idea that purchased items were better than home-made, because the upper classes could afford to buy, while people living in a largely money-less economy of the lower classes had to make their own clothes from raw materials. Only in recent decades has the artisan begun to regain true appreciation by others.

In Lithuania, craftwork has survived on a wider scale than in many societies more deeply influenced by industrialisation, especially perhaps because commercial goods were so hard to come by during Soviet times. In the Soviet era, folk art and craft were encouraged by the state at the same time that industries, especially farming, were centralised. In 1985, as part of an ethnographic study of the

*Knitter Barutaitė Elena. 1939. Milžinkapiai farmstead, Šiaulėnai rural district, Šiauliai county. BB*

Soviet peoples, a Russian atlas was published that shows regional crafts in Lithuania, Latvia, and Estonia. It includes information on the distribution of local design on knitted gloves and mittens, taken from surveys of various time periods from the mid-nineteenth century to the 1950s. When I asked a friend in England to help translate the Russian text, he was amused and rather puzzled by the description of a motif as "India rubber." As it turned out, this referred to the diagonal motif across the back of mittens, such as those from the Šiauliai region.

# Craft Groups

Groups of craftspeople meet all over Lithuania. Some artisans belong to branches of the Lithuanian Folk Artists Union (Lietuvos Tautodailininkų Sąjunga). The society organises retail shops in the major towns and cities, in addition to a programme of publications, exhibitions, and a system of "masters." Weaving dominates the textile crafts, because it supplies fabric for the regional costumes worn at events, particularly the biennial national song festivals. These gatherings, involving a strong sense of national identity, became significant in ending the Soviet era in the Baltic States, as people poured their feelings of solidarity and national pride into music. The events between 1987 and 1991 that led to the restoration of the independence of Estonia, Latvia and Lithuania are now known as "The Singing Revolution." People dress up to participate in the song festivals, adding to the women's basic bodice and skirt or the men's jacket and trousers an abundance of folk textiles: woven sashes, elaborate aprons, embroidered linen shirts, a rich variety of head gear, and felt coats and boots.

Some interesting crossover has taken place between textiles and other folk-art traditions. Another form of folk art used wood and metal, for which both Christian and pagan symbols provide traditional subjects. Wooden crosses topped with ironwork can be seen beside roads and in village centres.

An amazing example of this practice of installing crosses in public locations is Lithuania's famous Hill of Crosses (Kryžių kalnas), near Šiauliai, which has become a national shrine. During the Soviet era, when religion was banned, crosses were added, including many commemorating the death of a child. Although crosses were repeatedly removed by the authorities, people persisted in erecting more. The site now attracts thousands of pilgrims and tourists, who add to the innumerable collection of crosses, which range from the elaborate to the flimsy. On my first visit I was delighted to find two knitted crosses!

The local museum in the former palace at Alanta has a display of small wooden figures carved by Jonas Matelionis which depict the everyday activities of traditional village life. I particularly like the one depicting Father Christmas driving a sled pulled by an elk.

Craftsman in Pociūnėliai fixes an iron cross onto a wooden base. JLH.

Knitted crosses at Kryžių kalnas, 2004. JLH.

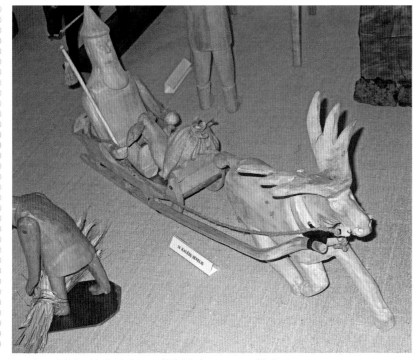

*Carving of sled with "Kalėdų Senelis" (Christmas Grandfather). JLH.*

*Toma Garuckas, with bundles of willow ready to sell to basket makers. JLH.*

Baskets are widely used throughout Lithuania. They range from tiny, distinctive "berry" baskets to large containers, made from willow. The Garuckas family of Pociūnėliai grow willows for basket makers in Kaunas.

The painting of landscapes in all seasons, of scenes of village life, of farming, and of folk tales is part of the Lithuanian tradition, much of it in naïve style. Among the most celebrated Lithuanian painters is Magdalena Stankunienė, born in the village of Ozeli, in the Šunskai region, in 1925. She studied art and textiles in Germany and England, and emigrated to the United States of America. Her work includes charming scenes of rural life, and can be seen in the Vilkaviškis Regional Museum, in her native area (see more on page 99).

Ceramics are well represented in folk art, with a distinctive Lithuanian style that can be seen in many forms, from everyday pottery to elaborate tiles used for facing the large stoves in old houses. Throughout Europe, slipware is made for household pottery. The Lithuanian version is simple but distinctive. The folk-art school at Vilkija taught ceramics, as do some local schools. The children at Pociūnėliai School are always pleased to present visitors with examples of their creative work.

The last decade has seen a revival of the prehistoric style known as black pottery, made from Lithuanian clay and fired in open-air kilns at 950°C (1750°F) for up to fifteen hours. The wood smoke gives the pots their distinctive black finish.

As modern concepts of business, entrepreneurship, and marketing develop in post-Soviet society, initiatives to sell craftwork become more numerous. Groups of makers produce catalogues of their work, often funded by grants from government agencies.

# Festivals and Markets

Traditional outlets for craftwork include both local markets and special craft markets. The biggest special craft market, held annually in early March, is called Kaziuko Mugė (St. Casimir's Feast). It attracts makers from all over Lithuania, who come together to sell their best work in a glorious pageant of colour, set against the magnificent backdrop of the snow-covered Baroque architecture of Vilnius Old Town.

Although the festival brings an abundance of folk crafts to Vilnius, through most of the year the city's main street, Pilies Gatvė (Castle Street), offers products made of amber, leather, linen, wool, wood, basketry materials, and iron. Woollen gloves, mittens, socks, and hats can be found here, hand-knitted in traditional patterns. Even so, similar designs can be seen all over Lithuania, as previously distinct regional identities become merged. The symbolism of early designs has largely become generalised, and their significance forgotten.

Other towns hold folk markets throughout the year, in addition to regular produce markets. These outlets are not generally available to knitters in remote rural villages. Elderly women, in particular, are one of my concerns, because they have very few ways to earn money through their expertise. They have great resources— skill, experience, knowledge of traditional designs, and time—but they earn little income and often are experiencing failing health. Having spent most of their lives under the Soviet system, when initiative was discouraged, they find it difficult to think in terms of "business." I have tried to encourage some of these talented women to work together to market their work on the internet with the help of an "agent" (someone from the village who has computer skills and could do things like receive orders, commission work, and despatch goods), but they have difficulty with the notions of trusting someone else with their money— someone who would by necessity know about their own and other people's business.

*Easter palms for sale at St Casimir's Feast, Vilnius. JLH.*

They are quite happy for me to buy direct from them as individuals, and I do inevitably purchase examples of their excellent work in return for their generosity in sharing their skill and experience with me. However, this does not amount to a sustainable system. I have even arranged for representatives from the tax office to speak to groups of village women, to reassure them of their rights and responsibilities regarding sales of their knitted goods, but the older generation have too many fears. The idea of village cooperatives seems to them too much like the collective system of their past. Maybe the time will come when these deserving women will find the right outlet for their skill, time, and effort. If they could only work together to make gloves, scarves, socks, and sweaters, using designs which derive from their locality, their work could be recognised and promoted. They would benefit from their abilities in so many ways. Self-esteem, an independent income, and a sense of purpose would all follow and presumably enrich their lives.

## Not Your Grandmother's Knitting?

Of the excellent hand knitters throughout Lithuania, many are, like the women I have just described, elderly. Grandmothers knit for their grandchildren, but younger women are occupied with careers and families, and it is easier for them to buy ready-made clothes than to choose patterns, buy yarn, and find the time to sit still and knit.

*Knitter living near Ukmergė, typical of retired women holding the knitting traditions of rural Lithuania in their hands. JLH.*

Younger women prefer up-to-date fashions and clothes they can put into a washing machine. They have the means to buy, and the shops and markets have the goods to sell. Often, these are clothes made of synthetic fibers, imported from the Far East. Garments from other countries also intrigue them. Traders with secondhand and surplus clothes from other European countries visit villages. (I have seen many people wearing T-shirts with totally inappropriate slogans in languages obviously not understood by the wearer!)

Nowadays, knitting is undergoing a world-wide revival after a generation of disinterest. The tide is turning and the qualities of pure wool are once more being valued. Modern styles of knitted and crocheted clothing are interesting, can be varied to suit individual taste, and can be worn with pride. Knitting is seen to be adventurous, experimental, and fun. Most of the shops selling knitting yarn in Lithuania stock imported wool, much of it Merino from the Southern Hemisphere,

that has been processed in Italy. In addition, they offer a huge variety of fashion yarns, not only made of wool, but of other natural fibres including silk, cotton, linen, alpaca, camel, and more, as well as synthetics. In the last few years, books of knitting patterns have become more widely available in Lithuania, and the home-craft magazine Kraitė (The Craft Basket) contains many ideas for handicrafts, including knitting.

At the same time, native Lithuanian materials can be found by those who seek them out: I have bought Lithuanian wool in market stalls and from the mill at Lygumai (see page 66 in Chapter 5: The Wool).

It was within this context of folk knitting that I saw the Lithuanian knitters that I met during my travels. The following sections are a scrapbook of my travels and memories. I hope you will enjoy visiting different cities, towns, and villages in Lithuania with me and meeting the knitters who have been so kind and generous to share their work and love of knitting with me over the years.

*Naomi modelling knitwear by Aušra (pictured at right), at a fashion show in Mungrisdale, Cumbria, England. JLH.*

*Aušra Kaveckienė wearing her own knitting designs, at home in Kuršėnai, Lithuania. JLH.*

# Mes, vilnos gamintojai...

Tatjana RAMANAUSKIENĖ

Veronikai Barningem verpimo ratelis – mieliausias dr

„Jūsų ketinimai ir norai – garantija
štos kokybės rankų darbo gami-
ns“ – rašoma skelbime, kuris kovo
l dienomis kvietė dalyvauti seminare,
tame tradiciniam vilnos apdirbimui
įu sąlygomis. Seminaras vyko Vilki-
, Dalios ir Zigmo Kalesinskų aukštes-
oje liaudies amatų mokykloje,
loje jau prieš dvejus metus pirmuo-
seminarus vilnos augintojams,
ėjoms, mezgėjoms ir audėjoms vedė
nia iš Anglijos, menų magistrė ir avių
intoja Džiunė HOLL (June Hall). Šį
ą ji atvyko drauge su trimis kolegė-
Didžiosios Britanijos vilnos gamin-
gildijos narėmis. Seminaro metu
viai mokėsi paruošti nukirptą vilną,
ti rateliu ir verpstuku, megzti,
inosi dažymo ir audimo subtilybes.
cutinę seminaro dieną dalyviai įsteigė
os verpėjų, audėjų ir mezgėjų gildiją –
ą tokią organizaciją ne tik Lietuvo-
bet ir visoje Rytų Europoje.

Džiunė Holl nuo mažens moka visus darbus, susijusius su avimis ir vilnomis.

D. ir Z. Kalesinskų mokyklos
dėstytoja Asta Vandytė išmoko
verpti ir rateliu, ir verpstuku.
„Mano siūlų sruogoje, gerai
įsižiūrėję, rastume labai lygiai
suverptų atkarpėlių,“ – juokėsi ji
paskutinę seminarų dieną.

Vakarų šalyse gildiją po-
irinanti Džiunė Hol ren-
ne tik seminarus, bet ir
os festivalius. Pernai ja-
dalyvavusi Vilkijos liau-
amatų mokykla pristatė
icinius pinikus, kuriais
šomėjo daugelis Vakarų
darbių mėgėjų.
Perskaitę skelbimą apie
narą ir gildijos steigimą,

rios tradicinių Lietuvos amatų grandys ilgainiui sunyko.
Tebeauginame avis, mokame
megzti, austi, daugelis dar
prisimena, kaip verpdavo jų
močiutės, ir tebesaugo jų
verpimo ratelius, bet karšti
vilnos namuose nebemokame.
XIX a. pabaigoje ir XX a.
pradžioje Lietuvoje buvo
įsteigta daug karšyklų ir ūki-

to pluoštas atsargiai skalauja-
mas ir džiovinamas. Kai rei-
kia sukaršti, imamos dvi
lentelės su standžios vielos
dantukais – tarp jų suspaus-
tos gijos pašomos tol, kol
gražiai išsikedena į tolygius,
verpti tinkamus kuodelius.
Iš keturių atvykusių seminaro vadovių geriausiai apie
vilnos paruošimą verpti iš-

gobeleno audimo kursus, ji
atsitiktinai pamatė ratelį ir
labai juo susidomėjo. Tuo-
met užsirašė į kitus kursus,
išmoko verpti rankomis ir
rateliu ir taip pamėgo šį
užsiėmimą, kad dabar be jo
nebeįsivaizduoja savo gyve-
nimo.
Mezgimo raštais ir pa-
slaptimis seminare dalijosi

Jaunos lietuvaitės uoliai atkuria prarastąją na

# Knitters in Žagarė

Žagarė is a village that holds a special place in my heart. It is a border town with a lively history, located on the northern boundary of Lithuania, with Latvia lying directly north of it. It lies on a long-established trade route that runs north and south through the Baltic states, connecting Warsaw in the south to Tallinn in Estonia, almost directly north, and to St. Petersburg to the northeast. Traffic along this path also travelled west across the Baltic Sea to the Scandinavian countries. The village grew up at the crossing of the River Švėtė, and the bridge across that river joins old and new Žagarė.

Ancient earthworks and a rare geological exposure of dolomite give the landscape round Žagarė a distinctive character. Merchants and craftspeople, most of them Jewish, lived here in the early twentieth century, and Žagarė thrived with a population of around fifteen thousand people until World War II. Over the course of the war, the population shrank to around twenty-five hundred inhabitants living near a mass grave of Jewish victims.

Žagarė became impoverished. Until 1998, only sixty percent of its houses had electricity. In 2004, there were a total of around two thousand residents, of whom about half were pensioners and thirty percent of the rest were unemployed. Over the last decade, many changes have been made to improve the quality of life for the residents, and the natural beauty of the area remains. In 2009, Lithuania Link handed over its funds and mandate to the newly formed Žagarė Club in Vilnius, where natives of Žagarė who live and work in the capital continue to interest themselves in the welfare of their hometown.

The older generation of women in Žagarė are skillful knitters. I interviewed some of them in 2008, including Eugenija. She has lived a full life, part of it in Latvia. Although she suffers from diabetes, which limits what she can do, she happily demonstrates plying yarn on her blue-painted spinning wheel. Her old carders are unused, because she no longer spins her own yarns. When she was young, people kept sheep and she used to spin wool. Now there are few sheep. She has some yarn from the old times, but now her daughter-in-law buys wool yarn for her. She shows me items she has knitted. There are mittens with entrelac cuffs; socks, their heels reinforced with handspun fox hair; and lacy sweaters and shawls.

Eugenija learned to knit from her mother when she was seven years old and made dresses for her dolls, using needles made from the wood of fir trees. Since then she has always knitted—dresses, socks, gloves—for her family and sometimes for other people. She knits much less now, however, because of her weak health.

*Žagarė. JLH.*

Eugenija plying yarn. JLH.

Mittens. JLH.

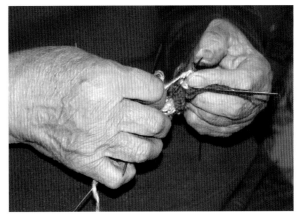

Eugenija knitting. JLH.

Entrelac mitten cuffs. JLH.

Socks with fox hair heel. JLH.

Another woman I met is Stanislava, or Stasė, who has knitted since she was six years old. She says, "I taught myself. It was very interesting." She knits for her family, especially her grandchildren. Earlier, she knitted clothes and sold them. Though she does not knit as much as she used to, because she has a problem with her eyes, she says, "I always knit. I knit various types of clothes, shawls, tablecloths, serviettes [napkins], socks, gloves, and also neckties for men. I knit because I am interested. I always have to be doing something. I experiment. I am a 'seeker.'"

Stasė buys wool from the village shop, or wool is given to her. Until she was twenty-two, she lived in the country, and she learned to spin. Later, there was no time to spin, but she still has her wheel, which she brings out of storage to show me. Her best room is filled with a display of her work.

Another of the Žagarė knitters is Bronislava, or Bronė. In her seventies, she has been knitting all her life; her mother taught her when she was very young. She knits for her children, grandchildren, relatives, and friends. She buys wool at the local shop or at market, but doesn't spin. She knits because she loves it, and she would knit more if she had better health.

And there is Janina-Marija, who has knitted since childhood, especially socks. Her mother died young and she was brought up by her father, who taught her to knit. The first socks she made had holes in them, but she soon learned to join the heels securely.

"I knitted everything. About eight years ago I was asked to knit an owl. Now I knit animals to order: horoscope signs, cockerels, monkeys, rats, or whatever people want. For the Žagarė Cherry Festival, I knitted cherries. I knit for pleasure. I take part in various exhibitions and knitting shows. I am a member of the craft club. Women need to sell their work. At home, I have a lot of yarn. I can't use the best, most expensive, yarn—I buy too much! I buy affordable yarn in the shops and maybe at market. I was given a bag of yarn at the craft club."

Women in Žagarė and other communities in northern Lithuania used to be able to buy wool from a representative of a company called Texrena. The company produced 100 percent wool as well as wool-acrylic blend yarn, that was sturdy, soft, and affordable. Each week, the salesman came to take orders, and on the next visit he delivered the yarn. The company is no longer in business, so this useful service has ceased.

*Stasė with her spinning wheel. JLH.*

*Janina-Marija with her work. JLH.*

*Crocheted table centre, linen, by Stasė. JLH.*

*I ordered wool from the salesman, in the square at Žagarė. 2006. JLH.*

*Bronė with hats, gloves, socks, and mittens, at a meeting we held to discuss possibilities for marketing hand-knitted products. JLH.*

# From My Notebook— 1 May 2004

This was the day when Lithuania became part of the European Union. It was a day of celebration in Žagarė, as in most other Lithuanian communities. I was there, with my sister and with representatives of Lithuania Link. We had stayed the night in a modernised forest lodge, previously part of the Žagarė manor and later used by the Žagarė National Park.

After a walk into the town, we visited an exhibition of old photographs of Žagarė, then arrived in the square where a stage was ready for the day's events. The youth-club leader, Tomas, aged seventeen, had planned the programme of music, dance, song, and speeches. He not only hosted the show, but also planned and hosted a concert in the evening.

We were guests at a banquet where a special cake was cut to round off the celebrations.

*Celebration cake—"Mes esame Europoje!" ("We are in Europe").*

# Knitters in Pociūnėliai and Baisogala

On my first working visit to Lithuania, in 2003, I was introduced to the community of Pociūnėliai, a village eight kilometres (five miles) along what was at the time an unsurfaced road through forest and farmland. Women brought their knitting and other needlecraft to show me. Roma, the mayor (seniūnė) for the rural district, introduced me, and Ona, an English teacher at the school, translated. Roma was totally committed to improving the lives of her community members, especially of the women, and saw rural tourism and economic independence as the way to a better future. The fifteen women at the meeting found it difficult to obtain materials for textile work. Only one woman could spin and no one locally kept sheep. These women belonged to a Lithuanian craft organisation but would have liked to be in touch with a wider scene.

Since that first meeting, both my sister Vivien and I have worked with Roma, the school, and the village, where we have always received great kindness and the warmest of welcomes.

To encourage the women to knit traditional patterns in pure wool, I arranged a visit to the M. K. Čiurlionis National Art Museum in Kaunas, to examine the reserve collections of historic knitting.

(The museum was named for Mikalojus Konstantinas Čiurlionis, see page 95.) Janina, curator of textiles, made gloves and mittens available for the women to chart on the squared paper of their notebooks.

One of the knitters, Bronė, came from the next village, Baisogala. She invited me to meet her village knitters, which I was pleased to do. Again, the women exhibited their handiwork and the meeting ended with a delicious tea, as I found most meetings in Lithuania tend to do. This event led to many more visits to Baisogala, which I came to know well. On one occasion, I was there at Easter, which Bronė's family

*First meeting with Pociūnėliai women, 2003. JLH.*

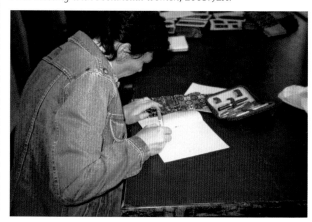

*Giedrė (from Pociūnėliai) chart patterns from her area from resource materials in the M. K. Čiurlionis National Art Museum, 2004. JLH*

celebrated with local customs: dyed eggs; a birch branch decorated with tiny wooden rabbits and eggs, which would remain in the home until the leaves sprouted; and an Easter breakfast—a lavish spread of traditional foods.

On the following Sunday, I was invited to join the "Second Easter" (the Sunday after Easter), celebrated in the culture house, or community centre, where the older generation gathered for a feast, games (including egg rolling), accordion music, and dancing. The "Easter Mother" presided over the occasion and I was presented with a crocheted egg cosy in the shape of a hen's head.

Another gift was a copy of an old book of knitting patterns, with black-and-white photographs. The cover was missing, and one page had been torn and then carefully sewn together again. I discovered that this was the Tamošaitis book, *Mezgimo-nėrimo raštai*, full of patterns based on the knitting collection in the M. K. Čiurlionis National Art Museum. Bronė knitted a pair of socks for me, from the book: they have lace-up fronts.

*Dyed eggs for Easter, at the Damanauskas home, Baisogala. JLH.*

*Easter breakfast at the Damanauskas family home, Baisogala. JLH.*

*Egg cosy for Easter. JLH.*

*Easter Mother, Baisogala, 2005. JLH.*

*Laced socks knitted by Bronė of Baisogala, from early twentieth-century pattern. JLH.*

# Knitters in Šiauliai

When I asked to see the knitting collection in the Aušros Museum, in the city of Šiauliai, I met Audronė Tamulienė, who translated for me. She is the librarian and translator at this republican museum, and she speaks fluent English. This was the beginning of a firm friendship.

The collection of knitted gloves and mittens, which date from the early to the mid-twentieth century, contains interesting examples. As with most gloves, there is very little representation of animal life, but plenty of stylised foliage and flowers. Most decoration takes the form of geometric symbols and abstract patterns.

One exception is a pair of mittens bordered with delightful ducks and chickens.

Several pairs of gloves and mittens in the collection are made of undyed wool, in creamy white and dark brown. Patterns are similar to those on handwear knitted from dyed wool, particularly the stylised tulip and eight-pointed star. Some pairs are lined for extra warmth, constructed with thicker yarn for the outer layer and finer-spun yarn inside. Some of the early examples are made from handspun yarn. While some pairs have natural colour for decoration, others are self-coloured, featuring panels of textured stitches that would have been described in early Lithuanian books as raised knitting but that would be more familiar to English-speaking knitters as cables, on the backs of the hands.

Nijolė, who lives a little way out of the city, knitted some replicas of these gloves and mittens for me. I appreciated these very much. She does not have a great deal of time to knit, as she runs a dairy farm and makes delicious cheese which she sells in the market at Šiauliai.

Nijolė showing her knitted mittens. JLH.

Mittens with cuff design featuring domestic fowl. DC.

Replicas of natural wool gloves from the Aušros Museum, in Šiauliai, knitted by Nijolė. JLH.

*Genovaitė Žukauskienė, left, wearing a dress she knitted, and holding a copy of* 500 Knitting Patterns. *Audronė Tamuliene, right. JLH.*

*Gauntlet mittens knitted by Anelė Mocevičiūtė. JLH.*

Genovaitė Žukauskienė was a museum curator in Šiauliai. When we visited her home, she greeted us wearing an elegant black dress, which she had knitted herself. In the hall stood the family's spinning wheel, and we browsed through her collection of knitting pattern books. One of the books she showed me was *500 Knitting Patterns*, by Zita Morkūnaitė. Later, I met the author in Kaunas.

Audronė, my friend in Šiauliai, comes from a family of knitters. She was born in Rumšiškės. Her grandmother, Julija Bunevičiūtė-Mocevičienė, who came from the Alytus region, spun wool yarn (see page 55). In the 1990s Audronė's aunt, Anelė Mocevičiūtė, knitted a pair of mittens with gauntlets, then fashionable throughout Europe. Unusually, they are decorated with a pattern of squirrels.

Audronė's mother was also a great knitter. This frail old lady died in 2013, but two years earlier, she could still remember how to knit, and was proud of the lovely clothes she had made for the family over the years.

Audronė's husband, Jonas Tamulis, has memories of gloves and mittens from his childhood in the mid-twentieth century. He remembers that gloves and mittens were made for specific purposes. Fine gloves were worn in church with best clothes. He says, "Viskas buvo geriausa," everything was the best, "to meet God." Gloves suited winter church-going better than mittens, because the separate fingers made it easier to turn pages and feel the rosary. Yet because of the cold, people often walked to church with an extra layer of mittens covering their gloves.

For work outdoors, people needed warm and thick mittens. Mittens in the Šiauliai area often had vertical stripes on the cuffs and horizontal decorations on the backs of the hands. Ties in the cuffs were decorated with two or three pompoms of different colours. For forest work—using axes and carrying wood, for example—mittens had leather from cows or from bull calves sewn on the palms, that would be replaced when worn out.

Thicker handspun wool was used for socks (three-ply) and for gloves (two-ply). Jonas remembers his mother dyeing wool with chemical dyes she bought at the market in Šiauliai. The coloured yarns she made, in red, yellow, and green, decorated mittens and gloves of natural white and brown wool from their own sheep.

Socks and mittens were knitted large, then felted by rubbing them on a washboard with soap and hot water. The felting made them both stronger and warmer. Scarves were never felted. Woollen gloves, mittens, and scarves were knitted as gifts from young women to young men. Jonas still has the scarf Audronė knitted for him when they were courting.

*Audronė, wearing a coat knitted by her mother about twenty-five years earlier. JLH.*

*Audronė's mother, knitting in 2010, with some of the garments she had made. The family's dog, Ausis ("long-eared") keeps her company. JLH.*

# Knitters in Vilkija

Vilkija and its school of folk-crafts (D. ir Z. Kalesinskų Liaudies Amatų Mokykla) have occupied a large part of my work in Lithuania. In fact, the school has almost become a home from home. Before I went there for the first time, I had been told about a school where traditional textile crafts were taught, but did not know what to expect. When I stepped off the bus with a student from Kaunas who had volunteered to translate for me, I found a steep road that led up to a gracious, old wooden house, painted deep yellow. Inside, we were welcomed by the smiling director, Zigmas Kalesinskas.

This unusual school, independent but recognised by the state, provided craft-teaching and folklife studies for students who could then progress to the art academies. It was set up in the early 1990s, after Independence, when property was restored to the families who had owned it before Soviet times. Zigmas's wife, Dalia, was a co-heiress and art teacher. Together, they realised her dream and Zigmas gave up his career as a veterinarian to administrate the school. Sadly, Dalia died in 1996, but the school continued under Zigmas's direction until 2007.

Weaving was always the main textile craft taught, but interest in hand-spinning and knitting were included. It was here that I organised a spinning school for students and the public in 2006 (see page 71).

Zigmas now runs a two-week summer academy each year, to teach young people between eight and eighteen years old about traditional crafts and folklore. In 2009, I taught knitting at this academy. We enjoyed using two needles made from broom handles, cut in two and sharpened to a point, to knit fabric with about twenty lengths of yarn held together to make a thick strand. The students worked in pairs, choosing the colours of wool and supporting the needles for each other. It was great fun and the results became bags, cushions, mats, and wall hangings. I had knitted an example to show them the kind of thing they could make with these tools and materials: a rug for Zigmas's young dog, Kaukas—a delightfully mischievous puppy who wanted to chew his gift, and could not keep still to have his photograph taken.

*Zigmas shows me hand weaving on my first visit to the school, 2004. JLH.*

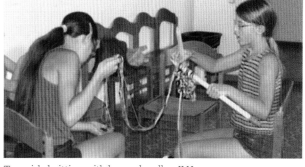

*Two girls knitting with broom handles. JLH.*

*Children selecting coloured yarns. JLH.*

*Kaukas and his new rug. JLH.*

My sister and I established a scholarship for one young person to attend the summer academy each year, in memory of our mother, Lenna, who was a painter in her later years. She was never able to visit Lithuania to see the land of her ancestors.

Zigmas and some of his teachers, Asta, Rasma, and Birutė, and Lina, a friend of his who is an artist, have all travelled in the other direction as well, to Cumbria in northwest England, where I live. At Woolfest, a fiber-oriented event held each June, they wore their colourful national costumes and demonstrated weaving braid, beaded knitting, and sprang, which is an ancient form of textile construction used in Lithuania to make head-dresses. To work in sprang, the craftsperson stretches threads between two bars that keep them under tension. The structure is made by the simple (but not easy) method of crossing these stretched threads over each other in elaborate patterns. Because the threads are secured at each end, every set of crosses (made in the middle) affects the strands at either end.

Zigmas and Asta have researched, catalogued, and published two collections covering the folk textiles in the Marijampolė Local Lore Museum, which are woven sashes and aprons.

The steep back lane from the Vilkija Folk Art School and Zigmas's home is delightful at all times of year. In the spring, it is full of blossom; in autumn, bright apples roll about; and in winter, it becomes a glistening passageway of snow and ice. When it's sparkling with cold, I have had many a perilous scramble down the lane in a hurry to catch a bus. When spring comes again, a trip down the lane reveals a garden that contains an old wooden house with a porch, surrounded by fruit trees and flowers. This was the home of folklore collectors Antanas and Jonas Juška. The building now houses the A. and J. Juškos Ethnic Culture Museum. Here I have seen examples of local gloves.

Textile historian Inga Nenienė, whose doctoral studies involved examining the woven shawls women used to wear, discussed the gloves with me. She also showed me gloves knitted in the region by her grandmother and great-grandmother, both from the Rokiškis region.

One night, I visited the Juška museum to meet the curator, and was treated to a memorable musical experience. Standing in a room lit by only one candle, a musician played a huge wind instrument which reached from his head to his toes. The music, eerie and exciting, made a deep bubbling sound that seemed to come from far away.

*Vilkija comes to Woolfest: Rasma, Asta, Zigmas and Birute with their exhibition. JLH.*

# Knitters in Kaunas

Kaunas was the capital of Lithuania from 1919 to 1939, and still retains the feeling of an important centre of culture, commerce, and city life. Beginning from the domed Catholic church of St. Michael the Archangel, a long pedestrian walkway leads down the arrow-straight Laisvės Alėja (Liberty Avenue) to the cobbled Kaunas Old Town, the ancient settlement. Built near the confluence of the Nemunas and Neris rivers, with the ruined castle testifying to the city's strategic position, Kaunas is a thorough mixture of ancient and modern standing side by side. A wide road beside the water, always busy with traffic, skirts the Old Town. Airy bridges span the river, and blocks of flats, modern shopping malls, and car parks rise above the centuries-old brick buildings.

## M. K. Čiurlionis National Art Museum

Kaunas is the home of the M. K. Čiurlionis National Art Museum, named in honour of artist Mikalojus Konstantinas Čiurlionis (1875–1911). Čiurlionis lived in Druskininkai and for a while in Vilnius (his homes there are now museums, too). He was one of those rare people of genius who express themselves in several art forms, and he excelled in music, painting, and poetry. He lived at a time when nationalistic feelings rose throughout Europe. Finland had Sibelius, England had Elgar, and Lithuania had Čiurlionis—all wrote music which appealed to a sense of national pride and aroused an emotional response. Čiurlionis's tone poems "Miške" (In the Forest) and "Jūra" (The Sea) convey what it is to love one's country—a yearning for a homeland. Surprisingly, this beautiful and emotional music is hardly known in Western Europe.

*Kaunas Old Town. JLH.*

*Giedrė, left, and Bronė, right, examine traditional mittens from their region, in the national collections, Mikalojus Konstantinas Čiurlionis National Art Museum, Kaunas. Dr. Janina Savickienė, Keeper of Textiles, explains regional characteristics. JLH.*

Čiurlionis's paintings are unlike those of any other artist of his time. Abstract evocations of a cosmic spirituality, they are small in size but wide and deep in content. They are both decorative and memorable.

# Kaunas Art Academy

The Kaunas Faculty of Vilnius Academy of Arts has developed a strong textile-art department. Textiles have until recently been regarded as applied art. It has taken the art world a long time to accept textiles as a medium for fine art, and the Kaunas Faculty, along with the Vilnius Academy of Art, has played a significant part in that achievement.

In 2010, Birutė, a teacher, weaver, and folklorist who taught at the Folk Art School of Vilkija and was part of the Lithuanian delegation that came to Woolfest in England, celebrated her fiftieth birthday by weaving fifty traditional sashes. Sashes are an essential part of the national costume and their design varies from region to region. Birutė's gorgeous and impressive project was exhibited in Kaunas. Flowers, speeches, food, music, and dancing made the exhibition opening and preview a splendid and memorable occasion.

In Kaunas Old Town, a shop called Rūta Žalioji specialises in national costume, offering everything from complete outfits with accessories to materials for making garments. Knitted riešinės (wrist warmers) can be bought here.

Book cataloguing decorative woven aprons in Marijampolė Museum, compiled by Zigmas Kalesinskas and Asta Vandytė. JLH.

# Conference on Crafts at the Lithuanian University of Agriculture

In 2004, the year Lithuania entered the European Union, a conference was held at the Lithuanian University of Agriculture (recently renamed Aleksandras Stulginskis University). The theme was the preservation of ethnic folk culture in a widening world. The question was how to develop public appreciation of craftsman-made goods in an age of factory production. Academics and politicians gave papers on the historical background of folk art and presented information on grants and schemes available for promoting traditional skills. I was invited to speak about the problem from an outside perspective.

# Knitters in Marijampolė

The Hand in Glove exhibition, consisting of my re-creations of traditional handwear along with panels explaining their cultural contexts, was shown in the Marijampolė Local Lore Museum in 2005. Alongside my exhibition, the museum displayed its own collection of regional knitting, and twenty-two local women knitted new items specially for the occasion. For many of them, this was the first time that their work was shown in a public setting that honoured it as fine craft.

The exhibition opening, a formal occasion, included speeches, thanks, and refreshments, and the press was in attendance. Some women wore expertly hand-knitted suits. Accompanying me were the teachers who had come from England to help with the spinning course at Vilkija. Each of us waspresented with a single flower taken from a huge vase full of bright red tulips, along with a charming ceramic sheep as a memento of the occasion.

The exhibit went on to be shown in six other Lithuanian museums.

Exhibit open, Marijampolė, showing knitters, tulips, and ceramic sheep. JLH.

Opening of Hand in Glove exhibition. June, left; Zigmas 2nd left; with Museum director and two knitters. JLH.

Ceramic sheep. JLH.

Press cutting of opening. JLH.

# Knitters in Vilkaviškis

The town of Vilkaviškis has undergone great modernisation since our first visit in 2001. The Vilkaviškis Regional Museum is in a grand palace in gracious parkland. The collections, which reflect the social history of the Suvalkija region in southwestern Lithuania, include a selection of knitwear. Two examples that I especially remember were gauntlets knitted in 1938, and a pair of lily-patterned mittens knitted in 1957.

An interesting group of woodcut prints illustrates rural life in this district in the first half of the twentieth century. The artist of these and other works on display is Magdalena Birutė Stankūnienė, born in 1925 in Oželiai farmstead, near Vilkaviškis. While she now lives in Chicago, Illinois, she still enjoys visits to her homeland.

*Print by artist Magdalena Birutė-Stankūnienė in the Vilkaviškio krašto muziejus (Vilkaviškis Regional Museum), JLH.*

*Knitting in the Vilkaviškis Regional Museum. JLH.*

Woman at loom. JLH.

Crocheted birds. JLH.

Onutė spinning. JLH.

In the culture house, or community centre, there is a workshop where a cooperative of twelve women learn to weave. They only have to pay for electricity. A woman named Marija has been weaving here for four years, on her mother's loom. Her mother wove all her life, using handspun yarn. Now, Marija weaves fabric in the Suvalkija style, for national costume, mainly skirts and aprons, using factory-spun wool yarn.

One of the women in the cooperative has her own sheep in the countryside, one Lithuanian Black Face and the rest white sheep. She uses their wool, handspun and hand-dyed. She has been told that during the nineteenth century, wool was imported into Lithuania from England.

Another weaver was producing braid incorporating the word Lietuva (Lithuania) on an inkle loom.

At the hospital in Vilkaviškis, a women's group helps patients with special needs to make craftwork for sale. Leaders Albina Tiunaitienė and Irena Kaminskienė showed us their work, mainly knitting and crochet. I could not resist buying three small crocheted birds, complete with feather tails.

Outside the town of Vilkaviškis, in the village of Vartai, a woman named Onutė, who was born in 1947, spins wool on a modern wheel made by the Canadian company Lendrum. A woman named Daiva, who lives in Kaunas, has prepared fibers sent from Norway for women to earn money by spinning. Onutė was spinning alpaca when we visited. She also spins wool from her own small flock of ten Lithuanian Black Face sheep, which she uses for knitting socks. Her aunt taught her to spin when she was a child; because she was part of a family of nine children, her mother had little time to teach her. After World War II, the whole family was exiled to Siberia, Novosibirsk, near the town of Tomsk. They had a number of difficult years there, but were able to return to Lithuania in 1956.

# Knitters in Panevėžys, Anykščiai, and Biržai

## Panevėžys

In Lithuania's fifth largest city, Panevėžys, the Local Lore Museum has a good folklife collection. Daina, who takes care of the ethnology collection, showed me plenty of examples of locally knitted gloves and mittens. They reflect the style of Aukštaitija, Lithuania's northeastern cultural region.

During one of my first visits to Lithuania, I received an email from Maeve McMahon, a professor in the Department of Law and Legal Studies at Carleton University in Canada, who was spending an academic year in Lithuania researching issues related to justice. She told me that the women's prison for Lithuania, located in Panevėžys, had a knitting programme and needed wool. The prisoners knit clothes for babies and small children, their own and other people's, including for young ones in orphanages. This gives them something constructive and productive to do with their time. Back home in Cumbria, I appealed to members of the Eden Valley Guild of Spinners, Weavers, and Dyers, who kindly donated nine large bags of beautiful yarn. I took the bags to the coast, where the Eimskip shipping line took them in hand for complimentary transport to Lithuania. The English donors received a grateful letter of thanks from the prison governor in appreciation of the sixty kilograms (133 pounds) of wool for "our inventive imprisoned women."

*Young knitter in Biržai, with her knitted rabbits. JLH.*

*Gloves from Anykščiai region. JLH.*

## Biržai

Biržai is located in the far northeast of Lithuania, near the Latvian border. Housed in a medieval castle surrounded by great banks of earth, the local museum tells, in part, the story of troubled times when Swedish armies conquered the town. There are also natural-history and folklife collections, and the museum hosted one of the Lithuanian showings of the Hand in Glove exhibition.

I visited Biržai again a few years after that event, in 2010, this time to visit Kristina Milišiūnienė and see her flock of milk sheep. Her youngest daughter, at the time aged twelve, is the knitter of the family and was pleased to show me the rabbits she had made.

## Anykščiai

Anykščiai is a region of beautiful landscape, much of it forest, and is famous for its literary connections and its horses. Earlier (see Chapter 4, page 59), I mentioned Žilvinas Augustinavičius, a veterinary surgeon who is active in the Lithuanian Sheep Breeders Association, and who has his own flocks here. He showed us his sheep, a type of Lithuanian Black Face, and a great deal of wool! Fleece was piled high in a building that was formerly part of a collective farm. At the time I was there, in 2009, there was little demand for Lithuanian wool. Fortunately, the situation has improved and farmers can now sell all the wool they produce.

Žilvinas had arranged for Donna and me to meet some local women who brought their knitting to show us in the community hall. We were invited to the home of one woman who willingly brought out her knitting, mostly gloves and mittens in the regional style, which she charted by hand in a notebook, and insisted on presenting us each with a pair of gloves.

*Mittens knitted in Anykščiai, 2009. JLH.*

# Knitters in Mažeikiai

The town of Mažeikiai is in another border region of Lithuania, this time in the northwest. Folk art and textiles are well represented in the Mažeikiai Museum. The series of museum publications includes illustrated catalogues of handwoven linen and cotton hand towels; wristlets, mittens, and gloves (written after the Hand in Glove exhibition appeared here); and woven bed-spreads. When the museum installed the Hand in Glove exhibition in October 2006, the curators used the opportunity to augment the display with examples of knitting from the museum's collections and with the work of local women.

One of the local knitters, Marija, invited me to her home in a modern apartment block. On a wet Sunday afternoon, we approached her flat, climbing two flights of concrete stairs past non-descript doors on each landing. Marija opened the door into her home, and it was an enchanting place into which she welcomed us with a beaming smile. She had prepared a little table, covered with a hand-crocheted cloth, with home-baked apple fritters and coffee in china cups. The aromas and that vision drew us in, and they were only the start of the delights she shared. Photographs of her grandchildren filled one wall. Marija's hands cannot wait to knit. She showed us her works in progress: one sock finished and the second started, plus another complicated tablecloth.

She has a garden not far from the flats and likes to spend time there, where she can be "out of civilisation—no telephone, no electricity, no television." On summer nights, she even sleeps in the garden house.

Here is Marija's life story, translated by her daughter, who is an English teacher.

*Marija was born in 1945, in a peasant family. Her mother was a weaver and wove various patterns: ornaments, stars. Marija watched her mother's work. Her mother knitted, too. She showed her how to hold the needles, that is all. Marija taught herself knitting. When Marija was nine, once her mother went shopping in town. Marija hid under the weaving machine, took a little sweater, unravelled it, and used the yarn to knit gloves, complete with fingers.*

*Initially, Marija worked as a sales assistant and knitted only for her family. Later she started knitting for other people as well.*

*Knitting is her hobby. She knits to relax, to rest, not to think about anything.*

*Now she knits a lot of stockings and gloves. She started knitting them after the exhibition in the museum. Then these things had a great success.*

*She owns an old knitting book with ornaments, designs, and patterns, from which she gets ideas. Sometimes she uses knitting magazines, but most often she devises models for sweaters or other things herself. She creates her own ornaments for her stockings and gloves, sometimes basing them on ornaments for weaving, either reduced or enlarged. She even uses ornaments from candy wrappers.*

*She can't spend a minute without holding needles in her hands.*

Obviously, Marija is an independent and creative knitter. She sometimes designs work using an album of charts she has compiled, with motifs of rabbits, cats, stars, and more. Her book of reference for weaving patterns is *Audimas* (Weaving), by Olga Lapienytė (1982), and her main knitting book is *Didžioji Mezgėja* (The Great Knitter), by Rasa Lipskytė-Praninskienė (1994).

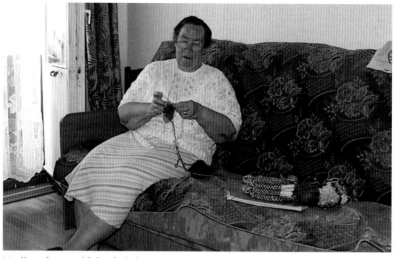

*Marija at home with her knitting. JLH.*

Mažeikių muziejuje

# PARODA

## „Tradicinis mezgimas Lietuvoje ir Anglijoje"

Paroda iš Vilkijos atkeliauja 2005 spalio 13 d. 15 val.
Lapkričio mėnesį išvyks į Panevėžį.

Paskubėkite aplankyti...

*Hand in Glove exhibition on display at the Mažeikiai Museum. JLH.*

# Knitters in Palanga

Palanga is the great seaside resort of Lithuania. The wide, sandy beach stretches for miles north and south along the Baltic coast. In fine weather, the town and beach are crowded with Lithuanians enjoying a holiday in the fresh air and sunshine. In summer, there is a carnival atmosphere in this leafy, elegant town, where entertainment, food kiosks, and fun fill the streets. One day, as a huge orange sun set in the west, I was surprised to see the wide wooden steps that stretch over the dunes to the beach filled with people as if in a theatre, watching the spectacular performance of the setting sun, which turned the sea into a fiery expanse like beaten copper.

By way of contrast, on one winter weekend I was taken to Palanga in wild, stormy weather. The beach was deserted and the sea tumbled in, wave upon wave of white foam spreading in huge fans over the sand.

Palanga is a spa town with many clinics and treatment centres. Here, too, is the Palanga Amber Museum, with every possible shade of amber from black to white, green to gold, from all over the world.

The sea has influenced folk art over the centuries, moving cultural ideas around within Scandinavia, Western Europe, and beyond. The Baltic Sea was a great trading highway, especially active from the Viking era through the medieval period and the domination of the Hanseatic League, and into modern times. Over the centuries, great quantities of linen and timber left the shores of Lithuania from the principal port on the Baltic coast, Klaipėda.

In Palanga, a craft and ethnology group called Mėguva meets regularly, led by Zita Baniulaitytė. They have a dedicated workspace, funded by several grant-making bodies. It is a centre for teaching traditional textile skills and for recognising the value of the rare sheep breed of the area, the Lithuanian Black Face.

The programme of seminars sponsored by Mėguva includes traditional weaving techniques, sash weaving, sewing, knitting, felt-making, spinning and yarn-dyeing. The group acts as consultant for national costume re-creators who want to make items of traditional dress using motifs relating to their own local customs. They also advise on sheep-

Brochure of Mėguva. JLH.

breeding programmes. Children's workshops are an important part of the group's efforts to ensure that traditional crafts survive.

Near Palanga, one man is using wool to make felted yurts. Yurts are the traditional homes of nomadic people of the central Asian desert. Felt panels are fixed to a wooden frame to create a warm, weatherproof house. The whole structure can be dismantled and transported from one site to the next. Felt is the oldest known textile in the world, discovered through the exploitation of a process which occurs naturally on the backs of wool-bearing animals. Yurts have recently found popularity in Western countries among people who want to lead a life of self-sufficiency, or like to have a form of temporary house in their garden or as a studio.

# Knitters in Vilnius

Irena Juškienė is the type of person who is instantly likeable and whose company I have enjoyed every time we have met. Born in 1943 in the village of Kemešys, in the Utena region, Irena has had a life-long practical interest in folklore, especially singing, dancing, and storytelling.

In 1996, she began a project to knit replicas of every pair of wrist warmers she could locate in Lithuania's museum collections. Along the way, she discovered the characteristic styles and techniques of each region of the country. The results of this huge undertaking resulted in an exhibition which toured Lithuania and was followed by a book, *Riešinės* (Wrist Warmers), initially published in 2005, with a second edition in 2009. Although the text is in Lithuanian, it provides summaries in German and English. The book charts one hundred examples—complete with historical context of— charming and varied wrist warmers, many of them beaded, from the different cultural regions of Lithuania.

When I was preparing the Hand in Glove exhibition, I asked Irena if she would like me to include four pairs of her wrist warmers and she happily lent them to me. Irena's work, exhibition, and book have brought this important detail of regional costume into prominence after almost a century of obscurity. Wrist warmers are once again fashionable to wear and to knit. Irena shares her knowledge by regularly teaching in yarn shops.

*Irena Felomena Juškienė, Riešinės, 2005. ISBN 9955 668 30 X. JLH.*

*Irena and wrist bands. JLH.*

# Lithuanian Art Museum Collections

The store of textiles contains many examples of knitting, including: mittens (double or lined) from Žemaitija, and brown mitts, with tan flowers and roses on the cuffs. The museum documentation says they were knitted from the wool of ožkavilnė avis (goat-woolled sheep), possibly referring to mohair or to fibre from another type of goat.

Many examples of beaded wrist warmers are in this collection. Asked why these were so popular in the early twentieth century, the curator of textiles, Dalia Bieliauskienė, told me they covered soiled shirt cuffs, or protected clean ones. She then added, in delightful English, "I put them on, and I am a nice girl."

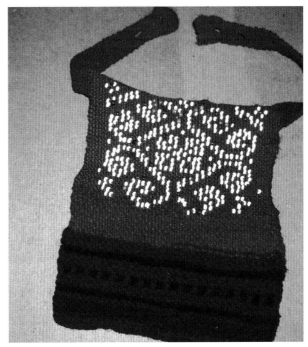

*Collar fronts. Used in winter to fill the neck of a coat. Worn for warmth and ornament and to lend variety to a plain dress. Beaded examples. JLH.*

*Stockings, women's, mid-twentieth century. Plain for every day. Patterned stockings were worn for church. JLH.*

*Felted coats, c. 1900–1910. These long, elegant coats are natural grey wool. They were woven, then felted with rollers containing stones. JLH.*

# Lithuanian Folk Art Guild

The headquarters of the Guild of Lithuanian Folk Artists is located in Vilnius Old Town. A shop, office, and gallery occupy an old building in the picturesque Stiklių gatvė (Glaziers Street). Nearby, weavers' workshops supply fabric for national costume to be worn especially at the biennial song festivals. The society in its present form was founded in 1966, but it grew out of an earlier organisation that had its roots in an exhibition held as long ago as 1901. The society promotes many forms of folk art, and I took part in a conference organised to discuss the inclusion of knitting in the country's folk-art conservation programme.

The society also sponsors regular exhibitions of work by individual artists. We were invited to the opening of an exhibition of iron crosses by Vytautas Paukštys. We enjoyed a very jolly evening with speeches, wine, food, accordion music, and impromptu dancing. Society publications include regular newsletters, catalogues of members and their work, and books about the lives and work of important artists. Each of the organisation's six regional branches, located throughout Lithuania, has its own shop and gallery, and all sell knitwear made by members.

The palms we saw on the streets that day are an unusual form of folk craft, unique to Vilnius. They are made in nearby villages, woven from dried flowers, grasses, and ears of wheat and barley. The top of the assembly is often trimmed with a plume of feathers.

## From My Notebook, Palm Sunday, 2004

Vivien and I arrived in Vilnius last night and stayed at the Litinterp guest house on Bernardinų Gatvė (Bernardine Street). Alex met us, as arranged, at the Gates of Dawn, just before midday. The street was filled with people emerging from the churches to the sound of bells, from deep, sonorous tones to light ringing notes. On every corner, people were selling palms. Everyone seemed to be carrying one. There was even a dog with a palm in its mouth.

*Palm bought in Vilnius. JLH.*

# Lithuanian Institute of History

As an academic establishment, full of archives and photographs, publications, and research papers, The Lithuanian Institute of History is a great source of reference material and expertise. The series of ethnological studies published by the institute includes these two books, relevant to knitting history and its place in society:

Number 3. Irena Regina Merkienė and Marija Pautieniūtė-Banionienė, *Lietuvininkų Pirštinės: Kultūrų Kryžkelėje* (Gloves of Lithuania Minor: At the Crossroads of Cultures, 1998)

Number 8. Auksuolė Čepaitienė, *Verpimas Lietuvoje: Liaudies Kultūros Likimas* (Spinning in Lithuania: The Fate of Folk Culture, 2001)

Both are well illustrated and have summaries in English.

# National Museum of Lithuania

In the main galleries of the National Museum of Lithuania, there is a permanent display of home textile processing, including tools for working with both wool and linen. The archives and collections contain many examples of antique hand tools (drop spindles, carders, spinning wheels, wool winders, etc.) and textiles. Blankets form a large group, illustrating regional variations in weaving designs and techniques.

*Teresė working on the costumes.*

# Folk Art Centre

The Lietuvos Liaudies Kultūros Centras (Lithuanian Folk Culture Centre) is focused on academic research. Teresė Jurkuvienė, manager of the Folklore division and Junior Research Fellow at the Lithuanian Culture Research Institute, has written the most recent authoritative book on Lithuanian national costume, *Lietuvių tautinis kostiumas*. She has researched and worked with textile specialists to create accurate replica costumes using authentic methods—not only for the tailoring, but for the weave of the fabric, embroidered embellishments, and knitted accessories. For the book, which provides a vivid picture of the regional styles, the costumes, were beautifully photographed on live models in countryside locations.

Teresė regrets that not many people want to spin and weave in the truly traditional way. Few of the summer camps where children used to be taught take place anymore, and most people who weave do so in their free time from paid work. There is a shortage of skilled teachers. "We are dying now," Teresė told me in 2005.

# The Antanas ir Anastazija Tamošaičiai Gallery "Židinys"

## (Antanas and Anastazija Tamošaitis Gallery "Hearth")

This husband-and-wife team worked hard to keep traditional textile skills alive between World War I and World War II. They exhibited, taught, and collected examples of regional costumes from all over Lithuania. Because of their work, some designs were identified and officially recorded for the first time. Now the centre named in their honour displays traditional costumes and has a weaving workshop. Antanas wrote for magazines and helped to popularise folk art. He revived interest in traditional textiles and the practice of skills needed to construct them, and adapted them to the needs of his time.

The books that Antanas and Anastazija Tamošaitis wrote, were directed at village craftworkers, to help them value their products and so continue the traditions. Antanas was, said Teresė Jurkuvienė, "the father of our profession."

*Marija, a knitter from Mažeikiai, showing June and Donna how she knits (see page 103). DC. Facing page from left to right: Knitting on double-pointed needles; Working a Baltic Braid; Decreasing.*

# Chapter 7:
# Lithuanian Knitting Techniques

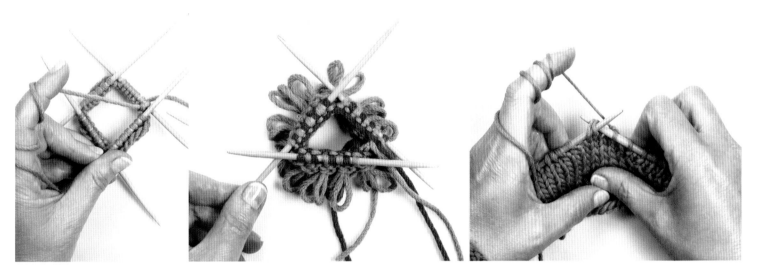

What makes knitting Lithuanian? Is it special techniques that are used? A unique way to hold the yarn and needles? Certain combinations of colors? Interesting pattern stitches? The answer is all of these things, and more.

The special techniques I've included in this chapter are all based on vintage accessories in museum collections, reproductions of Lithuanian national costume ensembles, or folk art pieces made by contemporary knitters. These instructions are adapted from *Mezgimas* (Knitting) by Anastazija Tamošaitis and other Lithuanian knitting books in my library, along with tips I've picked up from Lithuanian friends. I've modernized instructions and made other adjustments to make the techniques easier for contemporary knitters.

On the following pages, you'll find instructions for:

### Special Techniques

Bulgarian Cast On
Fringe Edge
Baltic Braid

### Sock Techniques

Sizing
Cuff
Leg
Heel
Foot
Toes

### Glove and Mitten Techniques

Sizing
Cuff
Thumbs
Mitten Tip Decreases
Glove Fingers
Lining Mittens

### Beaded Wrist Warmer Techniques

Knitting with Beads
Crochet Borders

For basic techniques as well as more detailed tutorials with photos and videos, visit my website: **www.lithuanianknitting.com.**

# Special Techniques

## Bulgarian Cast On

This is a variation of the long-tail cast on, so pull out a long tail of yarn—about four times the width of the piece you'll be knitting, or about 1 inch (2.5 cm) for each stitch you need to cast on. Triple the length of the tail and fold it into thirds. Do not make a slipknot.

Hold the yarn with the triple strands over your thumb and the single strand over your index finger, as shown. This will create two loops around the needle, which count as the first two stitches.

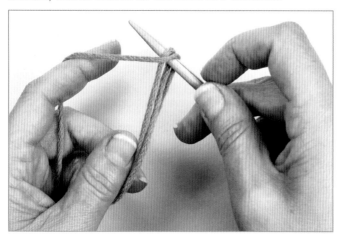

Make the next stitch as you would in a long-tail cast on, treating all three strands of yarn around the thumb as a single loop.

Remove your thumb and wrap the yarn around it in the opposite direction. Then make the next stitch by inserting the needle under the strands of yarn at the back of the thumb, between the thumb and index finger, and drawing the working yarn through.

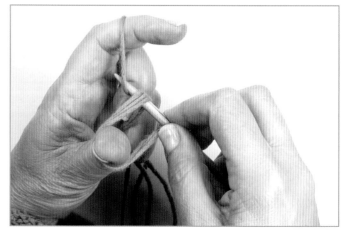

Continue to alternate between these two maneuvers, and cast on an even number of stitches. If your pattern calls for an odd number of stitches, just work an increase or a decrease in the first row.

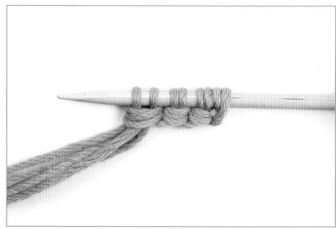

# Knitted Fringe

Mittens are commonly edged with a round of fringe around the cuff. In most cases, the fringe is knit in just after the cast on.

To work a looped fringe, cast on the desired number of stitches. Join to knit in the round. Purl 1 round or work 2 or more rounds in k1, p1 ribbing as indicated in the pattern you're working on.

Turn the knitting so it's inside out and you can work on the inside (WS) of the mitten.

**Rnd 1 (WS):** Knit around, wrapping the working yarn around the needle and one or two fingers 2 or 3 times for each stitch.

*Note: If you carry the working yarn in your right hand, use the fingers of your left hand to make the loops.*

**Rnd 2 (WS):** Knit around, working each stitch together with all its loops as a single stitch. If necessary, give a little tug on the fringes to even them out as you go.

# Baltic Braid

This decorative braid is popular in both Lithuania and Latvia. It is worked by making three rounds with two colors, changing colors after every stitch. The first round is knit and the second two rounds are purled. On the purl rounds, the floats create the braid pattern. It is very important to pick up the new color in the proper position in order to create the braid.

**Setup rnd:** (K1 MC, k1 CC) around.

**Braid rnd 1:** Bring both yarns to the front. (P1 MC, p1 CC) around, always bringing the new color from *under* the old color.

This will twist the yarns. Don't worry. The next rnd will untwist them.

**Braid rnd 2:** (P1 MC, p1 CC) around, always bringing the new color from *over* the old color.

# Sock Techniques

## Sizing

To make a sock at a custom size and gauge, you only need a few measurements. Many sock knitting reference books provide tables listing different gauges, sizes and stitch multiples, but I think it's easier to figure out the numbers on your own than to dig through a spreadsheet.

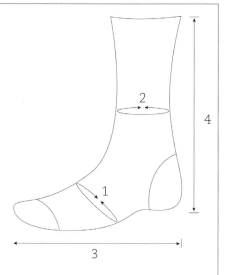

First you need to measure your foot:

1. **Foot Circumference**—measure at widest point at ball of foot
2. **Ankle Circumference**—measure just above the ankle bone
3. **Foot Length**—measure from back of heel to tip of toe
4. **Sock Length**—measure from top of cuff to floor
5. **Calf Circumference**, for knee socks—measure at widest point

Subtract about 5% for colorwork socks and 10% for other socks for negative ease so the socks fit snugly.

Next you need to measure your gauge:

_____ stitches and _____ rounds = 4 inches/10 cm

_____ size needle used to make swatch

_____ pattern stitch used for swatch

Your main number for working the socks is the number of stitches per inch times the number of inches in the circumference on your foot after subtracting for negative ease.

Round this up or down a few stitches so your pattern stitch fits.

**Main number:** _____ stitches per inch × _____ circumference

Rounded to multiple of _____: _____ stitches in ankle and foot (Round up for stranded colorwork; round down for other stitch patterns.)

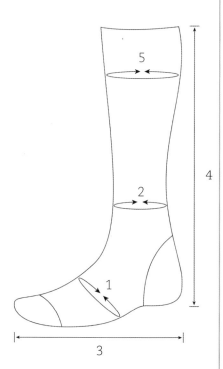

For the heel, you will work back and forth on about half of this number of stitches, plus or minus one or more stitches if you want to center the pattern a certain way.

For the toe, you will divide the stitches into 2, 4, or 8 equal sections.

# Cuff

**Ribbing:** Most Lithuanian socks are worked with a k1, p1 or k2, p2 ribbing stitch on the cuff. Often the ribbing is worked in bright, multicolored stripes.

**Folded Colorwork:** In this type of cuff, you work ribbing for ½ to 1 inch, then work in a colorwork pattern for 2 or 3 inches. After that, turn the sock inside out and double the length of the cuff by working with the main color in stockinette stitch or ribbing.

**Lace, Colorwork, and Other Cuffs:** Many types of cuffs that are used on mittens and gloves are also used on socks.

# Leg

**Crew (Mid-calf) Socks:** If you're making a short crew sock, after the cuff is complete you will work with no shaping until you are ready to make the heel.

**Knee Socks:** If you're making a knee sock, the number of stitches at the ankle will match the number of stitches in the foot of the sock, but you will need to cast on a larger number to accommodate the calf. You'll need to decrease between the cuff and the ankle to reach the desired number of stitches a few inches above the heel. Changing needle sizes and stitch patterns can also be used to shape the calf.

# Heel

In cuff-down socks, the most common types of heels are made of two parts: a heel flap and a heel turn. Each type of heel has a different technique used to knit the flap and the turn, and the two parts work together to create a unique heel shape.

**Note:** You can use use any heel flap pattern stitch with any heel turn technique. I have listed these in the combinations that are most common in Lithuanian socks.

# Dutch Heel

This heel is not unique to Lithuanian knitting. It is very common in English-language sock patterns. The heel is worked back and forth on half of the total number of stitches. Put one half of the stitches on one needle and put the other stitches on hold without working them while you work on the heel stitches.

**Heel Flap:** Work back and forth on the heel stitches in Heel Stitch or Eye of Partridge Stitch. End after working a WS row. Heel Stitch can be worked over an even or odd number of stitches.

**Heel Stitch**

**Row 1 (RS):** (Sl 1, k1) across. If you have an odd number of stitches, knit the last stitch.

**Row 2 (WS):** Sl 1, purl across.

Rep rows 1 and 2 for patt.

**Eye of Partridge Stitch**

**Row 1 (RS):** (Sl 1, k1) across. If you have an odd number of stitches, knit the last stitch.

**Rows 2 and 4 (WS):** Purl.

**Row 3:** (K1, sl 1) across. If you have an odd number of stitches, knit the last stitch.

Rep rows 1–4 for patt.

Continue in pattern of choice until the heel is a square or the desired length. End after working a WS row.

**Turning the Heel:** Divide the heel into three even sections, separated by markers. If there is an odd stitch, place it in the center section. The heel turn is worked back and forth in short rows, with decreases before each turn creating the corners that cause the heel to curve around and create a right angle.

**Next row (RS):** Sl 1, knit to second marker, slip marker, ssk, turn.

**Next row (WS):** Sl 1, purl to second marker, slip marker, p2tog, turn.

Rep last 2 rows until all sts have been used. Sl 1, knit across.

## Easy Lithuanian Heel

*Easy Lithuanian Heel.*

The heel is worked back and forth on half of the total number of stitches. Put one half of the stitches on one needle and put the other stitches on hold without working them while you work on the heel stitches.

**Heel Flap:** Work back and forth on the heel stitches in stockinette stitch, with garter stitch (all knit) or reverse garter stitch (all purl) edges.

**Row 1 (RS):** Sl 1 kw, p2, knit to last 3 sts, p2, k1.

**Row 2 (WS):** Sl 1 pw, purl.

Rep rows 1 and 2 until the heel is a square or the desired length. End after working a WS row.

**Turning the Heel:** Continue to work back and forth in pattern as set to turn the heel. Divide the heel stitches into three sections, with half of the stitches in the center between two markers and one-quarter on each side. For a narrower heel, divide the stitches into three equal sections as for the Dutch Heel. (Vintage books instruct the knitter to divide the stitches onto three double-pointed needles and to use a fourth to knit back and forth on the heel stitches. I've found it much easier to use two needles and stitch markers.)

**Row 1 (RS):** Work to 2 sts before first marker, k2tog, slip marker, work to next marker, slip marker, ssk, work to end of row.

**Row 2 (WS):** Work to 2 sts before first marker, ssp, slip marker, work to next marker, slip marker, p2tog, work to end of row.

Continue working back and forth in this manner, noting that all the decreases are outside the markers, so you will have fewer and fewer stitches outside the markers until only 1 stitch remains on each side. The number of stitches in the center does not change. End after working a WS row when 1 stitch remains on each side outside the markers.

## T-Heel

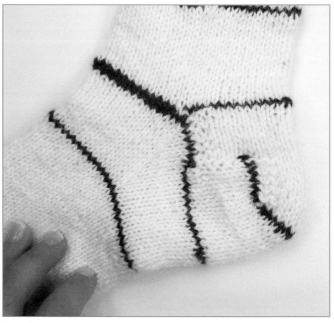

*T-Heel.*

The heel is worked back and forth on half of the total number of stitches, with reverse garter stitch (all purl) edges. Put one half of the stitches on one needle and put the other stitches on hold without working them while you work on the heel stitches. It's most fun if you work the heel flap and heel turn in different colors.

**Heel Flap:** Work back and forth on the heel stitches as follows.

**Row 1 (RS):** Sl 1 kw, p2, knit to last 3 sts, p2, k1.

**Row 2 (WS):** Sl 1 pw, purl.

Repeat rows 1 and 2 until the heel is HALF of the desired length. End after working a WS row.

Count the number of slipped stitches on one side of the heel.

Work this number of stitches at the beginning of the row and put those stitches on a holder or spare needle. Work until the same number of stitches remains at the end of the row. Put those remaining stitches on a holder or spare needle.

On the center stitches that are still on the working needle, continue in the heel pattern as above until you have worked the same number of rows as in the first portion of the heel. End after working a WS row.

**Turning the Heel:** Break the yarn. With RS facing, join the desired color of yarn at the bottom of the heel center on the right edge. Pick up 1 stitch in each edge stitch up the side of the heel center, knit across the center stitches, and pick up 1 stitch in each edge stitch down the other side of the heel center. Do not turn.

**Row 1 (RS):** Sl the first st from the held sts kw and pass the last picked-up st over it. Turn.

**Row 2 (WS):** Sl 1 pw, purl across to the held sts on the other side, sl the first held stitch pw and pass the last purled st over it. Turn.

**Row 3:** Sl 1 kw, knit across to the held sts, sl 1 and pass the last knit st over it. Turn.

Rep rows 2 and 3 until all sts are worked, ending after working row 2 (a WS row). Turn.

# Garter Stitch Short-Row Heel

This is a short-row heel that also has instep shaping. All of the Lithuanian short-row heel instructions I have seen include a section that is worked back and forth on two needles before the short-row section is begun.

The heel is worked back and forth on half of the total number of stitches. Put one half of the stitches on one needle and put the other stitches on hold without working them while you work on the heel stitches.

**Heel Flap:** Work in St st, slipping the first stitch of every row, for about ½–1 inch (1–2.5 cm), ending after working a WS row.

**Short-Row Heel Turn:** Begin working short rows in garter stitch as follows.

**Every Row:** Sl 1 kw wyib, knit to 1 st before end of row, turn.

Continue in this fashion, slipping the first stitch and working 1 fewer stitch in each row.

When ⅓ of the heel stitches remain unworked in the center of the heel, begin working 1 more stitch in each row as follows.

**Every Row:** Sl 1 kw wyib, knit to the last of the worked/center sts, sl the last center st kw, k1 (first stitch of unworked sts), turn.

When all stitches have been worked, end after completing a WS row. Note that this leaves a line of decorative holes on the sides of the heels.

*Garter Stitch Short-Row Heel.*

# Gusset Shaping

After completing the heel, you return to knitting in the round.

**Setup rnd:** Knit across heel stitches. Pick up and knit 1 stitch in each slip-stitch chain along the side of the heel. Work across the instep stitches (previously put on hold) in pattern. Pick up and knit stitches in the chains along the other side of heel. Knit across half of the heel stitches. Place marker for the end of the round; this is the center of the bottom of the foot.

Continue to work in the round in patterns as established, decreasing as follows.

**Dec rnd:** Knit to last 3 sts on sole, k2tog, k1, work instep sts; on sole, k1, ssk, knit to end of rnd.

**Plain rnd:** Knit.

Repeat these 2 rnds until you are back down to your original number of sts.

# Foot

On the spiral toe and the wedge toe, 4 stitches are decreased every other round until half the stitches remain, then 4 sts are decreased every round until about 8 stitches remain for closing the toe.

To estimate the length the toe will be, subtract 8 from your total number of stitches. This is how many stitches you need to decrease. Divide by 4 to get the total number of decrease rounds to be worked. Then take this number and multiply it by 1.5 to get the total number of rounds worked in the toe.

For example, if you have 48 sts, you will need to decrease 40 stitches, which means you will have 10 decrease rounds. Multiply that by 1.5 to get 15 rounds total in the toe. And then multiply this by your row gauge. That is the length of the toe. Subtract this from the total length to determine when to stop knitting the foot.

# Toes

In cuff-down socks, toes are easier to knit than heels. They are made simply by decreasing in some pleasing pattern until you have few enough stitches to gather in and fasten off (or to join with grafting).

The only exception is the short-row toe, which is not traditionally used in Lithuania but would be worked exactly the same as the Garter Stitch Short-Row Heel on page 117, excluding the flap.

## Spiral Toe

The most basic sock toe, and the type used most frequently in Lithuanian socks, is similar to the type of shaping used for hats in many English-language patterns.

Divide the stitches evenly into four sections.

For a left-slanting spiral, k2tog at the end of each section as follows.

**Rnd 1:** *Knit to the last 2 sts in the section, k2tog, rep from * 3 more times.

**Rnd 2 (and all even rnds):** Knit.

Continue in this fashion, dec at the end of each section every other rnd, with 1 fewer st before the dec in each section. When half of the original number of sts remain, dec every rnd. When 8 sts remain, cut the yarn, run the tail through the remaining sts, and pull gently to close up the toe.

For a right-slanting spiral, ssk at the beginning of each section as follows.

**Rnd 1:** *Ssk, knit to the end of the section, rep from * 3 more times.

**Rnd 2 (and all even rnds):** Knit.

Continue to dec every other rnd and finish off as for left-slanting spiral.

*Spiral Toe.*

*Wedge Toe.*

## Wedge Toe

With the stitches divided equally into two sections, with half of the stitches in the sole and half in the top of the foot and the beginning of the round at the middle of the sole, work as follows.

**Dec Rnd:** *Knit to last 3 sts in sole, k2tog, k1; on instep, k1, ssk, knit to last 3 sts on instep, k2tog, k1; on sole, ssk, knit to end of rnd at center of sole.

**Next Rnd:** Knit.

Decrease every other rnd until half of the original number of sts remain, then dec every rnd until about 8 to 12 sts remain. Close toe with Kitchener stitch or gather in and secure. (Kitchener stitch instructions can be found just about anywhere on the Internet and in basic sock knitting books.)

# Tips for Arranging Stitches on Different Kinds of Needles

As you work on your sock, you will need to rearrange the stitches on the needles for several parts of the project to make the work easier to manage. The setup is different depending on whether you are working on double-pointed or circular needles.

## Double-Pointed Needles

**Cuff and leg:** Divide stitches into three or four equal sections (or almost equal if necessary to keep full repeats on each needle).

**Heel:** Put the heel stitches on one needle and divide the remaining stitches equally on two needles to be worked later.

**Gusset shaping:** Divide the sole (including the gusset stitches picked up on each side of the heel) on two needles; the end of the round should be in the center of these two needles. Put the instep stitches on one or two needles; you will work gusset decreases on each of the sole needles on the ends farthest away from the center of the heel.

**Foot and toe:** Keep the instep on one or two needles and the sole divided equally on two needles.

## Two Circular Needles or Magic Loop

**Cuff and leg:** Divide the stitches in half with the back of the leg on one needle or section and the front of the leg on the second needle or section.

**Heel:** Put the heel stitches on one needle or section and the remaining stitches on the other needle or section to be worked later.

**Gusset shaping:** Beginning at the center of the heel, put half of the stitches (up to the center of the instep) on one needle or section and the second half of the stitches (from the center of the instep to the center of the heel) on the second needle or section, placing markers between the sole and instep on each side; you will work gusset decreases in the middle of each section. Place markers to denote the break between the sole and the instep.

**Foot and toe:** Divide the stitches in half, placing the sole stitches on one needle or section and the instep stitches on the second needle or section.

## One Short Circular Needle

If you're working on one short circular, there's no trick. All of the stitches flow around the needle automatically. When working the heel, put the unworked stitches on scrap yarn or leave them on the needle while working back and forth on the heel stitches only. When working the foot and toe, place markers to divide the instep from the sole.

# Glove and Mitten Techniques

## Sizing

To make a mitten or glove at a custom size and gauge you only need a few measurements.

First you need to measure your hand:

1. **Circumference**—measure around your palm, then add about 10 to 15% for positive ease
2. **Hand Length**—measure from your wrist to the tip of your longest finger
3. **Cuff Length**—measure from your wrist to the end of the cuff on your arm

Next you need to measure your gauge:

_____ stitches and _____ rounds = 4 inches/10 cm

_____ size needle used to make swatch

_____ pattern stitch used for swatch

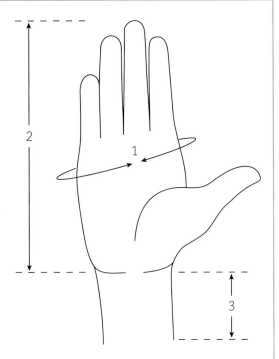

Your main number for working the mittens is the number of stitches per inch times the number of inches in the circumference on your hand.

Round this up or down a few stitches so your pattern stitch fits. Remember, the most important thing for getting the right size is to have the correct number of stitches at the given gauge. It is less important to fit a complete pattern repeat. In many folk art and vintage knitting samples, the round ends in the middle of a repeat. Modern knitters are less forgiving, perhaps because we are used to manufactured and mass-produced clothing being "perfect." Of course, if you must have a full repeat, then you can change needle sizes and adjust your gauge

**Main number:** _____ stitches per inch × _____ circumference

**Rounded to multiple of ____:** ____ stitches in hand

# Cuff

Lithuanian knitters used a variety of interesting techniques to make cuffs on gloves and mittens.

## Ribbing

Some gloves and mittens, particularly those for everyday wear, were made with simple ribbing. The patterns were k2, p2 ribbing or k1, p1 ribbing.

Twisted ribbing is made by working the knit stitches through the back loop.

## Colorwork and Pattern Stitches

When mitten cuffs are worked in color or texture patterns rather than ribbing, they are not smaller or tighter than the remaining part of the mitten.

## Picot Hem

A delicate picot hem is used on many gloves and mittens and is especially nice on lined mittens, because it creates an elegant way to turn the hem and attach the lining. Begin by using a regular long-tail cast on worked over two needles to cast on an even number of stitches. Working with needles one or two sizes smaller than your main needle size, knit several rounds, or about ½ inch (1.25 cm). On the next round, work (yo, k2tog) around. This creates the turning ridge. Change to larger needles and knit several rounds plain before you begin working a plain stockinette stitch or colorwork cuff.

## Lined Openwork

A very common cuff design consists of a simple diagonal openwork pattern with a contrasting color lining. Begin by casting on an even number of stitches and joining to work in the round. With the contrasting color, work 1–2 inches in stockinette stitch. Change to the main color. Knit 1 round, then purl 1 round. Change to the second contrasting color and begin working the diagonal openwork.

### Diagonal Openwork

(even number of sts)

**Rnd 1:** (K2tog, yo) around.

**Rnd 2:** *Knit across sts on the needle, then knit the first st of the next needle. Rep from * around. This will shift the beginning of the rnd 1 st to the left as the pattern moves diagonally across the end of rnd.

Repeat rnds 1 and 2 until the cuff is about 2 rnds shorter than the lining. This will allow you to stitch the lining hem to the solid portion of the mitten or glove.

## Trinity Stitch

Sometimes Trinity Stitch is worked instead of the diagonal openwork pattern. You work this stitch from the wrong side, so turn the knitting inside out after working the cuff lining, work the cuff, then turn it right side out again to work the remainder of the mitten or glove.

### Circular Trinity Stitch

(multiple of 4 sts)

**Rnd 1 (WS):** *(K1, p1, k1) into same st, p3tog; rep from * around.

**Rnds 2 and 4:** Knit.

**Rnd 3:** *P3tog, (k1, p1, k1) into same st; rep from * around.

Rep rnds 1–4 for patt.

## Lace

Sometimes more elaborate lace patterns were used for glove and mitten cuffs without a lining. When I use this technique, the lace instructions are included in the pattern.

## Long (Gauntlet) Mittens

Gauntlet mittens with long cuffs that were worn outside an overcoat, reaching almost to the elbow, were popular in Lithuania in the middle of the twentieth century. These cuffs begin with up to three times the number of stitches needed for the wrist and hand, and are decreased every few rounds as you work down toward the wrist.

# Thumb

All Lithuanian mittens and gloves are worked with no gusset shaping for the thumb. This type of thumb is sometimes called a "peasant thumb." When the hand is the desired length to the thumb opening, simply work approximately ⅕ of the total number stitches with scrap yarn for the thumb opening at the desired location (or as instructed in my patterns). Slip these stitches back onto the left needle and work them again with the working yarn.

For the thumb opening, you will work a number of stitches on the palm with scrap yarn. The opening should be worked over approximately ⅕ of the total number of stitches. For example, if have a total of 48 sts, ⅕ of the stitches is 9.6 so work the thumb opening over about 10 or 11 stitches. If you have a total of 72 stitches, ⅕ of the stitches is 14.4 stitches, so work the thumb opening over about 14 to 16 stitches.after the beginning of the palm stitches and end it 1 or 2 stitches before the center of the palm for the right hand. Begin the thumb opening 1 or 2 stitches
after the center of the palm and end it 1 or 2 stitches before the end of the palm for the left hand.

When the glove or mitten is complete, remove the scrap yarn, carefully placing the live stitches onto needles, pick up an extra stitch at each "corner," and work the thumb in the round, decreasing the tip as for a glove finger (see page 123).

**Mitten Palm with Thumb Placement**

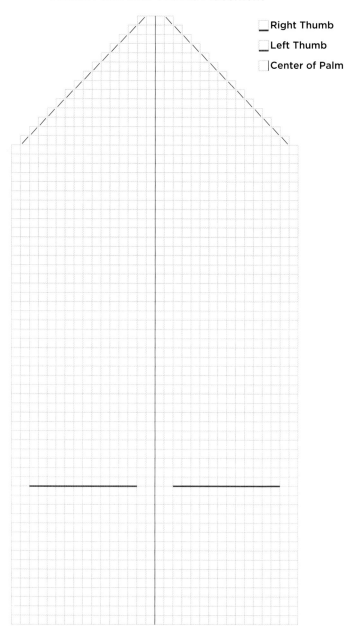

☐ Right Thumb
☐ Left Thumb
☐ Center of Palm

# Lining Mittens

Mitten linings are worked following the same basic instructions as for the outer mitten, using a thinner yarn and larger needles to obtain a softer fabric at the same gauge as the outer mitten. The outer mitten must be worked at a large enough size to fit with the lining tucked inside. After the outer mitten is complete, weave in the ends. Begin the outer mitten with a long-tail cast on worked over two needles. Use the lining yarn to pick up and knit 1 stitch in each cast-on stitch after the outer mitten is complete. Then work the lining as for the outer mitten, making the thumb a tiny bit shorter, and tuck the ends between the layers after the lining is complete. Push the lining inside the outer mitten, inserting your hand to force the thumb lining inside the thumb. (If you know how to work a provisional cast on, you can begin the outer mitten with that technique and remove the provisional cast on to have live stitches for knitting the lining.)

# Glove Fingers

Work even on the hand after the thumb opening for about 1½ inches (3.75 cm) or until knitting reaches the space where the little finger separates from the ring finger.

## Arranging the Stitches

**Little finger:** Work the little finger, setting aside the remaining hand stitches for the other fingers to be worked later.

Work half of the required number of stitches from the palm and half from the back
of the hand, plus CO 2 or 3 stitches to join. If desired, decrease 1 stitch over the join on the first round, then work even until the finger is about ¼ inch (0.5 cm) shorter than desired length or to the middle of the fingernail bed, then shape tip (see below) and fasten off.

After the little finger is complete, put the remaining hand stitches back on the needles, pick up and knit 2 or 3 stitches over the join and work a few rounds before beginning the other fingers.

**Ring finger:** Work half of the required stitches from the palm, CO 2 or 3 stitches over the gap, work half of required stitches from back of hand, then pick up and knit 2 or 3 stitches between ring finger and little finger.

Put the remaining stitches on hold and work as for little finger.

**Middle finger:** Work as for ring finger with 1 more stitch on each half.

**Index finger:** Use the remaining stitches and pick up and knit 2 or 3 stitches between the index finger and the middle finger.

## Shaping the Fingertips

Fingertips can be shaped with round or pointed tips just as for mittens.

### Mitten Tip Shaping

For mitten tip shaping, you will divide the stitches into 2, 4, or 8 equal sections. If it's 2 sections, half are on the palm and half on the back of the hand. If 4 or 8 equal sections, start the divisions at the end of the round.

**Pointed tips:** Divide the stitches into 2 equal sections with half on the palm side and half on the back of the hand. On each section: ssk, knit to last 2 sts, k2tog. Decrease every row until 6 or 4 sts rem.

**Round tips:** Divide the stitches into 3 equal sections. On each section: knit to the last 2 sts, k2tog. Decrease every row until 6 sts rem. For a reverse swirl, work ssk at the beg of each section.

**Tapered tips:** Divide the stitches into 8 equal sections. On each section: knit to the last 2 sts, p2tog. Work the same number of rows with no shaping as you worked stitches before the decrease. The number of stitches before each decrease and the number of rows between decrease rounds will be 1 less each time.

# Finger Placement

For a glove, work the thumb the same as for a mitten. To calculate how many stitches you need for each finger, divide the number of stitches in the palm by 4. Then subtract 1 for the little finger and ring finger, and add 1 for the middle finger and index finger. You will take this number of stitches from both the palm and the back of the hand for each finger.

For example, if you have 72 stitches in your glove, half of those, or 36 stitches, form the palm. Dividing 36 by 4, you get 9. Subtract 1 and you have the number of stitches for the little finger and ring finger: 8. Add 1 and you have the number of stitches for the middle finger and index finger: 10.

_____ **Total number of stitches**

_____ **Number of stitches in palm**
(half of total)

_____ **Palm stitches divided by 4** for
number of stitches in ring finger

_____ **Subtract 1** for number of stitches
little finger

_____ **Add 1** for number of stitches middle
finger and index finger

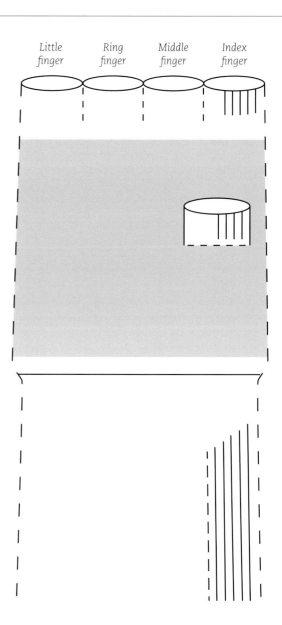

**Glove Finger Placement**

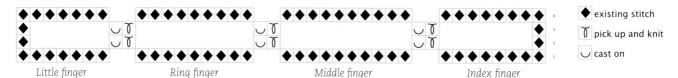

| | | | |
|---|---|---|---|
| ◆ existing stitch | | | |
| Ⴀ pick up and knit | | | |
| ᴗ cast on | | | |

Little finger      Ring finger      Middle finger      Index finger

# Wrist Warmers

## Sizing Tips

For wristers knit in the round, see Mitten Sizing Tips on page 120. Beaded wristers are worked sideways in rows. Work until you have enough rows to reach around your wrist.

## Knitting with Beads

**Stringing Beads**

Lithuanian beaded wristers are worked with the beads pre-strung on the yarn and a bead pushed up to the knitting at each point indicated in the chart.

To pre-string the beads, use a beading needle or a plastic dental floss threader with a big eye and thread. Thread the knitting yarn through the loop or needle eye and pick up beads with the single end of the needle. Slide the beads over the loop and onto the yarn.

### Knitting with Beads

Beads are worked on WS, and RS are worked plain with no beads. Following the chart, alternate between plain and beaded rows as follows.

**Bead Row (WS):** Sl 1 kw wyif for a slip-stitch edge (optional). When you come to a black square on the chart, slip a bead up to the needles and knit the next stitch, pulling it tight to hold the bead in place. This counts as one bead stitch.

The bead sits between two stitches on the needles and will naturally go to the back of the work, which is why we knit in the beads on the WS rows.

## Crochet Borders

If desired, you can crochet a border on your wristers, with or without incorporating additional beads into the design. Use a crochet hook that is close to the size of the knitting needle you used to make the wristers.

### Single Crochet

Working from right to left, insert the crochet hook into the next stitch on the edge of the piece. Pull the working yarn through to the front. Two loops are now on the hook. Pull the working yarn through both loops on the hook. One loop remains on the hook. Repeat until you have worked across the entire edge.

### Crochet Shells

Join the yarn to the knitting (this counts as the first single crochet). *Skip 2 sts, work 5 double crochets into next st, skip next 2 sts, single crochet into next st, rep from * to end. Slip st to first single crochet to join and fasten off.

### Beaded Picots

Attach the yarn as for other crochet trims. *Slide 5–9 beads up to the edge of the wrister, then work a single crochet. Pull the loop very large and draw the whole ball of yarn through it as if you're fastening off. Repeat from * all the way around. After the last stitch, cut the yarn and pull the tail through, to actually fasten off.

For basic techniques as well as more detailed tutorials with photos and videos, visit my website: **www.lithuanianknitting.com**.

- Grandmother's Knitting
- Decreases
- Casting On
- Fringe Edge
- Baltic Braid
- Knitting in the Round
- Sock Construction and Sizing
- Glove and Mitten Techniques
- Wrist Warmers
- Knitting with Beads
- Crochet Stitches

*The Green Bridge in Vilnius. Facing page from left to right: Suvalkija Beehives, page 158; Little Lithunia, page 165; Market Socks, page 178.*

# Chapter 8: The Patterns

# Market Mittens

These mittens are inspired by the many pairs of colorful mittens knitted with floral motifs found in the tourist markets in Vilnius. Floral designs are often knitted in shades of pink, yellow, and blue on a white or black background, or in undyed grey or brown wool on a cream background. Made with worsted weight yarn on fairly large needles, these mittens knit up quite quickly, making them profitable to sell in quantity by the market vendors, and great for gift knitting as well.

The fringe cuff and the multiple shades of the same colors used to paint the leaves and flowers are traditional Lithuanian style, as is the use of a simple check pattern on the palm and the simple peasant thumb. The mittens sold in the markets almost always have a pointed fingertip shape, reminiscent of Scandinavian designs, although the older mittens in museum collections more frequently have rounded fingertip shaping.

Interestingly, all of the mitten charts I've seen in Lithuanian knitting books—both vintage and contemporary publications—show the pointed tips, even when a photograph of the actual project has a rounded shape. I've included these mittens here because they were the first designs I saw when I visited Vilnius as a tourist in 2007. Made with heavier yarn and bigger needles than most of the projects I've designed, they make a good introductory project for those of you who may be new to knitting in the round with multiple colors.

## Experience Level

Intermediate

## Finished Measurements of Sample

8" (20.5 cm) palm circumference

11½" (29 cm) hand length from cast on to tip

For sizing tips, see page 120.

## Materials

Worsted weight wool yarn, approx 200 yds/182 m MC and 50 yds/46 m each of multiple contrasting colors

Sample shown in Cascade 220 (worsted weight; 100% Peruvian wool; 220 yds/ 200 m per 100 g skein)

**A:** 8555 (charcoal); 1 skein

Approx 50 yds/46 m of each of the following contrast colors:

**B:** 8910 (light green)

**C:** 7814 (medium green)

**D:** 9430 (dark green)

**E:** 4147 (pale yellow)

**F:** 7826 (pale orange)

**G:** 7825 (orange)

Scrap yarn

## Needles

US size 5 (3.75 mm) needles for working in the round: DPNs, 1 long circular or 2 short circulars

Tapestry needle

## Gauge

26 sts and 28 rnds = 4"/10 cm over stranded colorwork

## Special Techniques

Knitted Fringe, see page 113.

Baltic Braid (optional), see page 113.

Peasant Thumb, see page 122.

Pointed Mitten Tip, see page 123.

# Instructions

## Cuff

With color D, loosely CO 48 sts. Join to knit in the round, being careful not to twist sts.

Purl 1 round. Turn the knitting around so you so you can work on the inside (WS) of the mitten.

**Rnd 1:** *K1, wrapping the working yarn around the needle and your index finger 2 or 3 times. Repeat from * around.

**Rnd 2:** Knit, catching all of the loops from a fringe in each stitch. If necessary, give a little tug on the fringes to even them out as you go.

Turn the knitting so you are again working on the outside (RS) of the mitten. Knit 3 rnds.

**Cuff rnd:** Work Cuff chart twice around.

Work as set until Cuff chart is complete.

Baltic Braid Option if desired, on rnds 5–7 and rnds 13–15 of chart, substitute Baltic Braid as shown on page 113.

**Setup rnd (Cuff rnds 5 and 13):** (K1 MC, k1 CC) around.

**Braid rnd 1 (Cuff rnds 6 and 14):** Bring both yarns to the front. (P1 MC, p1 CC) around, always bringing the new color from under the old color. This will twist the yarns. Don't worry. The next rnd will untwist them.

**Braid rnd 2 (Cuff rnds 7 and 15):** (P1 MC, p1 CC) around, always bringing the new color from over the old color.

## Hand

Knit 1 rnd in MC, inc 4 sts evenly around—52 sts.

Work Hand chart on first 26 sts, Palm chart on second 26 sts. Work as set until rnd 14 is complete.

## Thumb Opening

**Right mitten:** Work Hand chart across first 26 sts; work 2 sts of Palm in pattern as set; with scrap yarn k9, slip these 9 sts back onto right-hand needle and knit them again with working yarn following chart pattern, work to end of rnd in pattern.

**Left Mitten:** Work Hand chart across first 26 sts; work 15 sts of Palm in pattern as set; with scrap yarn k9, slip these 9 sts back onto right-hand needle and knit them again with working yarn following chart pattern, work to end of rnd in pattern.

Continue even in patterns until chart row 40 is complete and mitten measures approx 9" (23 cm) from cast-on edge.

## Finger Tip Shaping

This mitten has pointed mitten tip shaping with solid bands on the side edges. Continue following chart pattern, working decreases as shown.

When chart is complete, break yarn and thread tail through rem sts and pull gently to fasten off.

## Thumb

Remove the scrap yarn from the thumb opening. With A, pick up 9 sts above and below the thumb opening and pick up 2 on both sides—22 sts.

**Rnd 1:** Knit, working k2tog at each "corner"—20 sts.

Knit even until thumb meas 1¾" (4.5 cm) or reaches to middle of thumbnail.

**Dec rnd:** *SSK, k to last 2 sts of first half of sts, k2tog; rep from * once more on second half.

Repeat dec rnd until 8 sts remain.

Break yarn and thread tail through rem sts and pull gently to fasten off.

## Finishing

Weave in ends, wash and dry flat to block.

*This sample made with yarn from the Siūlas mill in Lygumai (see page 66).*

## Cuff Chart

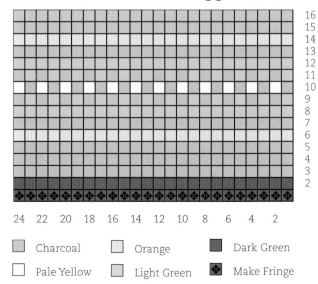

16
15
14
13
12
11
10
9
8
7
6
5
4
3
2

24  22  20  18  16  14  12  10  8   6   4   2

☐ Charcoal   ☐ Orange   ☐ Dark Green
☐ Pale Yellow   ☐ Light Green   ✛ Make Fringe

# Hand Chart

# Palm Chart

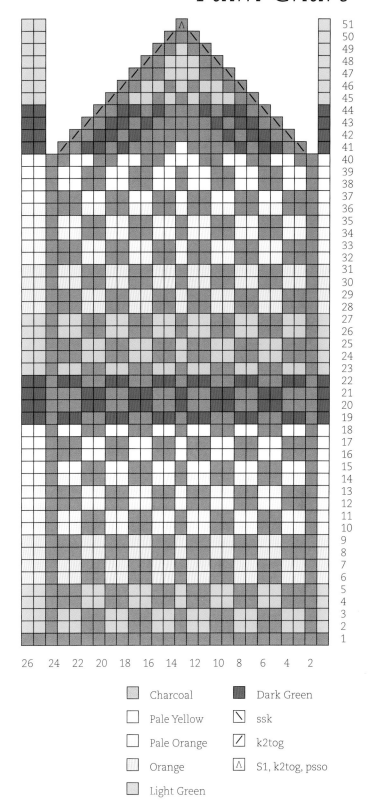

Charcoal

Pale Yellow

Pale Orange

Orange

Light Green

Dark Green

ssk

k2tog

S1, k2tog, psso

# Židinys: Hearth

Handwoven fabrics, knitted socks and gloves, natural dyes, handspun yarns, decorative carpets, colorful wall-hangings, lithographs, and paintings: these comprise the legacy of Anatstazija and Antanas Tamošaitis. Sometimes called the matriarch and patriarch of Lithuanian textiles or champions of Lithuanian folk art, the couple spent their lives studying and reproducing traditional clothing as well as creating contemporary tapestries and paintings.

Although rarely mentioned, both partners wrote books about knitting in the 1930s. Reserved for making socks, gloves, mittens, and other small items in Lithuania, knitting is usually overlooked in a discussion of national costume, with the focus being placed on larger items of clothing. The Tamošaitis family collected and documented colorwork and lace motifs from regions around Lithuania, and Anastazija wrote instructions for knitting a variety of accessories using traditional motifs and colors. These mittens are made with a geometrical pattern from Antanas's book of charted knitting patterns. The techniques of most of the projects in this book were included in Anastazija's book of knitting techniques.

Anastazija passed away in 1991 in Canada. In 2000, Antanas returned to Vilnius, where he founded the Anastazija and Antanas Tamošaitis Gallery Židinys (Hearth), and donated the couple's collection of folk art, original creations, and books to the gallery. Today, the gallery is run by the Vilnius Academy of Arts.

## Experience Level

Intermediate

## Finished Measurements of Sample

8¾" (22.5 cm) palm circumference

11" (28 cm) hand length from cast-on to tip

For sizing tips, see page 120.

## Materials

Fingering weight wool or wool-blend yarn, approx 200 yds/182 m in each of 2 colors.

Sample shown in Teksrena Wool Yarn (100% wool; 380 yds/350 m per 100 g ball); 1 ball each in:

**MC:** Burgundy

**CC:** Mauve

Scrap yarn

## Needles

US size 3 (3.25 mm) needles for working in the round: DPNs, 1 long circular or 2 short circulars

US size 2 (2.75 mm) needles for working in the round: DPNs, 1 long circular or 2 short circulars

Tapestry needle

## Gauge

32 sts and 33 rnds = 4"/10 cm over stranded colorwork with larger needles

## Special Techniques

Ribbed Cuff, see page 121.

Peasant Thumb, see page 122.

Pointed Mitten Tip, see page 123.

# Instructions

### Cuff

With smaller needles and CC, loosely CO 64 sts. Join to knit in the round, being careful not to twist sts.

Work in K2, P2 ribbing, following Cuff chart for stripe pattern.

### Hand

Change to larger needles and with MC, knit 1 rnd, inc 6 sts evenly around—70 sts.

Work Hand chart twice around. Work as set until rnd 29 is complete.

### Thumb opening

**Right mitten:** K3 in patt, with scrap yarn knit the next 13 sts, slip these sts back to the left needle and knit them again with the working yarn in patt, work to the end of the round.

**Left mitten:** K20 in patt, with scrap yarn knit the next 13 sts, slip these sts back to the left needle and knit them again with the working yarn in patt, work to the end of the round.

Continue following chart to row 64.

### Finger Tip Shaping

Continue following chart pattern, working decreases as shown.

When 6 sts remain, break yarn and thread tail through rem sts and pull gently to fasten off.

### Thumb

Remove the scrap yarn from the thumb opening. With MC and larger needles, pick up 13 sts above and below the thumb opening and pick up 1 st on both sides—28 sts.

Knit, working k2tog at each "corner"—26 sts.

Work Thumb chart twice around. Work as set until Thumb chart is complete—6 sts rem.

Break yarn and thread tail through rem sts and pull gently to fasten off.

### Finishing

Weave in ends, wash and dry flat to block.

## Cuff Chart

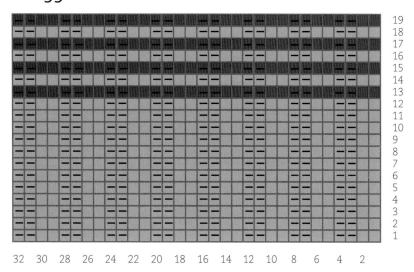

19
18
17
16
15
14
13
12
11
10
9
8
7
6
5
4
3
2
1

32  30  28  26  24  22  20  18  16  14  12  10  8  6  4  2

▢ Rose

▨ Burgundy

⊟ Purl

## *Hand Chart*

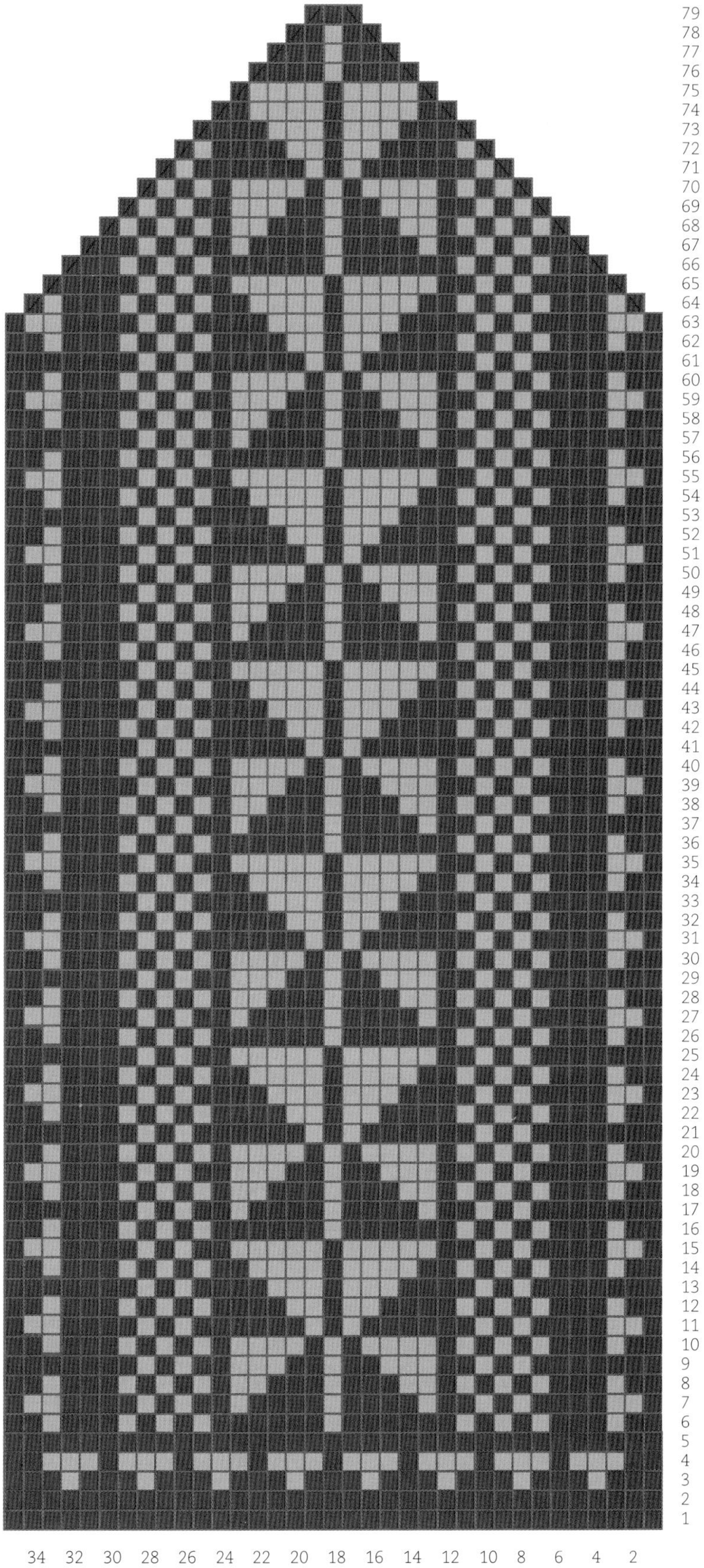

## *Thumb Chart*

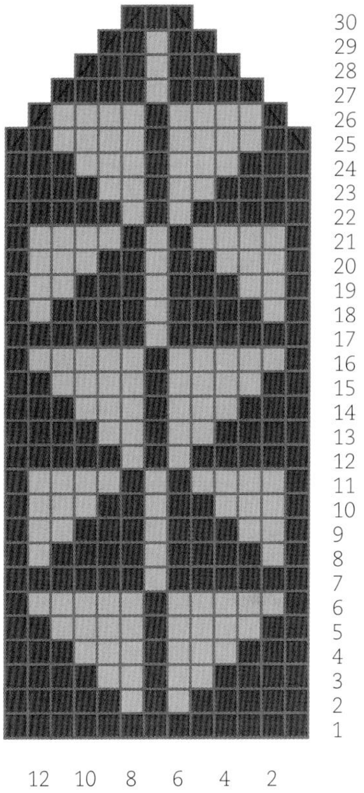

- Rose
- Burgundy
- K2tog
- SSK

# Warp and Weft to Knit

The geometric motif on these mittens is actually a weaving pattern that has been used by Lithuanian weavers for centuries, perhaps even for millennia. Weaving is revered in Lithuania, while knitting is considered a lowly craft. Why? Likely because weaving takes longer, requires more expensive, bigger equipment, and today is worked only by a small number of skilled craftsmen and -women. Knitting is a homey craft that everyone knows how to do. The difference in prestige may also be due to the fact that a much larger amount of woven fabric was needed in days gone by, both for traditional clothing and for home decor items including table linens, bed sheets, curtains, and more. The small amount of knitting used to make hand and foot coverings took up a relatively small amount of each women's time. To honor knitting as it should be, I've designed this pair of mittens that ties together the mystique of weaving patterns with the simplicity of the knit stitch. Because there are no long floats and the cuff, thumb, and fingertips are all very simple and worked with one color at a time, these are great mittens for anyone who is new to knitting with stranded colorwork.

## Experience Level

Beginner

## Finished Measurements of Sample

8" (20.5 cm) palm circumference

10" (25.5 cm) hand length from bottom of cuff to tip, with cuff folded up

For sizing tips, see page 120.

## Materials

Fingering or sock weight wool or wool-blend yarn, approx 200 yds/182 m in each of 2 colors

Sample shown in Knit Picks Stroll (75% Merino, 25% Nylon; 231 yds/211 m per 50 g ball); 1 ball each in:

**MC:** Eggplant #25606

**CC:** Sprinkle Heather #24595

Scrap yarn

## Needles

US size 3 (3.25 mm) needles for working in the round: DPNs, 1 long circular or 2 short circulars

US size 2 (2.75 mm) needles for working in the round: DPNs, 1 long circular or 2 short circulars

Tapestry needle

## Gauge

28 sts and 31 rnds = 4"/10 cm over stranded colorwork with larger needles

## Special Techniques

Ribbed Cuff, see page 121.

Peasant Thumb, see page 122.

Rounded Mitten Tip, see page 123.

# Instructions

### Cuff

With smaller needles and MC, loosely CO 64 sts. Join to knit in the round, being careful not to twist sts. Work in K2, P2 ribbing for 5" (12.5 cm).

### Hand

Change to larger needles and knit 1 rnd. Follow all rows of Hand chart on palm and back of hand; after completing 20 rows of Hand chart, make thumb opening on palm as follows.

### Thumb Opening

**Right mitten:** Work 3 sts in pattern as set, with scrap yarn, k12 sts, slip these sts back to the left needle and work them again following chart; work in pattern as set to end of round.

**Left mitten:** Work in pattern as set to last 15 sts of round; with scrap yarn, k12 sts, slip these sts back to the left needle and work them again following chart; work in pattern as set to end of round.

Continue following chart until row 43 is complete.

## Finger Tip Shaping

Change to stripe pattern as charted and arrange sts evenly into 4 sections.

K2tog at the end of each section every rnd until 8 sts rem.

Break yarn and thread tail through rem sts and pull gently to fasten off.

## Thumb

Remove the scrap yarn from the thumb opening. With MC and using larger needles, pick up 12 sts above and below the thumb opening and pick up 1 on both sides—26 sts.

Work thumb in stripe pattern as for tip of fingers. When thumb measures 1½" (4 cm) or middle of thumbnail, dec as foll:

**Rnd 1:** K2tog around—13 sts rem.

**Rnd 2:** Knit.

**Rnd 3:** K2tog at end of rnd—12 sts rem.

**Rnd 4:** K2tog around—6 sts rem.

Break yarn and thread tail through rem sts and pull gently to fasten off.

## Finishing

Weave in ends, wash and dry flat to block.

■ Eggplant

▨ Sprinkle Heather

☑ K2tog

# Hand Chart

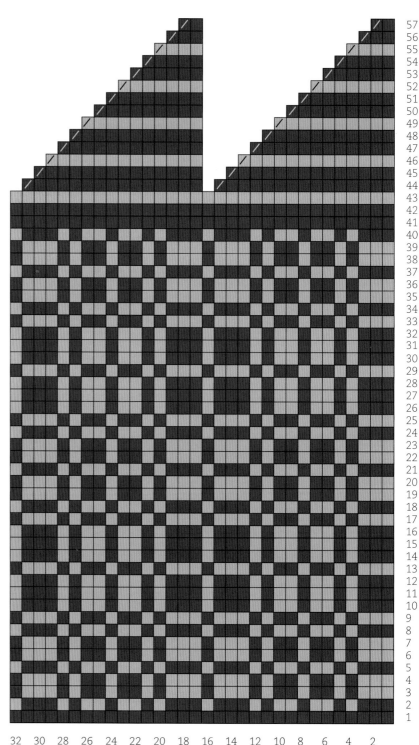

138.

# Rustic Fences

The colorwork pattern on these mittens, documented by Antanas Tamošaitis, knit in neutral colors reminds me of the rustic fences used in the Lithuanian country-side, and of the beautiful wooden fences at the traditional houses in the Open Air Museum of Lithuania in Rumšiškės. I love the way the vertical and diagonal lines interact with each other, drawing your eye first in one direction and then in another. I used horizontal stripes on the cuff to anchor the design, just as a fence is anchored in the earth.

## Experience Level

Intermediate

## Finished Measurements of Sample

8" (20.5 cm) palm circumference

10" (25.5 cm) hand length from from cast on to tip

For sizing tips, see page 120.

## Materials

Fingering weight wool yarn, approx 200 yds/182 m in each of 2 colors

Sample shown in Jamieson's Shetland Spindrift (100% wool; 115 yds/105 m per 25 g ball):

**MC:** Rust #578, 2 balls

**CC:** Natural White #104, 2 balls

Scrap yarn

## Needles

US size 3 (3.25 mm) needles for working in the round: DPNs, 1 long circular or 2 short circulars

US size 2 (2.75 mm) needles for working in the round: DPNs, 1 long circular or 2 short circulars

Tapestry needle

## Gauge

36 sts and 38 rnds = 4"/10 cm over stranded colorwork with larger needles

## Special Techniques

Ribbed Cuff, see page 121.

Peasant Thumb, see page 122.

Pointed Mitten Tip, see page 123.

# Instructions

### Cuff

With smaller needles and MC, loosely CO 64 sts. Join to knit in the round, being careful not to twist sts.

Work in K2, P2 ribbing following charted stripe pattern until all rows of chart are complete—72 sts.

### Hand

Change to larger needles.

Work Hand chart across first 36 sts, work Palm chart around next 36 sts.

Continue in patterns as set until 20 chart rounds are complete.

### Thumb Opening

**Right mitten:** Work 3 sts in pattern as set, with scrap yarn, k13 sts, slip these sts back to the left needle and work them again following chart; work in pattern as set to end of round.

**Left mitten:** Work in pattern as set to last 16 sts of round; with scrap yarn, k13 sts, slip these sts back to the left needle and work them again following chart; work in pattern as set to end of round.

Work even in patterns until 20 rows of pattern have been worked after thumb opening.

### Finger Tip Shaping

Work Finger Tip chart twice around, working decreases as charted.

When 8 sts remain, break yarn and thread tail through rem sts and pull gently to fasten off.

## Thumb

Remove the scrap yarn from the thumb opening. With MC, pick up 13 sts above and below the thumb opening and pick up 1 on both sides—28 sts.

Work Thumb chart around, decreasing as charted—4 sts rem.

Break yarn and thread tail through rem sts and pull gently to fasten off.

## Finishing

Weave in ends, wash and dry flat to block.

# Cuff Chart

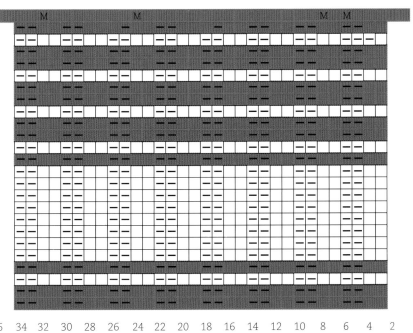

| | White |
|---|---|
| | Rust |
| − | Purl |
| M | M1 |

## Palm Chart

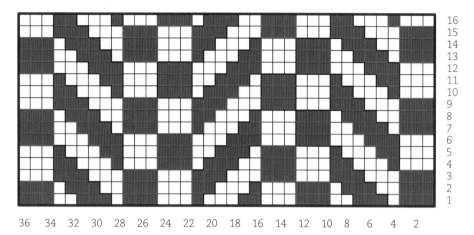

16
15
14
13
12
11
10
9
8
7
6
5
4
3
2
1

36  34  32  30  28  26  24  22  20  18  16  14  12  10  8  6  4  2

## Thumb Chart

30
29
28
27
26
25
24
23
22
21
20
19
18
17
16
15
14
13
12
11
10
9
8
7
6
5
4
3
2
1

14  12  10  8  6  4  2

## Hand Chart

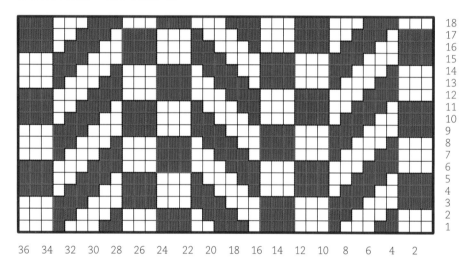

18
17
16
15
14
13
12
11
10
9
8
7
6
5
4
3
2
1

36  34  32  30  28  26  24  22  20  18  16  14  12  10  8  6  4  2

◻ White

◼ Rust

⟍ SSK

⟋ K2tog

## Finger Tip Chart

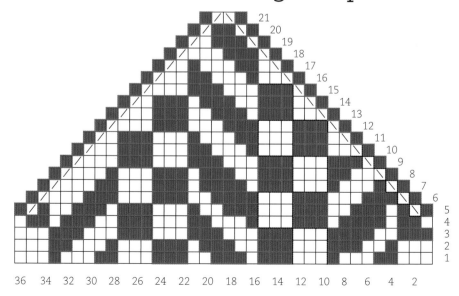

21
20
19
18
17
16
15
14
13
12
11
10
9
8
7
6
5
4
3
2
1

36  34  32  30  28  26  24  22  20  18  16  14  12  10  8  6  4  2

# Rumšiškės in Summer Mittens

The Rumšiškės Open Air Museum, situated on a main road between Vilnius and Kaunas, is like Colonial Williamsburg in Virginia, Old Beth Page Village on Long Island, or the Shelburne Museum here in Vermont. These places reproduce buildings, tools, and villages from times gone by. They give us a way to remember and relive the past so we can recall a way of life that has largely been lost to time. At these places we can see reminders of traditions and crafts we may want to re-store to our own lives, as well as of the dangers and hardships that we can be glad to leave behind.

Although mittens are worn in winter, the colors and motifs on these are meant to evoke visions of summer in the countryside. In July and August, Lithuanians stream out of the cities and flock to the Kaimas (countryside), to the Ežeras (lake) and to Palanga and Nida, vacation towns on the Baltic Sea. Because winters are long and summers are short, every warm and sunny day is a gift to be appreciated and savored.

## Finished Measurements of Sample

8" (20.5 cm) palm circumference

11" (28 cm) hand length from cast-on to tip

For sizing tips, see page 120.

## Materials

Fingering weight wool yarn, approx 200 yds/182 m of main color and 100 yds/91 m each of 4 contrasting colors

Sample shown in Teksrena Wool Yarn (100% wool; 380 yds/350 m per 100 g ball); 1 ball each in:

**MC:** Charcoal

**Right mitten:**

　**A:** Green

　**B:** Light Pink

　**C:** Dark Pink

　**D:** Burgundy

**Left mitten:** reverse B and D

　**B:** Burgundy

　**D:** Light Pink

Scrap yarn

## Needles

US size 1.5 (2.5 mm) needles for working in the round: DPNs, 1 long circular or 2 short circulars

Tapestry needle

## Gauge

34 sts and 36 rnds = 4"/10 cm over stranded colorwork

## Special Techniques

Peasant Thumb, see page 122.

Pointed Mitten Tip, see page 123.

# Instructions

With MC, loosely CO 70 sts. Join to knit in the round, being careful not to twist sts. K1 rnd, then k2tog around—35 sts. Make sure you have a multiple of 5 sts on each needle.

Work 7 beginning entrelac triangles as follows.

**\*Row 1 (RS):** K2, turn.

**Row 2 (WS):** Sl 1, p1, turn.

**Row 3:** Sl 1, k2, turn.

**Row 4:** Sl 1, p2, turn.

**Row 5:** Sl 1, k3, turn.

**Row 6:** Sl 1, p3, turn.

**Row 7:** Sl 1, k4, turn.

**Row 8:** Sl 1, p4, turn.

**Row 9:** Sl 1, k5, turn.

**Row 10:** Sl 1, p5, turn.

**Row 11:** Sl 1, k5, do not turn.

Move over to next sts and start again from \*. Work until you have 7 triangles total. Turn.

### WS Rectangles

\*With WS facing and B, with right-hand needle, pick up and purl 5 sts along the edge of the adjacent triangle (you are picking up sts from the WS, insert the needle from the BACK, and pull the working yarn through to the RS as if you are purling). Turn.

**Row 1 (RS):** Sl 1, k4, turn.

**Row 2 (WS):** Sl 1, p3, p2tog (1 st from rectangle and 1 st from triangle), turn.

Rep the last 2 rows until all sts from triangle are joined to rectangle. Don't turn after last row.

Rectangle complete. Move over to next triangle and rep from \* until 7 rectangles have been worked.

## RS Rectangles

*With RS facing and C, pick up and knit 5 sts on edge of adjacent rectangle.

**Row 1 (RS):** Sl 1, p4, turn.

**Row 2 (WS):** Sl 1, k3, ssk (1 st from new rectangle and 1 st from rectangle on prev rnd), turn.

Rep the last 2 rows until all sts are joined to adjacent rectangle. Don't turn after last row.

Rectangle complete. Move over to next triangle and rep from * until 7 rectangles have been worked.

**WS rectangles:** Rep WS rectangles with D.

**RS rectangles:** Rep RS rectangles with C.

**WS rectangles:** Rep WS rectangles with B.

## Ending Triangles

*With RS facing and A, pick up and knit 5 sts along edge of adjacent rectangle. Turn.

**Row 1 (WS):** Sl 1, p4, turn.

**Row 2 (RS):** Sl 1, k3, ssk, turn.

**Row 3:** Sl 1, p3, turn.

**Row 4:** Sl 1, k2, ssk, turn.

**Row 5:** Sl 1, p2, turn.

**Row 6:** Sl 1, k1, ssk, turn.

**Row 7:** Sl 1, p1, turn.

**Row 8:** Sl 1, ssk, turn.

**Row 9:** Sl 1, turn.

**Row 10:** Ssk.

Rep from * around.

## Hand

**Inc rnd:** With MC, (K1, m1) working around the top edge of all ending triangles—70 sts.

**Next rnd:** Knit around, dec 2 sts—68 sts.

**Right Hand round:** Work Floral Entrelac Hand chart twice around.

**Left Hand round:** Work Floral Entrelac Hand chart twice around, reversing positions of colors B and D.

Work as set until rnd 34 of chart is complete.

## Thumb Opening

While working chart rnd 35, make thumb opening as follows.

**Right mitten:** K2 in patt, with scrap yarn knit the next 12 sts, slip these sts back to the left needle and knit them again with the working yarn in patt, work to the end of the round.

**Left mitten:** K20 in patt, with scrap yarn knit the next 12 sts, slip these sts back to the left needle and knit them again with the working yarn in patt, work to the end of the round.

Continue with Floral Entrelac Hand chart through rnd 55.

## Finger Tip Shaping

Continue following chart pattern, working decreases as shown.

When 12 sts remain, cut yarn and use tapestry needle to run the tail through rem sts and gather in to fasten off.

Break yarn and thread tail through rem sts and pull gently to fasten off.

## Thumb

Remove the scrap yarn from the thumb opening. With MC and larger needles, pick up 12 sts above and below the thumb opening and pick up 1 st on both sides—26 sts.

Work in vertical stripes (k1 MC, k1 CC) to match wrist.

Knit until thumb meas 2¼" (5.5 cm) or to middle of thumbnail. Continue with MC only.

**Next rnd:** K2tog around—13 sts.

**Next rnd:** K1, k2tog around—6 sts.

Break yarn and thread tail through rem sts and pull gently to fasten off.

## Finishing

Weave in ends, wash and dry flat to block.

# Floral Entrelac Hand Chart

| | |
|---|---|
| ☐ | MC Charcoal |
| ▨ | A Green |
| ▨ | B Light Pink |
| ▧ | C Dark Pink |
| ■ | D Burgundy |
| ◩ | SSK |
| ◪ | K2tog |

# Larks in My Rose Garden

In the 1950s, mittens with long gauntlet cuffs became popular all over Lithuania. Some were made with drawstrings embellished with pompoms at the wrist, and many had fringe on the edge, as well. Realistic rose motifs also were popular for a period of time, some much more elaborate than this, knit in intarsia or added to knitting with duplicate stitch. Bird and animal motifs are also found on mittens and gloves in museum collections, but they are less common than geometric and floral designs. These are beautiful motifs in their own right, but they are not considered traditional by those who define these things.

These mittens are in the collection of the Vilkaviškio krašto muziejus (Vilkaviškis Area Museum), one of the first small regional museums I visited on our tour of Lithuania in 2008. Scattered throughout the country, it seems like every city, town, and village has its own historical or ethnographic museum where you can learn about the traditions and lifestyle of the region. Most feature exhibits of items from the nineteenth century, but some—especially those near archaeological digs— have objects from settlements and graveyards dating back to the Stone Age.

## Experience Level

Intermediate

## Sizes

Child (Adult)

## Finished Measurements of Sample

6 (8)" [15 (20.5) cm] palm circumference

8 (9)" [20.5 (23) cm] hand length from stripe at wrist to tip

For sizing tips, see page 120.

## Materials

Fingering weight wool for child's mittens or sport weight wool for adult's, approx 400 yds/365 m of MC and 30–50 yds/ 27–45 m each of 4 contrasting colors.

Child's sample shown in Brown Sheep Nature Spun Fingering (100% wool, 310 yds/283 m per 50 g skein) in:

**MC:** #N04 Blue Night, 2 skeins

Approx 50 yds/45 m each of:

**A:** #115 Bit of Blue

**B:** #155 Bamboo

**C:** #N44 Husker Red

**D:** #123 Saddle Tan

Adult's sample shown in Brown Sheep Nature Spun Sport (100% wool, 184 yds/168 m per 50 g ball) same colors as fingering: 3 balls of MC and approx 50 yds/45 m of each CC

Scrap yarn

## Needles

**Child:** US sizes 3 (3.25 mm), 2 (2.75 mm), and 1 (2.25 mm) needles for working in the round: DPNs, 1 long circular or 2 short circulars

**Adult:** US sizes 5 (3.75 mm), 4 (3.5 mm) and 3 (3.25 mm) needles for working in the round: DPNs, 1 long circular or 2 short circulars

Tapestry needle

## Gauge

40 (32) sts and 44 (36) rnds = 4"/10 cm over pattern stitch using smallest needles for your size

## Special Techniques

Gauntlet Cuff, see page 121.

Peasant Thumb, see page 122.

Round Mitten Tip, worked in pattern, see page 123.

# Instructions

## Cuff

With MC and largest needles for your size, loosely CO 80 sts. Join to knit in the round, being careful not to twist sts.

Knit 2 rnds.

Work rnds 13–23 of Rosebuds Motif chart.

Work all rnds of Rosebuds with Birds chart once.

Change to medium needles for your size.

**Dec rnd:** With MC, (k8, k2tog) around—72 sts rem.

Work 2 rnds even with MC.

Work rnds 13–23 of Rosebuds Motif chart.

Change to smallest needles for your size.

**Dec rnd:** With MC, (k7, k2tog) around—64 sts rem.

## Hand

**Next rnd:** With B, knit.

**Next rnd:** (K1 A, knit 1 MC) around.

**Next rnd:** With B, knit.

**Next 5 rnds:** With MC, knit.

Work all rows of Rosebuds Motif chart once, then work rows 1–11 once more.

## Thumb opening

Working rnd 12 (plain rnd) of chart, make thumb opening as follows.

**Right mitten:** K 34 sts; with scrap yarn, k12 sts, slip them back to the left needle and knit them again with MC, k to end of rnd.

**Left mitten:** K to last 14 sts of rnd; with scrap yarn, k12 sts, slip them back to the left needle and knit them again in MC, k last 2 sts.

Work even in Rosebuds Motif patt until a total of 3 repeats of chart have been worked from start of hand.

## Finger Tip Shaping

Divide sts into 8 sections of 8 sts.

With MC only, work as follows.

K2tog at the end of each section every other rnd until 8 sts rem.

Break yarn and thread tail through rem sts and pull gently to fasten off.

## Thumb

Remove the scrap yarn from the thumb opening. With MC, pick up 12 sts above and below the thumb opening and pick up 2 sts on both sides—28 sts.

**Rnd 1:** (K5, k2tog) 4 times—24 sts.

Knit 2 rnds.

Work rnds 13–19 of Rosebuds Motif chart.

Knit even until thumb meas 1¾" (4.5 cm) or reaches to middle of thumbnail.

Divide sts into 4 sections of 6 sts.

K2tog at the end of each section every other rnd until 6 sts rem.

Break yarn and thread tail through rem sts and pull gently to fasten off.

## Finishing

Weave in ends, wash and dry flat to block.

Add fringe to CO edge if desired.

# Rosebuds Motif Chart

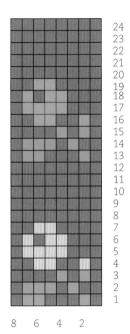

MC Midnight Blue

A Bit of Blue

B Bamboo

C Husker Red

D Saddle Tan

# Rosebuds with Birds Chart

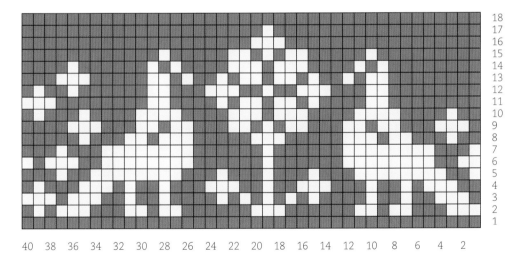

# Clover & Honey Bees

Visiting the museums around Lithuania and seeing the different styles of hand-knit accessories in each collection was one of my favorite parts of the research I did for this book. These mittens are based on a pair that June and I saw in the Šiaulių "Aušros" muziejus (Šiauliai Aušros Museum). The originals had a very odd, asymmetrical colorwork pattern above the cuff. I could not tell if it was meant to be a geometric design or a floral motif, or if, perhaps, a young girl was making one of her first pairs of mittens and had miscalculated when trying to knit a motif that was beyond her skill. Whatever the story behind these mittens might have been, I fell in love with their shape and colors and I knew I would make a pair for myself. To keep the design simple, I chose a tiny clover motif that allows the cuff colors to be repeated just above the wrist. There are only five rows of stranded knitting in the entire mitten, and the lacy cuff pattern is very simple, making this a perfect project for the new color or lace knitter. The clover motif reminds me of honey, and the shape of the mitten tips remind me of a honey pot. Honey is a popular natural treat in Lithuania and is sold at farmers markets every summer. Beehives are found all over the countryside and there is even a "Museum of Ancient Bee-keeping" (Senovinės bitininkystės muziejus) in the Aukštaitija National Park.

## Experience Level

Intermediate

## Finished Measurements of Sample

8" (20.5 cm) palm circumference

10" (25.5 cm) hand length from bottom of cuff to tip

For sizing tips, see page 120.

## Materials

Fingering weight wool yarn, approx 200 yds/182 m MC and 30 yds/27 m each of 2 contrasting colors

Sample shown in Jamieson's Shetland Spindrift (100% wool; 115 yds/105 m per 25 g ball):

   **A:** color #1340 Cosmos, 1 skein

Approx 30 yds/27 m of each of the following contrast colors:

   **B:** #587 (Madder)

   **C:** #350 (Lemon)

Scrap yarn

## Needles

US size 3 (3.25 mm) needles for working in the round: DPNs, 1 long circular or 2 short circulars

Tapestry needle

## Gauge

32 sts and 42 rnds = 4"/10 cm over stockinette stitch

## Special Techniques

Lined Openwork Cuff, see page 121.

Peasant Thumb, see page 122.

Tapered Mitten Tip, see page 123.

## Pattern Stitches

### Diagonal Lace Pattern

(worked over an even number of sts)

**Rnd 1:** (SSK, yo) around.

**Rnds 2 and 4:** Knit.

**Rnd 3:** Remove marker, sl1, replace marker, (ssk, yo) around.

Repeat rnds 3 and 4 for pattern, noting that the end of rnd moves 1 stitch to the left for each repeat worked.

## Instructions

With color C, loosely CO 60 sts. Join to knit in the round, being careful not to twist sts.

### Cuff

Mitten is worked with a lace cuff that is lined.

**Cuff lining:** Work even in St st until cuff measures 2" (5 cm).

**Turning ridge:** With A, k1 rnd, p1 rnd, k1 rnd.

**Outer cuff:** With B, work diagonal lace pattern for 2" (5 cm).

### Hand

With MC, k3 rnds, inc to 64 sts on 1st rnd.

Work all rnds of Tiny Clovers chart 8 times around hand.

With MC, work in St st.

When mitten measures 5" (12.5 cm) or desired length from turning ridge, make thumb opening as follows.

## Thumb Opening

**Right mitten:** With scrap yarn, k13 sts, slip them back to the left needle and knit them again with MC, k to end of rnd.

**Left mitten:** K to last 13 sts of rnd; with scrap yarn, k13 sts, slip them back to the left needle and knit them again in MC.

Work even in St st until mitten measures 2½" (6.5 cm) from thumb opening or desired length to finger tip shaping. (Remember that the Tapered Mitten Tip shaping creates a longer finger tip area than the round or pointed methods. The mitten tip will measure approx 2½" [6.5 cm] from first dec rnd to fastening off.)

## Finger Tip Shaping

Continue in St st and AT THE SAME TIME, divide sts into 8 sections of 8 sts.

**Dec rnd:** (K to last 2 sts before marker, p2tog) around.

Knit 6 rnds.

Repeat dec rnd. Knit 5 rnds.

Repeat dec rnd. Knit 4 rnds.

Repeat dec rnd. Knit 3 rnds.

Repeat dec rnd. Knit 2 rnds.

**Next rnd:** K2tog around.

Break yarn and thread tail through rem sts and pull gently to fasten off.

## Thumb

Remove the scrap yarn from the thumb opening. With A, pick up 13 sts above and below the thumb opening and pick up 1 st on both sides—28 sts.

**Rnd 1:** Knit, working k2tog at each "corner"—26 sts.

Knit even until thumb meas 1¾" (4.5 cm) or reaches to middle of thumbnail.

Divide sts into 3 equal sections.

SSK at the beg of each section every rnd until 6 sts rem.

Break yarn and thread tail through rem sts and pull gently to fasten off.

## Finishing

Fold up cuff and sew CO edge to inside of mitten on first row of MC above lace pattern.

Weave in ends, wash and dry flat to block.

## Tiny Clovers Chart

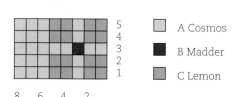

| | A Cosmos |
|---|---|
| | B Madder |
| | C Lemon |

# Lithuania Link

Inspired by mittens that June obtained during her travels in Lithuania, these remind me both of Lithuania and of England. I first saw two pairs of mittens made in this style when visiting June at her home in Cumbria. Later, I discovered the wide variety of pattern stitches in texture and color used to knit mitten and glove cuffs in Lithuania. Made with a trinity stitch cuff and a simple geometric design on the hand, this pair knits up quickly in sport weight wool. The lining is all stockinette stitch knit in fingering weight wool at the same gauge as the outer mitten. With the cold winters in Northern Europe, having the extra layer of insulation is definitely appreciated, and many of the colorwork mittens we saw in museum collections were fully lined with undyed wool yarn. June's mittens, and several pairs that I saw in museums, were made in a normal size and fit quite snugly with the extra layer of knitting inside. I made my pair in two sizes because I wanted an oversized pair to fit loosely, like one pair I saw during my research and a pair of commercial ski mittens I bought at a sporting goods store, so they can be worn with gloves inside them if desired. If you want your mittens to fit more snugly, make the smaller size. I added a drawstring at the wrist to keep the wind and snow out. Without the drawstring, the mittens fit nicely over the cuff of a parka or jacket.

## Experience Level

Intermediate

## Sizes

Normal (Oversized)

For sizing tips, see page 120.

## Finished Measurements of Sample

9 (10)" [23 (25.5) cm] palm circumference, outer mitten

8 (9)" [20.5 (23) cm] circumference, inside lining

10" (25.5 cm) hand length from bottom of cuff to tip, both sizes

## Materials

**Outer mitten:** sport weight wool, approx 180 yds/165 m of MC and 50 yds/46 m of CC

**Lining:** fingering weight wool, approx 180 yds/165 m

Sample shown in Brown Sheep Nature Spun Sport (100% wool, 184 yds/168 m per 50 g ball):

   **MC:** color #136 Chocolate Kisses, 1 ball

   **CC:** color #730 Natural, approx 50 yds/46 m

Brown Sheep Nature Spun Fingering (100% wool, 310 yds/283 m per 50 g ball):

   color #730 Natural, 1 ball

Scrap yarn

## Needles

US size 3 (3.25 mm) needles for working in the round: DPNs, 1 long circular or 2 short circulars

US size 5 (3.75 mm) needles for working in the round: DPNs, 1 long circular or 2 short circulars

Tapestry needle

## Gauge

28 sts and 32 rnds = 4"/10 cm over stockinette stitch with smaller needles and sport weight yarn; with larger needles and fingering weight yarn

## Special Techniques

Trinity Stitch Cuff, see page 121.

Peasant Thumb, see page 122.

Round Mitten Tip, see page 123.

Lining, see page 123.

# Pattern Stitches

### Trinity Stitch (circular)

Worked over a multiple of 4 sts.

**Rnds 1 and 3:** Purl all stitches.

**Rnd 2:** (P1, k1, p1) all in same stitch, k3tog.

**Rnd 4:** K3tog, (p1, k1, p1) all in same stitch.

Repeat rnds 1–4 for pattern.

# Instructions

## Outer Mitten

### Cuff

With MC and 2 larger needles held together and the long-tail cast on, loosely CO 60 (72) sts. Join to knit in the round, being careful not to twist sts.

Knit 1 rnd, purl 1 rnd, knit 1 rnd.

Work in Trinity stitch for 3" (7.5 cm).

### Hand

Knit 1 rnd.

Work Hand Pattern chart 5 (6) times around hand, completing rnds 1–14 once.

### Thumb Opening

While working chart rnd 15, which is a plain round, make thumb openings as follows.

**Right mitten:** K2, with scrap yarn knit the next 12 sts, slip these sts back to the left needle and knit them again with the working yarn, knit to the end of the round.

**Left mitten:** Knit to the last 14 sts, with scrap yarn knit the next 12 sts, slip these sts back to the left needle and knit them again with the working yarn, knit to the end of the round.

Work rnd 16 of chart, then rnds 1–16 once more, then rnds 1–9 once more.

### Finger Tip Shaping

Change to smaller needles.

Break CC. Divide sts into 4 equal sections. K2tog at the end of each section every other rnd until 36 sts rem. Then k2tog at the end of each section every rnd until 8 sts rem.

Break the yarn, draw the tail through the remaining sts, and pull gently to fasten off.

### Thumb

Remove the scrap yarn from the thumb opening. With MC and smaller needles, pick up 12 sts above and below the thumb opening and pick up 2 on both sides—28 sts.

**Rnd 1:** Knit, working k2tog at each "corner"—26 sts.

Work even until thumb meas 2¼" (5.5 cm) or reaches to middle of thumbnail.

Divide sts into 4 sections. K2tog at the end of each section every rnd until 6 sts rem.

Break yarn and thread tail through rem sts and pull gently to fasten off.

Weave in the ends on the outer mitten.

## Lining

With RS facing, using fingering weight yarn and smaller needles, pick up and knit 1 st in each st at the cast-on edge. Arrange the stitches evenly on the needles to work in the round.

Change to larger needles and work in St st until cuff reaches the end of the trinity stitch cuff on the outer mitten. Knit the remainder of the lining just as you did the outer mitten, making the thumb opening to line up with the thumb opening on the outer mitten. Check the fit as you go to make sure that it fits inside the outer mitten correctly.

Weave in ends on lining.

## Finishing

For oversized mittens, make two 12" (30.5 cm) long twisted cords and weave them in and out of the trinity stitch cuff near the wrist. Gather in slightly and tie to secure.

Wash and dry flat to block.

# Hand Pattern Chart

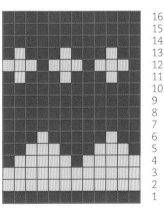

| | |
|---|---|
| Natural | Chocolate Kisses |

16 15 14 13 12 11 10 9 8 7 6 5 4 3 2 1

12 10 8 6 4 2

# Suvalkija Beehives

Suvalkija is named for a town that is now part of Poland. This southwestern region of Lithuania is small, with very few trees and soil free of rocks. Most of the region is quite flat and open, except for Vilkija, perhaps the hilliest town in Lithuania. Farming and agriculture have traditionally been quite important here, not only because of the quality of the soil, but also because serfdom was abolished here earlier than in other parts of Lithuania, enabling farm workers to have a greater degree of freedom and opportunity to make money for themselves. The people here are said to be clever and clear-thinking, but quite frugal. One story claims that Suvalkijans cut the tails off their cats in winter so they can pass through the door more quickly, thereby saving heat!

These gloves are made with a honeycomb pattern that was knit in Suvalkija, and pictured in vintage books about Lithuanian national costume. The patterning is always worked with slip stitches combined with rows of knits and purls, but different details create fabrics that vary from thick and cushy, as in these mittens, to thin and smooth, as in the Amber on My Mind Gloves on page 175.

## Experience Level

Beginner

## Finished Measurements of Sample

8" (20.5 cm) palm circumference

11" (28 cm) hand length from cast-on to tip

For sizing tips, see page 120.

## Materials

Fingering weight wool yarn, approx 200 yds/183 m in each of 2 colors

Sample shown in:

**MC:** Jamieson's Shetland Spindrift (100% wool; 115 yds/105 m per 25 g ball): color #1340 (Cosmos); 2 balls

**CC:** Kauni Wool 8/2 Effektgarn, (100% wool; 437 yds/400 m per 100 g ball); color EQ; 1 ball

Scrap yarn

## Needles

US size 3 (3.25 mm) needles for working in the round: DPNs, 1 long circular or 2 short circulars

US size 2 (2.75 mm) needles for working in the round: DPNs, 1 long circular or 2 short circulars

Tapestry needle

## Gauge

33½ sts and 50 rnds = 4"/10 cm over Honeycomb Stitch with larger needles

## Special Techniques

Ribbed Cuff, see page 121.

Peasant Thumb, see page 122.

Round Mitten Tip, see page 123.

# Pattern Stitches

### Honeycomb Stitch (circular)

Chart on page 160.

Worked over a multiple of 6 sts.

**Rnd 1:** With MC, knit.

**Rnds 2–3:** With MC, purl.

**Rnds 4–7:** With CC, (k4, sl2 wyib) around.

**Rnd 8:** With MC, knit.

**Rnds 9–10:** With MC, purl.

**Rnds 11–14:** With CC, (k2, sl2 wyib, k2) around.

Repeat rnds 1–14 for pattern.

# Instructions

Unwind the Kauni and make 2 balls of approx 65 g each with the sections of the colors you want to use for the mittens.

With MC and smaller needles, loosely CO 56 sts. Join to knit in the round, being careful not to twist sts.

### Cuff

Mitten is worked with a ribbed cuff in stripes.

Work in K2, P2 ribbing and stripe pattern as follows.

4 rnds MC, 2 rnds CC, 2 rnds MC, 6 rnds CC, 2 rnds MC, 6 rnds CC, 2 rnds MC, 2 rnds CC, 2 rnds MC.

### Hand

**Increase rnd:** (K14, m1) 4 times—60 sts.

Begin Honeycomb Stitch. Work rnds 1–14 three times, then work rnds 1 and 2 once more.

## Thumb opening

Working rnd 3 of Honeycomb Stitch (a purl rnd), make thumb opening as follows.

**Right mitten:** P1 in patt, with scrap yarn knit the next 12 sts, slip these sts back to the left needle and knit them again with the working yarn, purl to the end of the round.

**Left mitten:** Purl to last 13 sts, with scrap yarn knit the next 12 sts, slip these sts back to the left needle and knit them again with the working yarn, purl last st.

Work rnds 4–14 of Honeycomb stitch once, then work rnds 1–14 twice more, then work rnds 1–3 once more. Break MC.

## Finger Tip Shaping

Change to larger needles. Working with CC color only, divide the sts with markers into 4 sections of 15 sts each.

**Right mitten:** K2tog at the end of each section every rnd until 8 sts rem.

**Left mitten:** SSK at the beg of each section every rnd until 8 sts rem.

Break yarn and thread tail through rem sts and pull gently to fasten off.

## Thumb

Remove the scrap yarn from the thumb opening. With MC and larger needles, pick up 12 sts above and below the thumb opening and pick up 1 st on both sides—26 sts.

**Rnd 1:** Knit, working k2tog at each "corner"— 24 sts.

When thumb measures 2¼" (5.5 cm) or to middle of thumbnail, dec as follows.

Divide sts into 3 sections of 8 sts each with markers.

K2tog at the end of each section every rnd until 6 sts rem.

Break yarn and thread tail through rem sts and pull gently to fasten off.

## Finishing

Weave in ends, wash and dry flat to block.

# Honeycomb Stitch Chart

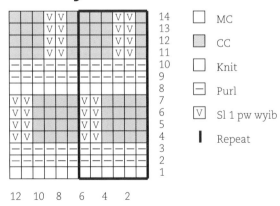

MC
CC
☐ Knit
⊟ Purl
V Sl 1 pw wyib
❙ Repeat

# Kaziuko mugė: St. Casimir's Feast

St. Casmir, the patron saint of Lithuania, is often depicted on stained glass windows in Lithuanian churches holding a lily. Every year on the first weekend in March, the streets of Vilnius are filled with stalls with craft vendors hawking their wares: woven baskets; ceramic bowls and vases; wooden spoons and utensils; iron crosses and jewelry; and knitted socks, mittens, and wrist warmers. Vilniaus verbos—bouquets of dried flowers—are also sold at the fair, in preparation for celebrating Palm Sunday and the coming of spring. Traditional foods are served by street vendors, singers and dancers perform age-old folk songs, and the streets are filled with tens of thousands of locals and visitors from near and far who have come to eat, drink, and be merry. This event is called Kaziuko mugė—St. Casimir's Fair—and it's been held annually since the early 1600s.

These gloves were inspired by the knitted accessories I saw for sale at this event, and by the hope for flowers to bloom not too far in the future.

## Experience Level
Advanced

## Finished Measurements of Sample
8¼" (21 cm) palm circumference

12" (30.5 cm) hand length from cast-on to tip of middle finger

For sizing tips, see page 120.

## Materials
Approx 400 yds/365 m of fingering weight wool yarn: 200 yds/182 m each of 2 colors and small amounts of 4 more colors for cuff

Sample shown in Rauma Finullgarn (100% wool, 191 yds/175 m per 50 g ball), 1 ball each in:

**MC:** 414 Grey

**CC:** 401 Natural

For stripes of cuffs, small amounts of:

483 Teal

498 Pea Green

494 Kelly Green

404 Baby Blue

Scrap yarn

## Needles
US size 0 (2 mm) needles for working in the round: DPNs, 1 long circular or 2 short circulars

US size 1.5 (2.5 mm) needles for working in the round: DPNs, 1 long circular or 2 short circulars

Tapestry needle

## Gauge
36 sts and 40 rnds = 4"/10 cm over stranded colorwork with larger needles

## Special Techniques
Ribbed Cuff, see page 121.

Peasant Thumb, see page 122.

Glove Fingers, see page 123.

# Instructions

With MC and smaller needles, loosely CO 64 sts. Join to knit in the round, being careful not to twist sts.

### Cuff
Work in K2, P2 ribbing for 36 rnds, working 4-rnd stripes in the following sequence: MC, Teal, MC, Pea Green, MC, Kelly Green, MC, Baby Blue, MC.

Change to larger needles and continue with MC.

### Hand
**Inc rnd:** (K4, m1) around—80 sts.

Work Checkers Chart for 23 rnds.

### Thumb Opening
**Left hand:** K23, k next 14 sts with scrap yarn, slip these sts back to the left needle and knit them again with the working yarn, complete round in pattern as set.

**Right hand:** K3, k next 14 sts with scrap yarn, slip these sts back to the left needle and knit them again with the working yarn, complete round in pattern as set.

Continue working Checkers chart as established and AT THE SAME TIME, on back of hand, after first 4 sts, pm, work 35 sts of Lily chart, pm, work rem sts in Checkers patt as set. When all rnds of Lily chart are complete, glove measures 8½" (22 cm) from cast-on edge, work fingers as follows.

### Fingers
Fingers are worked following Lice chart (page 164).

**Little finger:** Work 9 sts from the palm plus 9 sts from the back of the hand plus CO 3 sts in between the fingers—21 sts. Put rem 62 sts on hold.

Dec 1 st on first rnd—20 sts. Work 2" (5 cm) in Lice Patt. Change to MC only. Divide sts into 4 equal sections.

**Dec rnd:** (K to last 2 sts in section, k2tog) around—4 sts decreased.

Rep until 4 sts rem. Cut yarn and run tail through remaining sts. Pull gently to gather in and fasten off.

**Ring finger:** Work 9 sts from the palm, CO 3 sts between fingers, work 9 sts from back of hand, then pick up 3 sts between ring finger and little finger—24 sts. Put rem 44 sts on hold. Work 2¾" (7 cm), then dec and fasten off as for little finger.

**Middle finger:** Work 11 sts from the palm, CO 3 sts between fingers, work 11 sts from back of hand, then pick 3 sts between ring finger and little finger—28 sts. Put rem 22 sts on hold. Work 3¼" (8 cm), then dec and fasten off as for little finger.

**Index finger:** Work over the 22 rem sts and pick up 2 sts on side of middle finger—24 sts. Work for 3" (7.5 cm), then dec and fasten off as for little finger.

## Thumb

Remove the scrap yarn from the thumb opening. With MC and larger needles, pick up 14 sts above and below the thumb opening and pick up 1 st on both sides—30 sts.

Dec 2 sts in the first rnd—28 sts. Work even for 2" (5 cm), then dec and fasten off as for fingers.

## Finishing

Weave in ends, closing up the small holes between the fingers. Wash and dry flat to block.

# Checkers Chart

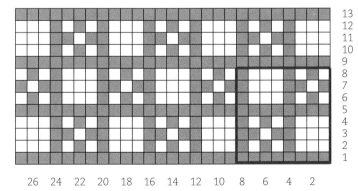

26  24  22  20  18  16  14  12  10  8  6  4  2

13
12
11
10
9
8
7
6
5
4
3
2
1

▨ Black

☐ White

❙ Repeat

# Lily Chart

| | | | | |
|---|---|---|---|---|
| | | 26 | | Black |
| | | 25 | | White |
| | | 24 | | Repeat |

Black
White
Repeat

26 25 24 23 22 21 20 19 18 17 16 15 14 13 12 11 10 9 8 7 6 5 4 3 2 1

34 32 30 28 26 24 22 20 18 16 14 12 10 8 6 4 2

# Lice Chart

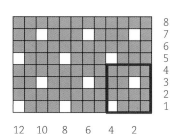

8 7 6 5 4 3 2 1

12 10 8 6 4 2

# Little Lithuania

The region on the western seacoast of Lithuania is called Mažoji Lietuva. Often translated as Lithuania Minor, I feel that it is more accurately described as Little Lithuania, in the same way that the Italian region in New York City is known as Little Italy. Historically part of East Prussia, with a strong German influence in its history and background, portions of the region are now within the political boundaries of Poland and Russia's Kaliningrad district.

Little Lithuana was very important in the development of the twentieth century Lithuanian national movement. During the period when printing books in the Latin alphabet was prohibited by Russia, many books were printed in East Prussia and smuggled into Lithuania. The most recognizable part of this region is the Baltic Sea Coast and the Curonian spit, a thin peninsula of sand dunes and pine forests that extends into the sea. For beach tourists, Palanga is the place to go for a "Coney Island" experience and party atmosphere. Nida, to the south, is the quiet destination of choice for nature lovers. The knitting in this region was especially rich and detailed, with large and small patterns and colorful striped cuffs on gloves and mittens. Some gloves were also made using Bosnian slip-stitch crochet.

The style of motif on these gloves was quite common in the region, and I've seen examples in several books as well as in museum collections. The motif is almost always worked in natural or white on a dark background.

## Experience Level

Advanced

## Finished Measurements of Sample

8" (20.5 cm) palm circumference

11½" (29 cm) hand length from cast-on to tip of middle finger

For sizing tips, see page 120.

## Materials

Approx 400 yds/365 m fingering weight wool; 200 yds/182 m each in MC and CC

Sample shown in Rauma Finullgarn (100% wool, 191 yds/175 m per 50 g ball), 1 ball each in:

**MC:** 136 Black

**CC:** 307 White

Scrap yarn

## Needles

US size 0 (2 mm) needles for working in the round: DPNs, 1 long circular or 2 short circulars

US size 1.5 (2.5 mm) needles for working in the round: DPNs, 1 long circular or 2 short circulars

Tapestry needle

## Gauge

36 sts and 40 rnds = 4"/10 cm over stranded colorwork with larger needles

## Special Techniques

Twisted Rib Cuff, see page 121.

Peasant Thumb, see page 122.

Glove Fingers, see page 123.

# Instructions

With CC and smaller needles, loosely CO 72 sts. Join to knit in the round, being careful not to twist sts.

## Cuff

**All rnds:** (K1-tbl, p1) around.

Alternate 3 rnds in MC and 3 rnds in CC until 33 rnds are complete, ending with 3 rnds MC.

Change to larger needles and with MC, knit 1 rnd.

## Hand

Work Little Lithuania charted pattern around on all sts and AT THE SAME TIME, when glove measures 2½" (6.5 cm) from top of ribbing, work thumb opening as follows.

## Thumb Opening

**Left hand:** On the palm, k20, k next 14 sts with scrap yarn, slip these sts back to the left needle and knit them again with the working yarn, complete round in pattern as set.

**Right hand:** On the palm, k2, k next 14 sts with scrap yarn, slip these sts back to the left needle and knit them again with the working yarn, complete round in pattern as set.

When all rnds of chart are complete, glove measures 8½" (22 cm) from cast-on edge.

## Fingers

Fingers are worked in MC and St st. Change to smaller needles.

**Little finger:** Work 9 sts from the palm plus 9 sts from the back of the hand plus CO 2 sts in between the fingers—20 sts. Put rem 54 sts on hold.

Work 2¾" (6 cm). Divide sts into 4 equal sections.

**Dec rnd:** (K to last 2 sts in section, k2tog) around—4 sts decreased.

Rep until 4 sts rem. Cut yarn and run tail through remaining sts. Pull gently to gather in and fasten off.

Continue working on the rem 54 on hold, pick up 2 sts in between the fingers—56 sts. Work 5 rnds in diamond pattern.

**Ring finger:** Work 8 sts from the palm, CO 2 sts between fingers, work 8 sts from back of hand, then pick up 2 sts between ring finger and little finger—20 sts. Put rem 40 sts on hold. Work 2½" (6.5 cm), then dec and fasten off as for little finger.

**Middle finger:** Work 10 sts from the palm, CO 2 sts between fingers, work 10 sts from back of hand, then pick up 2 sts between ring finger and little finger—24 sts. Put rem 20 sts on hold. Work 3" (7.5 cm), then dec and fasten off as for little finger.

**Index finger:** Work over the 22 rem sts and pick up 2 sts on side of middle finger—22 sts. Work and on fist rnd, dec 2 sts—24 sts. Work in patt until finger measures 2¾" (7 cm), then dec and fasten off as for little finger.

### Thumb

Remove the scrap yarn from the thumb opening. With MC and larger needles, pick up 14 sts above and below the thumb opening and pick up 1 st on both sides—30 sts.

Dec 2 sts in the first round—28 sts. Work even until thumb measures 2" (5 cm) or reaches to middle of thumbnail, then dec and fasten off as for fingers.

### Finishing

Weave in ends, closing up the small holes between the fingers. Wash and dry flat to block.

## Little Lithuania Chart

| | |
|---|---|
| ▨ | Black |
| ☐ | White |

# Vytis: Lithuania's Knight

*"Gules, a knight in full armour, riding on a horse, all argent, caparisoned azure, holding in the dexter hand sword above head in fess of the second, hilted and pommelled or, and at his sinister shoulder shield of the third, a double cross of the fourth; the horseshoes and bit, stirrup, spur and metal buckles."*

—The Lithuanian State Coat of Arms, President of the Republic of Lithuania website

The charging knight, called Vytis, was first used as the state emblem of Lithuania in 1366 during the reign of Grand Duke Algirdas. At the Battle of Grunwald in 1410, where the united Polish-Lithuanian army defeated the Teutonic Knights, Lithuanian regiments flew banners with the emblem of the charging knight. Coins featuring Vytis date from the late fourteenth century, and today the emblem is featured on all current Lithuanian coins, as well as on postage stamps and official documents. First interpreted as the ruler of the country, in later times the knight came to be seen as a hero, chasing intruders out of his country. This interpretation became especially popular in the nineteenth century during periods when Lithuania was occupied by the Russian Empire, the Soviet Union, and Nazi Germany.

Another popular medieval symbol that has been recreated in knitting is the Gediminas Tower. Both the knight and the Gediminas columns were symbols of the Lithuanian independence movement during the last years of the Soviet Union. Remembering the long history of Lithuania helped give hope for the dream of independence once again. That independence finally came in 1991.

## Experience Level
Advanced

## Finished Measurements of Sample
8" (20.5 cm) palm circumference

10" (25.5 cm) hand length from cast-on to tip of middle finger

For sizing tips, see page 120.

## Materials
Approx 400 yds/365 m of fingering weight wool yarn: 200 yds/182 m each of 2 colors

Sample shown in Rauma Finullgarn (100% wool, 191 yds/175 m per 50 g ball), 1 ball each in:

**MC:** A986 Yellow

**CC:** A83 Teal

Scrap yarn

## Needles
US size 0 (2 mm) needles for working in the round: DPNs, 1 long circular or 2 short circulars

US size 1.5 (2.5 mm) needles for working in the round: DPNs, 1 long circular or 2 short circulars

Tapestry needle

## Gauge
36 sts and 40 rnds = 4" (10 cm) over stranded colorwork with larger needles

## Special Techniques
Picot Hem Cuff, see page 121.

Peasant Thumb, see page 122.

Glove Fingers, see page 123.

# Instructions
With CC and smaller needles, loosely CO 72 sts. Join to knit in the round, being careful not to twist sts.

### Cuff
Knit for ½" (1.5 cm).

**Picot turning round:** (K2tog, yo) around.

Knit 3 rnds.

Change to MC and larger needles.

Work Diamond chart until cuff measures 2" (5 cm) from picot row.

### Hand
Continue working Diamond chart on palm and begin working Knight chart on back of hand until all rows of Knight chart have been worked. AT THE SAME TIME, when glove measures 1½" (4 cm) from top of ribbing, work thumb opening as follows.

### Thumb Opening
**Left hand:** On the palm, k20, k next 14 sts with scrap yarn, slip these sts back to the left needle and knit them again with the working yarn, complete rnd in pattern as set.

**Right hand:** On the palm, k2, k next 14 sts with scrap yarn, slip these sts back to the left needle and knit them again with the working yarn, complete rnd in pattern as set.

Continue until Knight chart is complete. Then return to working Diamond chart all around until glove measures 7" (18 cm) or desired length to beginning of fingers.

## Fingers

Fingers are worked following Diamond chart.

**Little finger:** Work 9 sts from the palm plus 9 sts from the back of the hand plus CO 2 sts in between the fingers—20 sts. Put rem 54 sts on hold.

Work 2¾" (7 cm) in Diamond patt. Change to MC only.

**Dec rnd:** *K2tog, k6, ssk; rep from * once more— 4 sts decreased.

Rep until 4 sts rem. Cut yarn and run tail through remaining sts. Pull gently to gather in and fasten off.

Continue working on the rem 54 on hold, pick up 2 sts in between the fingers—56 sts. Work 5 rnds in diamond pattern.

**Ring finger:** Work 8 sts from the palm, CO 2 sts between fingers, work 8 sts from back of hand, then pick up 2 sts between ring finger and little finger—20 sts. Put rem 40 sts on hold. Work 2½" (6.5 cm) in diamond patt, then dec and fasten off as for little finger.

**Middle finger:** Work 9 sts from the palm, CO 2 sts between fingers, work 9 sts from back of hand, then pick up 2 sts between ring finger and little finger—22 sts. Put rem 22 sts on hold. Work 3" (7.5 cm) in diamond patt, then dec and fasten off as for little finger.

**Index finger:** Work over the 22 rem sts and pick up 2 sts on side of middle finger. Work in diamond patt for 2¾" (7 cm), then dec and fasten off as for little finger.

## Thumb

Remove the scrap yarn from the thumb opening. With MC and larger needles, pick up 14 sts above and below the thumb opening and pick up 1 st on both sides—30 sts.

Work in diamond pattern, dec 2 sts in the first round—28 sts. Knit even until thumb meas 2" (5 cm) or reaches to middle of thumbnail, then dec and fasten off as for fingers.

## Finishing

Weave in ends, closing up the small holes between the fingers. Turn up hem at picot turning ridge and sew in place. Wash and dry flat to block.

# Diamond Chart

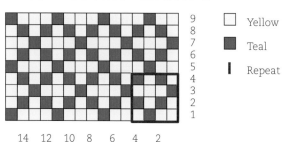

9
8
7
6
5
4
3
2
1

☐ Yellow

■ Teal

❘ Repeat

14  12  10  8  6  4  2

# Knight Chart

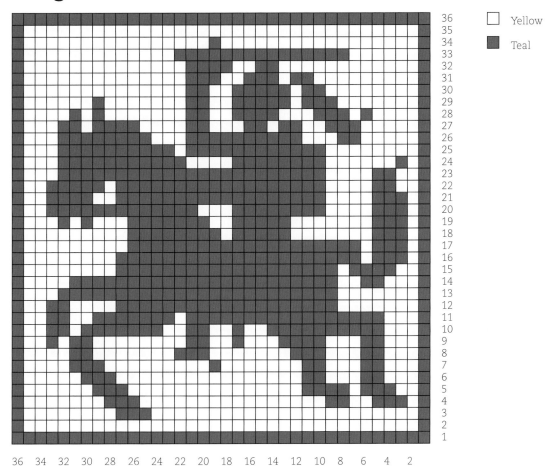

36
35
34
33
32
31
30
29
28
27
26
25
24
23
22
21
20
19
18
17
16
15
14
13
12
11
10
9
8
7
6
5
4
3
2
1

36 34 32 30 28 26 24 22 20 18 16 14 12 10 8 6 4 2

☐ Yellow

■ Teal

# Dzūkija Wedding Gloves

Dzūkija (or Dainava, Land of Songs) is spa country, with health resorts scattered throughout the region. In Dzūkija, people are known for their optimism and for preserving older traditions. The land is somewhat infertile, but covered with beautiful, dense forests where mushroom and berry picking are hobbies and businesses for many locals, who sell their fresh-pick from their cars on the side of the road. There are also a lot of bugs, and after spending an afternoon and evening outdoors in the southern resort town of Druskininkai at a wedding reception during one of my summer visits, I found my shoulders and legs covered with so many bug bites, I was afraid people would think I had the measles!

In 2009, I was honored to be invited to attend a wedding in Dzūkija. From the church, to a picnic on the river, to the reception at a Sodyba (country lodge), every moment was full of joy and beauty, and a celebration of nature, love, and life. These gloves, knit in bamboo rather than the traditional linen, remind me of that lovely wedding on a warm, sunny, summer day.

## Experience Level

Advanced

## Finished Measurements of Sample

8" (20 cm) palm circumference

10" (25.5 cm) hand length from cast-on to tip of middle finger

For sizing tips, see page 120.

## Materials

Approx 400 yds/365 m of fingering weight wool or wool-blend yarn

Sample shown in Crystal Palace Panda Silk Solid (52% bamboo/43% merino/ 5% silk, 204 yds/187 m per 50 g ball), 2 balls in 3204 Natural Ecru

Scrap yarn

## Needles

US size 0 (2 mm) needles for working in the round: DPNs, 1 long circular or 2 short circulars

US size 1.5 (2.5 mm) needles for working in the round: DPNs, 1 long circular or 2 short circulars

Tapestry needle

## Gauge

28 sts and 45 rnds = 4"/10 cm over zig zag pattern on smaller needles

36 sts and 40 rnds = 4"/10 cm over diamond lace stitch on larger needles

38 sts and 42 rnds = 4"/10 cm over stockinette stitch using larger needles

## Special Techniques

Lace Cuff, see page 121.

Peasant Thumb, see page 122.

Glove Fingers, see page 123.

## Chart Note

On Circular Diamond Lace chart, at the end of rnd 3, remove marker, k1, replace marker. The beg of the rnd moves 1 st to the left.

# Instructions

Using smaller needles, loosely CO 44 sts. Join to knit in the round, being careful not to twist sts.

### Cuff

Work Zig Zag Lace chart around. Work as set until 3 full repeats of chart are complete.

Change to larger needles.

**Next rnd, increase:** [K1, m1, (k2, m1) twice] 4 times, (k1, m1, k2, m1) 8 times—72 sts.

### Hand

**Next rnd:** Work Circular Diamond Lace chart 9 times around.

Work as set until all rows of chart have been worked twice.

### Thumb opening

**Right hand:** Work 38 sts in patt, k next 14 sts with scrap yarn, slip these sts back to the left needle and knit them again with the working yarn, work in patt to end of rnd.

**Left hand:** Work 56 sts in patt, k next 14 sts with scrap yarn, slip these sts back to the left needle and knit them again with the working yarn, work in patt to end of rnd.

Begin working 37 sts for back of hand following Flat Diamond Lace chart, keeping pattern aligned as set from Circular Diamond Lace, and work rem 35 sts for palm in St st. Work even in patts as established until glove measures 7" (18 cm) or desired length to beginning of fingers.

## Finger

This glove has fingers worked in St st.

**Little finger:** Work 8 sts from the palm plus 8 sts from the back of the hand plus CO 3 sts in between the fingers—19 sts. Put rem 56 sts on hold.

Dec 1 st on the first rnd—18 sts—and work 2¼" (6 cm). Divide sts into 2 equal sections split so half of the sts are on the palm side and the other half are on the back of the hand.

**Dec rnd:** *K2tog, knit to last 2 sts in section, ssk; rep from * once more—4 sts decreased.

Rep until 4 sts rem. Cut yarn and run tail through remaining sts. Pull gently to gather in and fasten off.

Continue working on the rem 56 on hold, pick up 3 sts in between the fingers—59 sts. Work 5 rounds in patts as established.

**Ring finger:** Work 8 sts from the palm, CO 3 sts between fingers, work 8 sts from back of hand, then pick up 3 sts between ring finger and little finger—22 sts. Put rem 40 sts on hold. Work 2½" (6.5 cm), then dec and fasten off as for little finger.

**Middle finger:** Work 10 sts from the palm, CO 3 sts between fingers, work 10 sts from back of hand, then pick up 3 sts between ring finger and little finger—26 sts. Put rem 20 sts on hold. Work 3" (7.5 cm), then dec and fasten off as for little finger.

**Index finger:** Work over the 20 rem sts and pick up 3 sts on side of middle finger. Dec 1 st on the first rnd—23 sts—and work for 2¾" (7 cm), then dec and fasten off as for little finger.

## Thumb

Remove the scrap yarn from the thumb opening. With MC and larger needles, pick up 14 sts above and below the thumb opening and pick up 1 st on both sides—30 sts.

Dec 2 sts in the first round—28 sts. Work even until thumb meas 2" (5 cm) or reaches to middle of thumbnail, then dec and fasten off as for fingers.

## Finishing

Weave in ends, closing up the small holes between the fingers. Wash and dry flat to block.

## Zig Zag Lace Chart

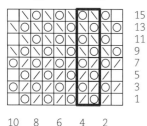

## Flat Diamond Lace Chart

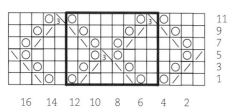

## Circular Diamond Lace Chart

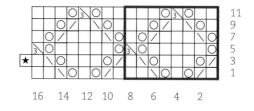

☐ Knit

☑ K2tog

◫ Sl1, k2tog, psso

◫ SSK

◉ YO

★ Remove marker, k1, replace marker

▮ Repeat

# Amber on My Mind

I can't think of the Baltic countries without thinking about amber. When my great-grandmother came to the United States at the beginning of the twentieth century, she brought with her two strands of golden pearls strung on silk with fourteen karat gold clasps. The pearls were made out of amber, most likely taken from the coast of the Baltic Sea. Their rich, butterscotch color is not found in today's jewelry, because amber is clarified by heating it in oil to fill any air pockets in the sap and create a transparent jewel; older amber beads were not treated this way and have a denser, opaque glow that I find beautiful and evocative of time gone by.

These gloves are knit in a variation of the honeycomb stitch used in the Suvalkija Beehive Mittens on page 158. Knit in shades of gold and orange, the finished result reminds me of the amber shops strung along Pilies gatvė (Castle Street) and scattered throughout Vilnius Old Town. Scrappy strings of leftover chips of amber are sold by street vendors, affordable mass-produced jewelry fill the shelves of souvenir shops, and hand-crafted jewelry can be found in a few high-end shops tucked into corners of the winding medieval streets.

## Experience Level

Advanced

## Finished Measurements of Sample

9" (23 cm) palm circumference

11" (28 cm) hand length from cast-on to tip of middle finger

For sizing tips, see page 120.

## Materials

Fingering weight wool yarn, approx 200 yds/182 m in each of 2 colors

Sample shown in:

**MC:** Jamieson's Shetland Spindrift (100% wool; 115 yds/105 m per 25 g ball): color #1340 (Cosmos); 2 balls

**CC:** Kauni Wool 8/2 Effektgarn, (100% wool; 437 yds/400 m per 100 g ball); color EQ; 1 ball

Scrap yarn

## Needles

US size 3 (3.25 mm) needles for working in the round: DPNs, 1 long circular or 2 short circulars

US size 2 (2.75 mm) needles for working in the round: DPNs, 1 long circular or 2 short circulars

Tapestry needle

## Gauge

29½ sts and 60 rnds = 4"/10 cm over Honeycomb Stitch on smaller needles

## Special Techniques

Twisted Ribbed Cuff, see page 121.

Peasant Thumb, see page 122.

Glove Fingers, see page 123.

# Pattern Stitches

### Honeycomb Stitch (Circular)

Chart on page 177.

(mutliple of 6 sts)

**Rnds 1–3:** With CC, (k5, sl 1 wyib) around.

**Rnds 4 and 8:** With MC, purl.

**Rnds 5–7:** With CC, (k2, sl 1 wyib, k3) around.

Repeat rnds 1–8 for pattern.

# Instructions

Unwind the Kauni and make 2 balls of approx 65 g each with the sections of the colors you want to use for the gloves.

With MC and smaller needles, loosely CO 56 sts. Join to knit in the round, being careful not to twist sts.

### Cuff

**All rnds:** (K1-tbl, p1) around.

Continue in ribbing as set and work stripe patt as foll: 3 rnds MC, *5 rnds CC, 1 rnd MC, 5 rnds CC*, 5 rnds MC, rep from * to * once more, 3 rnds MC.

Change to larger needles.

**Next rnd:** (K5, m1) 10 times, k to end—66 sts.

### Hand

Begin Honeycomb Stitch. Work rows 1–8 four times.

## Thumb Opening

Working rnd 1 of Honeycomb Stitch, make thumb opening as follows.

**Right hand:** K1 in patt, with scrap yarn knit the next 12 sts, slip these sts back to the left needle and knit them again with the working yarn, work in patt as established to the end of the round.

**Left hand:** Work in patt as established to last 13 sts, with scrap yarn knit the next 12 sts, slip these sts back to the left needle and knit them again with the working yarn, knit last st.

Work rnds 2–8 of Honeycomb Pattern once, then rnds 1–8 once more. Break MC.

## Fingers

Fingers are worked in MC and St st. Change to smaller needles.

**Little finger:** Work 6 sts from the palm plus 6 sts from the back of the hand plus CO 4 sts in between the fingers—16 sts. Put rem 54 sts on hold.

Work 1¾ inches (4.5 cm), on last rnd dec 1 st—15 sts. Divide sts into 3 equal sections.

**Dec rnd:** (K to last 2 sts in section, k2tog) around—3 sts decreased.

Rep every other rnd until 6 sts rem. Cut yarn and run tail through remaining sts. Pull gently to gather in and fasten off.

Continue working on the rem 54 on hold, pick up 2 sts in between the fingers—56 sts. Work 5 rounds.

**Ring finger:** Work 8 sts from the palm, CO 2 sts between fingers, work 8 sts from back of hand, then pick up 2 sts between ring finger and little finger—20 sts. Put rem 40 sts on hold. Work 2 inches (6 cm) in diamond patt, then dec and fasten off as for little finger.

**Middle finger:** Work 10 sts from the palm, CO 2 sts between fingers, work 10 sts from back of hand, then pick up 2 sts between ring finger and little finger—24 sts. Put rem 20 sts on hold. Work 2½ inches (6.5 cm), then dec and fasten off as for little finger.

**Index finger:** Work over the 20 rem sts and pick up 2 sts on side of middle finger. Work for 2 inches (5 cm), then dec and fasten off as for little finger.

## Thumb

Remove the scrap yarn from the thumb opening. With MC and larger needles, pick up 12 sts above and below the thumb opening and pick up 1 st on both sides—26 sts.

When thumb measures 2¼" (5.5 cm) or to middle of thumbnail, dec as for fingers.

Break yarn and thread tail through rem sts and pull gently to fasten off.

## Finishing

Weave in ends, closing up the small holes between the fingers. Wash and dry flat to block.

## Honeycomb Stitch Chart

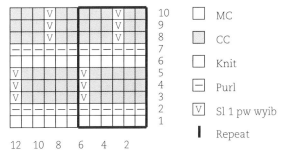

| | MC |
| - | - |
| | CC |
| | Knit |
| — | Purl |
| V | Sl 1 pw wyib |
| ❙ | Repeat |

# Market Socks

Like the Market Mittens (page 128), these socks are made in worsted weight yarn on fairly large needles, as are most of the socks sold in the tourist market in Vilnius. The motif on the leg is recognized as an eight-petal flower blossom in Lithuania, but if you look closely, you'll see that it is the same motif that is called a snowflake, a star, or a rose in other places. This eight-pointed motif is actually one of the most popular shapes wherever color work knitting is done. Today in the market, socks are usually made in white or cream yarn with one or two dark colors for patterning. Sometimes the market socks have the entire foot knitting in plain white yarn, as I've done on one example. Sometimes the colorwork pattern is repeated on the foot after the instep decreases are complete, as I've done on the second sample pair. The socks sold in the market include many different designs, some of which are not at all based on Lithuanian traditional patterns, and some of which are not even hand-knitted. This design is one that is knit by hand, but on a mass-produced level of production, and you can find socks with identical designs in many different booths. There are some sellers who make unique creations, and I have bought some one-of-a-kind socks that had extra yarn and the yarn label tucked inside the toe. This pair features a Dutch heel and a round toe, both frequently used on socks sold in the markets and on many of the socks in museum collections around the country.

## Experience Level

Intermediate

## Finished Measurements of Sample

8½" (22 cm) foot circumference

5½" (14 cm) leg length from CO to top of heel flap, not counting fringe

9" (23 cm) foot length from back of heel to tip of toe, or desired length

For sizing tips, see page 114.

## Materials

Approx 200 yds/181 m of DK or light-worsted weight wool yarn in A, 80 yds/73 m in B, and 40 yds/37 m in C and D (optional)

Sample (facing page) shown in Litwool classic colors (100% wool, 185 yds/170 m per 100 g skein); 1 skein each in Green, Black, Dark Red, and Light Red

Sample shown in Cascade 220 (worsted weight; 100% Peruvian wool; 220 yds/200 m per 100 g skein); 8010 Natural, and 2 contrasting colors of your choice

## Needles

US size 5 (3.75 mm) needles for working in the round: DPNs, 1 long circular or 2 short circulars

US size 6 (4 mm) needles for working in the round: DPNs, 1 long circular or 2 short circulars

Tapestry needle

## Gauge

24 sts and 25 rnds = 4"/10 cm over stranded color chart using larger needles

24 sts and 32 rnds = 4"/10 cm over stockinette stitch using smaller needles

## Special Techniques

Knitted Fringe, see page 113.

Dutch Heel, see page 115.

Spiral Toe, see page 118.

# Instructions

With B and smaller needles, loosely CO 52 sts. Join to work in the round being careful not to twist sts.

### Cuff

Purl 1 round.

Work knitted fringe as shown on page 113.

Change to A and larger needles.

### Leg

Work all rnds of Eight-Petal Rose chart once.

**Baltic Braid Option:** If desired, on rnds 5–7 and rnds 13–15 of chart, substitute Baltic Braid. See box on page 180.

Change to smaller needles. With A, k 1 rnd.

### Heel

The heel is worked on the first 26 sts. Place remaining sts on hold to be worked later.

### Heel Flap

**Row 1 (RS):** (Sl 1, k1) across.

**Row 2:** Sl 1, purl across.

Rep rows 1 and 2 until heel flap measures 2¼" (5.5 cm) long or desired length. End after working a WS row.

### Heel Turn

Divide the heel into 3 sections of 9, 8, and 9 sts, separated by markers.

**Next row (RS):** Sl 1, knit to second marker, slip marker, ssk, turn.

**Next row:** Sl 1, purl to second marker, slip marker, p2tog, turn.

Rep last 2 rows until all sts have been used. Sl 1, knit across.

### Gusset

Continue working with color A. Pick up 1 st in each slip st on first side of heel flap; knit across instep sts; pick up up 1 st in each slip st on second side of heel flap, knit to center of heel for new start of round.

Continue in St st and work gusset decreases every other rnd as follows until 52 sts rem.

**Dec rnd:** Knit to last 3 sts on sole, k2tog, k1, work instep sts; on sole, k1, ssk, knit to end of rnd.

## Foot

The foot can be worked in St st with A or, if desired, work Eight-Petal Rose pattern using larger needles, beginning with row 6 of chart. (Do not work Baltic Braids on foot.) Change to smaller needles and A after all rows of chart are complete.

Work even until foot measures 7" (18 cm) or approx 2" (5 cm) shorter than desired foot length.

## Toe

Divide sts evenly into 4 sections of 13 sts each with markers. Decrease every other rnd for spiral toe as follows.

**Left sock:** K2tog at the end of each section every other rnd until 8 sts rem.

**Right sock:** SSK at the beg of each section every other rnd until 8 sts rem.

Break yarn and thread tail through rem sts and pull gently to fasten off.

## Finishing

Weave in ends, wash and dry flat to block.

# Eight-Petal Rose Chart

☐ Natural  ■ Red

■ Navy  ✦ Make Fringe

## Chart Note

Colors shown as knit in sample on this page.

# Židinys: Hearth Socks

After the second World War, Anastazija and Antanas Tamošaitis worked in Vilnius, the restored capital of the nation, returned to Kaunas, and then spent time studying and working at a refugee camp in Austria and, later, at an art school in Germany. They finally moved to Canada in the late 1940s, where they later co-authored several books on Lithuanian folk art, including *Lithuanian Sashes*, *Lithuanian Easter Eggs*, and *Lithuanian National Costume*. They couple continued to promote Lithuanian folk art in the émigré community and to develop their own original works of art. During this period of their life, they worked separately on their art, and together on their books.

Their library, along with a collection of folk art, is housed at the Anastazija and Antanas Tamošaitis Gallery Židinys (Hearth) in Vilnius.

## Experience Level
Advanced

## Finished Measurements of Sample
8" (20.5 cm) leg circumference

8½" (22 cm) length cuff to top of heel flap

10½" (27 cm) foot length from back of heel to tip of toe, or desired length

For sizing tips, see page 114.

## Materials
Approx 600 yds/550 m of fingering weight wool yarn, 300 yds/275 m each in MC and CC

Sample shown in Teksrena Wool Yarn (100% wool; 380 yds/350 m per 100 g ball); 1 ball each in:

  **MC:** Rose, 1 skein

  **CC:** Burgundy, 1 skein

## Needles
US size 1 (2.25 mm) needles for working in the round: DPNs, 1 long circular or 2 short circulars

US size 2 (2.75 mm) needles for working in the round: DPNs, 1 long circular or 2 short circulars

Tapestry needle

## Gauge
36 sts and 38 rnds = 4" (10 cm) over stranded colorwork using larger needles

## Special Techniques
Ribbed Cuff, see page 115.

Easy Lithuanian Heel, see page 116.

Spiral Toe, see page 118.

# Pattern Stitches

### Salt and Pepper
**Rnd 1:** (K1 MC, k1 CC) across section.

**Rnd 2:** (K1 CC, k1 MC) across section.

Rep rnds 1 and 2 for patt.

# Instructions

With smaller needles and CC, loosely CO 72 sts. Join to knit in the round, being careful not to twist sts.

### Cuff

Work K2, P2 ribbing in stripe patt as follows: 2 rnds CC, (1 rnd MC, 1 rnd CC) twice, 12 rnds MC, (1 rnd CC, 1 rnd MC) twice, 2 rnds CC.

K 1 rnd in CC, inc 12 sts evenly around—84 sts.

### Leg

Change to larger needles. Work chart around. Work as set until chart is complete, and repeat rows 14–23 of chart until leg measures 8½" (22 cm) from CO.

### Heel

The flap is worked with MC, back and forth on 36 sts in Eye of Partridge with slip-st edges. Place remaining sts on hold to be worked later. Change to smaller ndls.

### Heel Flap

**Row 1 (RS):** (Sl 1, k1) across.

**Rows 2 and 4:** Sl 1, purl across.

**Row 3:** Sl 1, (k1, sl 1) to last st, k1.

Rep rows 1–4 until heel flap measures 3" (7.5 cm) or desired length. End after working a WS row.

### Heel Turn

The heel turn is worked in St st.

Divide the heel stitches into three sections as follows.

**Next row (WS):** Work 10 sts, place marker, work 16 sts, place marker, work 10 sts.

**Row 1 (RS):** Work in patt to 2 sts before first marker, k2tog, slip marker, work to second marker, slip marker, ssk, work to end of row.

**Row 2 (WS):** Work in patt to 2 sts before first marker, ssp, slip marker, work to the second marker, slip marker, p2tog, work to end of row.

Rep rows 1 and 2, slipping markers when you come to them, until 18 sts rem in heel. Remove markers.

### Gusset

Change to larger needles and break yarn, placing marker at center of heel.

Reattach CC at the end of the instep sts, at the top of the heel flap. Pick up 1 st in each slip st down this side of heel flap, k across heel sts, pick up 1 st in each slip st on the second side of the heel flap. With both yarns, work across instep in chart pattern as set.

Establish sole pattern and work gusset decreases as follows, until 72 sts rem:

**Rnd 1:** On sole, K1 CC, ssk CC, work Salt and Pepper to 1 st before marker at center of heel (bottom of foot), k2 CC, work Salt and Pepper to last 2 sts of sole, k2tog CC, k1 CC, work charted patt as established across instep sts.

**Rnd 2:** K2 CC, work Salt and Pepper to 1 st before marker, k2 CC, work Salt and Pepper to last 2 sts of sole, k2 CC, work charted patt as established across instep sts.

### Foot

Work even in patterns as established until foot measures 8½" (21.5 cm) or 2" (5 cm) shorter than desired foot length.

### Toe

Divide sts into 4 equal sections of 16 sts each, separated with markers.

With MC only, work toes as follows.

**Left sock:** K2tog at the end of each section every other rnd until 32 sts rem, then every rnd until 8 sts rem.

**Right sock:** SSK at the beg of each section every other rnd until 32 sts rem, then every rnd until 8 sts rem.

Break yarn and thread tail through rem sts and pull gently to fasten off.

### Finishing

Weave in ends, wash and dry flat to block.

## Leg Chart

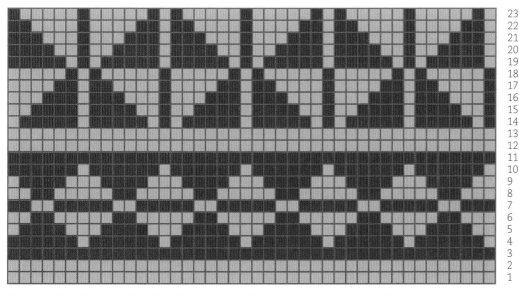

23
22
21
20
19
18
17
16
15
14
13
12
11
10
9
8
7
6
5
4
3
2
1

☐ Rose

■ Burgundy

⊟ purl

42  40  38  36  34  32  30  28  26  24  22  20  18  16  14  12  10  8  6  4  2

183

# Anklets for Anastazija

I love vintage knitting books and have my own small collection of nineteenth-century English-language books, but the earliest Lithuanian-language knitting books I've discovered so far were published almost a hundred years later. *Sodžiaus menas kn. 5: Mezgimo-nėrimo raštai* (Village Arts no. 5: Knitting patterns), by Antanas Tamošaitis, came out in 1933 and *Mezgimas* (Knitting), by Anastazija Tamošaitis, was published in 1935. Together, these two books form a wonderful foundation in Lithuanian knitting. Antanas wrote about the spiritual significance of folk art and documented colorwork motifs and mitten and sock designs from regions around the country, while Anastazija wrote instructions for knitting a variety of accessories using traditional motifs and colors.

These socks are adapted from a pair shown in a black and white photo in Anastazia's book, *Mezgimas*. I chose the colors to represent Baltic amber (gold), the Lithuanian forests (green), and the night sky (deep purple), to stand out in contrast against the natural undyed yarn of the rest of the sock.

## Experience Level

Advanced

## Finished Measurements of Sample

8" (20.5 cm) circumference over colorwork cuff

Approx 5" (12.5 cm) circumference on foot, stretches to fit a foot of up to 10" (25.5 cm) circumference

5" (12.5 cm) length cuff to top of heel flap, with cuff folded down

9" (23 cm) foot length from back of heel to tip of toe, or desired length

For sizing tips, see page 114.

## Materials

Wool or wool and nylon sock or fingering weight yarn, approx 400 yds/365 m total:

**Color A:** 300 yds/275 m

**Color B:** 100 yds/91 m

**Colors C and D:** 50 yds/46 m each

Striped sample shown in Shibui Sock (100% superwash merino wool, 191 yds/175 m per 50 g skein);

**A:** #2004 Ivory, 2 skeins

1 skein each:

**B:** #229 Mulberry

**C:** #1395 Honey

**D:** #7495 Wasabi

## Needles

US size 1 (2.25 mm) needles for working in the round: DPNs, 1 long circular or 2 short circulars

US size 3 (3.25 mm) needles for working in the round: DPNs, 1 long circular or 2 short circulars

Tapestry needle

## Gauge

32 sts and 38 rnds = 4"/10 cm over stranded colorwork on larger needles

36 sts and 48 rnds = 4"/10 cm over St st on smaller needles

## Special Techniques

Folded Colorwork Cuff.

> **Note:** The colorwork cuff has little or no give, while the ribbed portion of the sock is extremely stretchy. Take care to knit the cuff on larger needles so it will fit to pull the sock on over your heel.

Garter Stitch Short-Row Heel, see page 117.

Wedge Toe, see page 119.

# Instructions

With MC and smaller needles, loosely CO 60 sts. Join to knit in the round, being careful not to twist sts.

## Cuff

Work in K2, P2 ribbing for 1" (2.5 cm).

Change to larger needles. With A, k 1 rnd, inc 4 sts evenly around—64 sts.

Change to B, and beg working Folded Colorwork Cuff chart. After all rows of chart are complete, change to A and knit 1 rnd, dec 4 sts.

Turn cuff inside out and begin working in the other direction with the WS of the cuff on the outside of the tube. There will be a small hole where you turn, which you can sew up with the tails when you weave in the ends.

Work in K2, P2 ribbing for 1" (2.5 cm).

## Leg

Change to smaller needles and B. Continue in K2, P2 ribbing until cuff measures 9½" (24 cm).

Change to A and work in K2, P2 ribbing for ½" (1.25 cm).

## Heel

The heel flap is worked back and forth in K2, P2 ribbing on 30 sts. Place remaining sts on hold to be worked later.

## Heel Flap

Work in ribbing for ½" (1.25 cm). End after working a WS row.

## Heel Turn

The heel turn is worked in garter stitch, with short row turns.

**Every row:** Sl 1 kw, knit to 1 stitch before the end of the row, turn.

Work 1 stitch fewer in each row until 10 sts remain unworked in the center of the heel.

**Every row:** Sl 1 kw, knit to the last of the worked stitches in the center of the heel, sl the last center stitch kw, k1 (first stitch of unworked sts), turn.

Work 1 stitch further on each row. When all stitches have been worked, end after completing a WS row.

## Gusset

Knit across heel sts. Pick up 1 st in each slip st on first side of heel flap; continue ribbing pattern across instep sts; pick up 1 st in each slip st on second side of heel flap, knit to center of heel for new start of round. Work sole in St st and instep sts in ribbing.

Continue in patts as established and work gusset decreases every other rnd as follows until 60 sts rem.

**Dec rnd:** Knit to last 3 sts on sole, k2tog, k1, work instep sts; on sole, k1, ssk, knit to end of rnd.

## Foot

Work even in patterns until foot measures approx 7" (18 cm), or 2" (5 cm) shorter than desired foot length.

## Toe

Dec as follows every other rnd until 30 sts rem then every rnd until 8 sts rem.

**Dec rnd:** *Knit to last 3 sts in sole, k2tog, k1; on instep, k1, ssk, knit to last 3 sts on instep, k2tog, k1; on sole, ssk, knit to end of rnd at center of sole.

Break yarn, run end through remaining sts with a tapestry needle, and gather in to fasten off.

## Finishing

Weave in ends, wash and dry flat to block.

# Folded Colorwork Cuff Chart

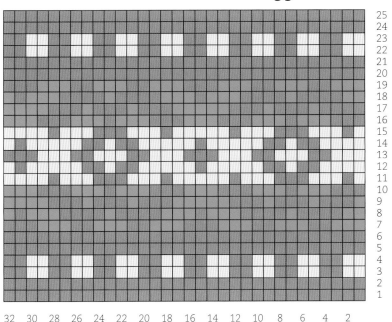

| | Mulberry |
| | Honey |
| | Wasabi |

# Marija's Kneesocks

June and I met Marija while visiting knitters throughout Lithuania in 2008. When we drove up to the Soviet-era apartment building where she lived, I could not imagine what it would be like inside. The outside of the building was plain concrete, with no beauty whatsoever. The hallways and stairs inside reminded me of the nineteenth-century railroad apartments where my grandmother lived in New York City. But once Marija invited us into her apartment, we found ourselves surrounded by beauty. Lace curtains, a vintage wooden sideboard, and all the comforts of home.

Marija's beautiful knitting, incorporating traditional Lithuanian motifs into modern garments and accessories, was such an inspiration! Like so many other wonderful knitters that we've met over the years (many of whom are featured in Knitters and Folk Art on pages 74–109) Marija makes both easy projects for sale in the market, and more complex ones for herself and her family. These socks are inspired by a pair she made, which used different motifs but featured the same method for shaping a knee sock by decreasing in salt-and-pepper columns between patterns of a traditional motif.

## Experience Level

Advanced

## Finished Measurements of Sample

8.5" (21.5 cm) foot circumference, unstretched

10" (25.5 cm) calf circumference, unstretched

10" (25.5 cm) foot length from back of heel to tip of toe, or desired length

12" (30.5 cm) length cuff to top of heel flap

For sizing tips, see page 114.

## Materials

600 yds/550 m of sock weight yarn: 300 yds/275 m each of 2 colors

Sample shown in:

**MC:** A Verb for Keeping Warm Creating (100% superwash merino, 385 yds/352 m per 100 g skein), color Thai Iced Tea, 1 skein

**CC:** Dream In Color Smooshy (100% superwash merino, 450 yds/ 411 m per 100 g skein), color Black Pearl, 1 skein

## Needles

US size 1 (2.25 mm) needles for working in the round: DPNs, 1 long circular or 2 short circulars

US size 3 (3.25 mm) needles for working in the round: DPNs, 1 long circular or 2 short circulars

Tapestry needle

## Gauge

28 sts and 30 rnds = 4"/10 cm over stranded colorwork using larger needles

## Special Techniques

Ribbed Cuff, see page 115.

Calf Shaping, see page 115.

Easy Lithuanian Heel, see page 116.

Wedge Toe, see page 119.

## Pattern Stitches

### Salt and Pepper

**Rnd 1:** (K1 MC, k1 CC) across section.

**Rnd 2:** (K1 CC, k1 MC) across section.

Rep rnds 1 and 2 for patt.

## Instructions

Using smaller needles and MC, loosely CO 88 sts. Join to knit in the round, being careful not to twist sts.

### Cuff

Work K2, P2 ribbing for 1" (2.5 cm).

### Leg

Change to larger needles. Knit 1 rnd. Follow Leg chart until all rounds of chart have been worked—60 sts rem. Work even in patts as established until leg measures 13" (33 cm) or desired length to heel.

### Heel

This sock is worked with an easy heel and flap. The heel is worked on 30 sts. Place remaining sts on hold to be worked later.

### Heel Flap

Work heel flap back and forth using Salt-and-Pepper Pattern until heel measures 2½" (6.5 cm) or desired length. End after working a RS row.

### Heel Turn

Divide the heel stitches into 3 sections as follows.

**Next row (WS):** Work 11 sts, place marker, work 8 sts, place marker, work 11 sts.

Continue working in color patt as established, and AT THE SAME TIME, work decreases to turn heel as follows.

**Row 1 (RS):** Work in patt to 2 sts before first marker, k2tog, slip marker, work to second marker, slip marker, ssk, work to end of row.

**Row 2 (WS):** Work in patt to 2 sts before first marker, ssp, slip marker, work to the second marker, slip marker, p2tog, work to end of row.

Rep rows 1 and 2 until 10 sts rem in heel.

### Gusset

Break both yarns. Starting at the end of the instep sts, rejoin MC and pick up 1 st in each slip st on first side of heel flap. Knit across heel sts. up 1 st in each slip st on second side of heel flap; rejoin CC and continue in patt as set across instep sts.

Sole is worked in Salt and Pepper pattern, instep is worked in chart pattern.

Continue in patts as established and work gusset decreases every other rnd as follows until 60 sts rem.

**Dec rnd:** Knit to last 3 sts on sole, k2tog, k1, work instep sts; on sole, k1, ssk, knit to end of rnd.

### Foot

Work even in patterns as set on rem sts until foot measures approx 8" (20.5 cm), or 2" (5 cm) less than desired length. End after working chart row 69.

### Toe

Work the toe as charted—12 sts rem. Break yarn and join with Kitchener stitch or run end through remaining sts with a tapestry needle, and gather in to fasten off.

### Finishing

Weave in ends, wash and dry flat to block.

## Toe Chart

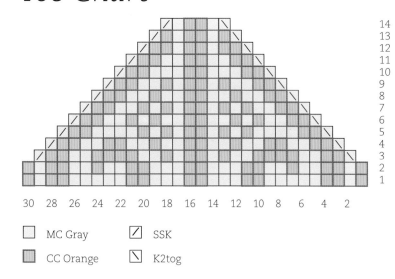

14
13
12
11
10
9
8
7
6
5
4
3
2
1

30 28 26 24 22 20 18 16 14 12 10 8 6 4 2

☐ MC Gray    ⟋ SSK

▨ CC Orange    ⟍ K2tog

# Leg Chart

Legend:
- ☐ MC Gray
- ▨ CC Orange
- ⧄ SSK
- ⧅ K2tog

# Rumšiškės in Summer Socks

These socks are made with true entrelac on the cuffs. Although this is not a technique that's traditionally recognized as a special Lithuanian technique, I have seen it on more than a few pairs of mittens in museum collections, as well as in vintage knitting books published in Lithuania and Russia.

One of my favorite parts of creativity is variations on a theme. Whether it's a jazz riff, a poem, a series of sketches, or even just doodles, there's something inspiring about seeing how one simple idea can be changed, expanded, revised, or turned upside down and inside out to create something that appears entirely different. I love experimenting with variations on a theme in my knitting, too. Take a pattern stitch and knit it up in lace-weight, worsted-weight, and super-bulky yarn, or use the same yarn and try the stitch out on three different sizes of needles. Sometimes I like to work the same design in solid, heather, and variegated yarns, or use the same pattern stitch on a pair of socks, gloves, and mittens in different colors, or on a sweater, a shawl, and fingerless gloves in yarns made from different fibers.

I love when things are related but not identical, and variations on a theme are used on many projects in this book. Several have companion accessories that play off of each other with a change in scale. Because I had so much yarn left over from the mittens on page 143, I could not resist making a matching pair of socks.

## Experience Level
Advanced

## Finished Measurements of Sample
9" (23 cm) circumference

7" (18 cm) length cuff to top of heel flap

10" (25.5 cm) foot length from back of heel to tip of toe, or desired length

For sizing tips, see page 114.

## Materials
Fingering weight wool yarn, approx 300 yds/182 m of main color and 100 yds/91 m each of 4 contrasting colors

Sample shown in Teksrena Wool Yarn (100% wool; 380 yds/350 m per 100 g ball);

  **MC:** Charcoal, 2 balls

1 ball each:

  **A:** Green

  **B:** Light Pink

  **C:** Dark Pink

  **D:** Burgundy

## Needles
US size 1 (2.25 mm) needles for working in the round: DPNs, 1 long circular or 2 short circulars

Tapestry needle

## Gauge
36 sts and 42 rnds = 4"/10 cm over stranded colorwork

36 sts and 48 rnds = 4"/10 cm over stockinette stitch

If you get a tighter gauge on stranded colorwork than you do in 1-color stockinette, go up 1 needle size for the colorwork sections.

## Special Techniques
Easy Lithuanian Heel, see page 116.

Spiral Toe, see page 118.

# Instructions
With A, loosely CO 45 sts. Join to knit in the round, being careful not to twist sts.

### Cuff
Work 9 beginning triangles with A, following the instructions for rows 1–9 of the mitten cuffs on page 144.

### Leg
**Inc rnd:** With MC, working around the top edge of all ending triangles, k4, m1 (k1, m1) to last 3 sts of rnd, k3—84 sts.

Knit 1 rnd in MC.

**Next 5 rnds:** (K1 MC, k1 CC) around, using B as CC on one sock and D on the other.

Knit 2 rnds in MC.

**Right Sock round:** Work Right Floral Entrelac chart twice around.

**Left Sock round:** Work Left Floral Entrelac chart twice around, reversing positions of colors B and D.

### Heel
This sock has an Easy Heel, with the flap worked in 2 color vertical stripes.

Knit 1 and work the heel back and forth on the following 41 sts, which will fall between the vertical columns of CC at the beg of each patt rep. Place rem 42 sts and the 1 st just knit on hold to be worked later.

### Heel Flap
Work heel flap back and forth using St st and vertical stripes as follows.

**Row 1 (RS):** Sl 1, (k1 CC, k1 MC) across.

**Row 2 (WS):** Sl 1, (p1 MC, p1 CC) across.

Repeat last 2 rows until heel flap measures 2¼" (5.5 cm) or desired length. End after working an RS row.

## Heel Turn

Divide the heel stitches into three sections as follows.

**Next row (WS):** Work 11 sts, place marker, work 19 sts, place marker, work 11 sts.

Continue working vertical stripe pattern as on flap and AT THE SAME TIME, work decreases to turn heel as follows.

**Row 1 (RS):** Work in patt to 2 sts before first marker, k2tog, slip marker, work to second marker, slip marker, ssk, work to end of row.

**Row 2 (WS):** Work in patt to 2 sts before first marker, ssp, slip marker, work to the second marker, slip marker, p2tog, work to end of row.

Rep rows 1 and 2 until 21 sts rem in heel.

## Gusset

Sl 1, (k1 CC, k1 MC) 5 times. This is the new start of round.

The 41 sts of the sole are worked in vertical stripes as set, changing colors as needed to match instep. The 43 sts of the instep (which were set aside during heel knitting) are worked following charted patt as established.

Continue in patts as established and work gusset decreases as follows.

**Rnd 1:** With A as CC, work in vertical stripe patt as established to last 3 sts of sole, k2tog CC, k1 MC, work across instep in charted patt as established, at beg of sole k1 MC, ssk CC, work in vertical stripe patt as established to end of rnd.

# Right Floral Entrelac Chart

| | |
|---|---|
| ☐ | MC Charcoal |
| | Light Pink |
| | Dark Pink |
| | Burgundy |
| | Green |

**Rnd 2:** Work patts as established.

Rep rnds 1 and 2 until 84 sts rem.

## Foot

Work even in patterns until foot measures 8" (20.5 cm) or approx 2" (5 cm) shorter than desired foot length, ending after any row of the chart that allows desired length.

## Toe

Begin working around in vertical stripe pattern as for heel. Divide sts into 4 equal sections of 21 sts each. Work 1 rnd in stripe pattern, then dec as follows:

**Dec rnd (LEFT sock):** *K to last 2 sts in section, k2tog; rep from * 3 more times.

**Dec rnd (RIGHT sock):** *Ssk, knit remaining sts in section; rep from * 3 more times.

Dec the same way every other rnd (on non-dec rounds, knit) until 42 sts rem, and then dec every rnd until 20 sts rem. K2tog around. Break yarn and thread tail through rem sts and pull gently to fasten off.

## Finishing

Weave in ends, wash and dry flat to block.

# Left Floral Entrelac Chart

| | |
|---|---|
| ☐ | MC Charcoal |
| ▨ | Light Pink |
| ▨ | Dark Pink |
| ■ | Burgundy |
| ▨ | Green |

# Aukštaitija Red and White Stripe Socks

The heart of ancient Lithuania is Aukštaitija, the highlands, a large region of dense forests and beautiful lakes. Located in the northeastern part of the country, this is where the Lithuanian state first coalesced, as many smaller tribes melded together and then, in the eleventh century, where the Grand Duchy of Lithuania was established. In this part of Lithuania, women's red or blue socks with white stripes were made in two different ways: with separate yarns of the two colors needed to create a stripe pattern, or with a single hand-dyed, self-striping yarn. When self-striping sock yarns became popular at the end of the twentieth century, I assumed this was a newly invented dye technique. But when I was looking through *Lithuanian National Costume* by Anastazija and Antanas Tamošaitis (1979), I saw a pair of socks that were clearly hand-painted in a self-striping pattern in a black and white photo. The caption said the socks were white with red stripes. The woman wearing them had simple crochet linen shoes, called čempės, indicating that she was a peasant or a poor farm laborer. The photo was from the late nineteenth century, but women in the rural areas of Lithuania wore these homemade shoes well into the twentieth century, to the 1940s in some areas. After the Second World War, leather and rubber boots were available to purchase in many larger stores. Because these are clearly socks made for everyday wear, I used the simplest heel and toe techniques. For an interesting twist, however, I made the right and left feet different. One toe is made with a clockwise spiral and the other is made with a counter-clockwise spiral.

## Experience Level

Beginner

## Finished Measurements of Sample

8" (20.5 cm) circumference

8" (20.5 cm) length cuff to top of heel flap

10" (25.5 cm) foot length from back of heel to tip of toe, or desired length

For sizing tips, see page 114.

## Materials

Wool or wool and nylon sock yarn, approx 400 yds/365 m

Samples shown in:

Hifa 2 Tykt (fingering weight, 100% Norwegian 2-ply Combed Long Fiber Wool, 425 m/100 g) in #808 red (MC) and #826 natural (CC), 1 skein each

Holiday Yarns Flock Sock (fingering weight, 75% superwash merino, 25% nylon, 400 yds per skein), color Candy Cane, 1 skein

## Needles

US size 0 (2 mm) needles for working in the round: DPNs, 1 long circular or 2 short circulars

Tapestry needle

## Gauge

40 sts and 54 rnds = 4"/10 cm over stockinette stitch

## Special Techniques

Ribbed Cuff, see page 115.

Easy Lithuanian Heel, see page 116.

Spiral Toe, see page 118.

## Pattern Note

This sock can be worked with two solid yarns or with a self-striping or hand-painted yarn for special effects. The pattern is written for working with 2 solid colors and stripes. When working with a single colorway of yarn, simply ignore the references to colors.

# Instructions

With MC, CO 80 sts. Join to knit in the round, being careful not to twist sts.

## Cuff

Work in K2, P2 ribbing in stripe patt as follows:

*4 rnds MC, 4 rnds CC, 4 rnds MC, 2 rnds CC, 2 rnds MC, 2 rnds CC

Work stripe pattern from * once more, then work the first 12 rounds again (or work until cuff measures 4" from CO edge if using self-striping yarn).

## Leg

Change to St st and larger needles and continue stripe patt as established.

Work even until leg measures approx 8" (20.5 cm) desired length to top of heel.

## Heel

Work the flap back and forth on 40 sts. Continue the stripe pattern as set throughout the heel flap. Place remaining 40 sts on hold to be worked later.

## Heel Flap

**Row 1 (RS):** Sl 1, knit across.

**Row 2 (WS):** Sl 1, knit 3, purl to last 4 sts, k4.

Repeat last 2 rows until heel flap measure 2¼" (5.5 cm) or desired length. Rep row 1 once more.

## Heel Turn

The heel turn is worked in CC.

Divide the heel stitches into three sections as follows.

**Next row (WS):** Work 14 sts, place marker, work 12 sts, place marker, work 14 sts.

Continue working garter stitch edges and AT THE SAME TIME, work decreases to turn heel as follows.

**Row 1 (RS):** Work in patt to 2 sts before first marker, k2tog, slip marker, work to second marker, slip marker, ssk, work to end of row.

**Row 2 (WS):** Work in patt to 2 sts before first marker, ssp, slip marker, work to the second marker, slip marker, p2tog, work to end of row.

Rep rows 1 and 2 until 14 sts rem in heel.

## Gusset

With color needed for next row of stripe patt on leg, knit heel sts. Pick up sts between garter ridges, one for each ridge, on first side of heel flap; knit across instep sts; pick up sts between garter ridges, one for each ridge, along second side of heel flap, knit to center of heel for new start of round.

Continue in patts as established and work gusset decreases every other rnd as follows until 80 sts rem.

**Dec rnd:** Knit to last 3 sts on sole, k2tog, k1, work instep sts; on sole, k1, ssk, knit to end of rnd.

## Foot

Work even in pattern as set until foot measures approx 8" (20.5 cm) or 2" (5 cm) less than desired length to toe.

## Toe

Work the toe continuing the stripe pattern. Divide sts into 4 equal sections of 20 sts each, separated with markers.

**Left sock:** K2tog at the end of each section every other rnd until 32 sts rem, then every rnd until 8 sts rem.

**Right sock:** SSK at the beg of each section every other rnd until 32 sts rem, then every rnd until 8 sts rem.

Break yarn and thread tail through rem sts and pull gently to fasten off.

## Finishing

Weave in ends, wash and dry flat to block.

# Knitting for a Folk Dance

Feather and Fan is the very first lace pattern I ever attempted to knit, and it's become one of my favorite stitches to knit. I use it every chance I get, so when I saw these lace socks in a book on Lithuanian national costume, I knew I would make a pair for myself. I ended up making two pairs: knee socks and crew socks. The originals were made in natural colored linen yarn for summer wear, but my versions are made in hand-dyed superwash merino wool to be more comfortable, and warmer for three-season wear, since I never wear socks in summer.

The crew socks are made with no shaping in the leg, and on the knee-high stocking, calf shaping is accomplished by changing pattern stitches and needle sizes. See page 115.

## Experience Level
Intermediate

## Sizes
Calf-length sock (Knee-high stocking)

## Finished Measurements of Sample
7" (18 cm) foot circumference, unstretched

9" (23 cm) foot length from back of heel to tip of toe, or desired length

7 (10)" [18 (25.5) cm] calf circumference, unstretched

6 (14)" [15 (35.5) cm] length cuff to top of heel flap

For sizing tips, see page 114.

## Materials
Wool or wool/nylon blend sock yarn, approx 400 (600) yds/365 (550) m

Samples shown in Madelinetosh Tosh Sock (100% superwash merino, 395 yds/170 m per 120 g skein); 1 (2) skeins in Medieval (Clematis)

## Needles
For sock: US size 1 (2.25 mm) needles for working in the round: DPNs, 1 long circular or 2 short circulars

For stocking: US size 1 (2.25 mm), US size 2 (2.75 mm) and US size 3 (3.25 mm) needles for working in the round: DPNs, 1 long circular or 2 short circulars

Tapestry needle

## Gauge
40 sts and 48 rnds = 4"/10 cm over feather and fan stitch using smallest needles

36 sts and 48 rnds = 4"/10 cm over stockinette stitch using smallest needles

## Special Techniques
Ribbed cuff, see page 115.

T-heel, see page 116.

Spiral toe, see page 118.

Calf shaping (stocking only), see page 115.

# Pattern Stitches

### Diagonal Lace
**Rnd 1:** (K2tog, yo) around.

**Rnds 2 & 4:** Knit.

**Rnd 3:** K1, (k2tog, yo) to last st, k1.

Repeat rnds 1–4 for pattern.

### Feather and Fan

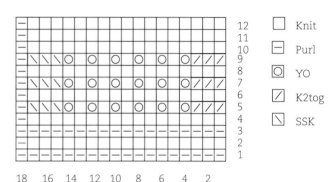

# Instructions

Using size 1 (2) needles, loosely CO 72 sts. Join to knit in the round, being careful not to twist sts.

### Cuff
Work K2, P2 ribbing for 1½" (4 cm).

### Leg
Work Diagonal Lace for 1½" (4 cm).

Knit 4 rounds.

**For sock only:** Work rnds 1–12 of Feather and Fan chart 4 times, then work rnds 1–4 once more.

**For stocking only:** Change to size 3 needles and work rnds 1–12 of Feather and Fan chart 3 times. Change to size 2 needles and work rnds 1–12 of Feather and Fan chart 3 times. Change to size 1 needles and work rnds 1–12 of Feather and Fan chart 3 times. then work rnds 1–4 once more.

## Heel

The heel is worked back and forth on first 35 sts, which will center heel between 2 purl columns. Place rem 37 sts on hold to be worked later.

### Heel Flap

**First half:** Work heel flap back and forth on 35 sts using St st with garter stitch edges for 20 rows as follows.

**Row 1 (RS):** Sl 1, knit across.

**Row 2 (WS):** Sl 1, k2, purl to last 3 sts, k3.

**Division:** Work across first 10 sts and set them aside on a spare needle. Knit 15. Place last 10 unworked stitches aside on a spare needle.

**Second half:** Work back and forth on the center 15 sts using St st with garter stitch edges as above for 20 rows.

### Heel Turn

**Row 1 (RS):** Knit across center 15 heel sts, pick up and knit 10 sts down the side of the heel center to the corner where the held sts are. Do not turn. Sl 1st held st kw, and pass the last picked-up st over it. Turn.

**Row 2 (WS):** Sl 1 pw, purl up side and across center of heel, pick up and purl 10 sts down other side of heel center. Do not turn. Sl 1st held st pw, and pass the last purled st over it. Turn.

**Row 3:** Sl 1 kw, k across to held sts, sl 1 pw and pass the last knitted st over it. Turn.

**Row 4:** Sl 1 kw, purl across to held sts, sl 1 pw and pass the last purled st over it. Turn.

Rep rows 3 and 4 until all sts are worked, ending after a WS row. Turn.

### Gusset

Sl 1, k across rem heel sts. Pick up 1 st in each slip-stitch chain on the side of the flap; continue patt as set across instep sts; pick up 1 st in each chain on the 2nd side of the flap, knit to center of heel for new start of round. Sole is worked in St st, instep is worked in Feather and Fan pattern.

Continue in patts as established and work gusset decreases every other rnd at beg and end of sole sts as follows.

**Dec rnd:** Knit to last 3 sole sts, k2tog, k1, knit across all instep sts, at beg of sole, k1, ssk, knit to end of rnd.

### Foot

When 72 sts rem, work even in patterns as established until foot measures approx 7" (18 cm), or approx 2" (5 cm) shorter than desired foot length.

### Toe

Divide sts into 4 equal sections of 18 sts each, separated with markers.

**Left sock:** K2tog at the end of each section every other rnd until 36 sts rem. Dec every rnd until 8 sts rem.

**Right sock:** SSK at the beg of each section every other rnd until 36 sts rem. Dec every rnd until 8 sts rem.

Break yarn and thread tail through rem sts and pull gently to fasten off.

### Finishing

Weave in ends, wash and dry flat to block.

# Miške: In the Forest

**[Miškai] ne tik didelis gamtos turtas, bet kartu ir mūsų krašto "plaučiai."**

*The forests are not only our national wealth, they are also our country's lungs.*
—*Enciklopedija vaikams apie Lietuvą* (Children's Encyclopedia about Lithuania)

Lithuanian forests are places of age-old magic and beauty that sustain not only humans, but also wildlife. With 60 species of mammals including wolves, foxes, otters, elk, wild boars, and European bison; and over 300 species of birds, including white and black storks, swans, owls, hawks, and cuckoos, Lithuanian wildlife is diverse and beautiful.

Mikalojus Konstantinas Čiurlionis (1875–1911) is Lithuania's most beloved composer and artist. His symphonic poem, "Miške" (In the Forest), captures the natural beauty of Lithuania in sound and portrays the emotional attachment of the people to the land. Written in 1901, "Miške" was the first symphony written by a Lithuanian composer.

Like Čiurlionis's symphonic poem, these socks represent the forest to me. The dark, variegated greens of the yarn representing the light flickering down through the leaves on the tall trees, and the diagonal lines of lace representing the shapes of the tree branches reaching to the sky overhead.

## Experience Level

Advanced

## Finished Measurements of Sample

8" (20.5 cm) foot circumference, unstretched

9" (23 cm) foot length from back of heel to tip of toe, or desired length

12" (30.5 cm) calf circumference, unstretched

14" (35.5 cm) length cuff to top of heel flap

For sizing tips, see page 114.

## Materials

Wool or wool/nylon blend sock yarn, approx 600 yds/550 m

Sample shown in Colinette Jitterbug (100% merino wool, 400 yds/356 m per 150 g skein), color Velvet Leaf, 2 skeins

## Needles

US size 1 (2.25 mm), US size 2 (2.75 mm), and US size 3 (3.25 mm) needles for working in the round: DPNs, 1 long circular or 2 short circulars

Tapestry needle

## Gauge

36 sts and 40 rnds = 4"/10 cm over Diagonal Lace pattern on smallest needles

32 sts and 44 rnds = 4"/10 cm over stockinette stitch on smallest needles

## Special Techniques

Bulgarian Cast On, see page 112.

Lace Cuff, see page 115.

Easy Lithuanian Heel, see page 116.

Wedge Toe, see page 119.

# Pattern Stitches

### Eyelet Ridges

**Rnds 1–2:** Purl.

**Rnd 3:** Knit.

**Rnd 4:** (YO, k2tog) around.

**Rnds 5–6:** Knit.

Rep rnds 1–6 for patt.

**Note:** there are no plain rnds on this lace motif.

# Instructions

### Cuff

CO 70 sts. Join to work in the round being careful not to twist sts.

Knit 2 rounds.

Work all rnds of Eyelet Ridges patt 3 times.

Purl 2 rounds.

Knit 2 rounds, inc 2 sts on last round—72 sts.

### Leg

Begin working Zig Zag Lace chart around all 72 sts (1 beginning stitch, seven 10-st repeats, 1 end st).

Work rnds 1–5 once, then rep rnds 6–23 four times, changing to medium needles after completing first repeat and to smallest needles after third repeat.

Work remainder of socks with smallest needles.

## Heel

Work 18 sts in pattern. Turn. Working back and forth on the next 36 sts, work heel flap as follows.

**Row 1 (WS):** Sl 1, knit 2, purl to last 3 sts, k3.

**Row 2 (RS):** Sl 1, knit.

Repeat last 2 rows until heel flap measure 2¼" (5.5 cm) or desired length.

## Heel Turn

Divide the heel stitches into three sections as follows.

**Next row (WS):** Work 13 sts, place marker, work 10 sts, place marker, work 13 sts.

Continue working garter stitch edges and AT THE SAME TIME, work decreases to turn heel as follows.

**Row 1 (RS):** Work in patt to 2 sts before first marker, k2tog, slip marker, work to second marker, slip marker, ssk, work to end of row.

**Row 2 (WS):** Work in patt to 2 sts before first marker, ssp, slip marker, work to the second marker, slip marker, p2tog, work to end of row.

Rep rows 1 and 2 until 12 sts rem in heel.

## Gusset

Knit heel sts. Pick up sts between garter ridges, one for each ridge, along first side of heel flap; k2, work Zig Zag Lace chart over the next 33 instep sts (1 beginning stitch, three 10-st repeats, 2 ending sts), k2; pick up sts between garter ridges, one for each ridge, along second side of heel flap, knit to center of heel for new start of round

Continue in patts as established and work gusset decreases every other rnd as follows until 72 sts rem.

**Dec rnd:** Knit to last 3 sts on sole, k2tog, k1, work instep sts; on sole, k1, ssk, knit to end of rnd.

## Foot

Work even in pattern as set until foot measures approx 7" (18 cm), or 2" (5 cm) less than desired length to toe.

## Toe

Dec as follows every other rnd until 36 sts rem then every rnd until 8 sts rem.

**Dec Rnd:** *Knit to last 3 sts in sole, k2tog, k1; on in- step, k1, ssk, knit to last 3 sts on instep, k2tog, k1; on sole, ssk, knit to end of rnd at center of sole.

Break yarn and thread tail through rem sts and pull gently to fasten off.

## Finishing

Weave in ends, wash and dry flat to block.

# Zig Zag Lace Chart

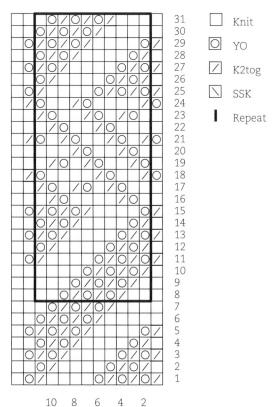

| | |
|---|---|
| ☐ | Knit |
| ⊡ | YO |
| ⧄ | K2tog |
| ⧅ | SSK |
| ❙ | Repeat |

# Megzkime Pačios—
# Let's Knit!

Most of the Lithuanian-language knitting books in my collection were published between 1959 and 1979, during the Soviet period. Most were written by Lithuanian authors, but others were translated from Russian. I found these books on eBay and at used book shops, street fairs, and flea markets in Lithuania. These books are quite similar to the vintage English-language knitting books I have from the same period. They include basic knitting and crochet instructions, a stitch library, and a collection of projects. Many of the books also include basic dressmaking information, along with tips for sizing garments which may be quite detailed or as vague as, "Models are given in one size. If you make a gauge swatch, it will be very easy to cast on for your own size."

I've been learning to read and speak Lithuanian, so at first it was a challenge to figure these books out. But since I am quite fluent in knitting and they all have lots of charts and diagrams, it's been a good way to learn the parts of the language related to knitting.

The stitch used on these socks is one I charted directly from the Lithuanian instructions in the book, *Megzkime Pačios* (O. Jarmulavičienė, Mintis, Vilnius, 1969). I used wool yarn that is coarser than many of the merino yarns used for making socks today, because I wanted these socks to be more like those that would have been knit by women and girls in Lithuania before the twentieth century using handspun yarn from their own sheep.

## Experience level

Advanced

## Finished Measurements of Sample

10" (25.5 cm) calf circumference, unstretched; 13" (33 cm) stretched

6" (15 cm) foot circumference, unstretched; 9" (23 cm) stretched

13" (33 cm) length cuff to top of heel flap

10" (25.5 cm) foot length from back of heel to tip of toe, or desired length

This sock fabric draws in like ribbing, creating a very stretchy fabric requiring extra negative ease. For sizing tips, see page 114.

## Materials

Approx 600 yd/550 m of sock weight wool yarn

Sample shown in Hifa 2 Tykt (100% Norwegian 2-ply Combed Long Fiber Wool, 464 yds/425 m per 100 g skein), color #826 natural, 2 skeins

## Needles

US size 5 (3.75 mm) needles for working in the round: DPNs, 1 long circular or 2 short circulars

Tapestry needle

## Gauge

24 sts and 40 rnds = 4"/10 cm over Lace pattern, stretched

24 sts and 38 rnds = 4"/10 cm over stockinette stitch

## Special Techniques

Lace Cuff, see page 115.

Easy Lithuanian Heel, see page 116.

Calf Shaping, see page 115.

Spiral Toe, see page 118.

## Instructions

Loosely CO 65 sts. Join to knit in the round, being careful not to twist sts.

### Cuff

Work following Cuff chart for 1½" (4 cm).

**Next rnd:** Purl, inc 1 st—66 sts.

**Next rnd:** (YO, k2tog) around.

**Next rnd:** Purl, dec 1 st—65 sts.

Knit 2 rnds.

### Leg

**Note:** Calf is shaped with decreases in pattern. Exact shaping used in the sample is shown on Calf Shaping chart.

Work Lace Pattern chart 8 times around.

Mark 33 sts for calf shaping, as indicated on Calf Shaping chart, paying careful attention to the repeat boxes as indicated below, and follow chart on these sts while maintaining main lace patt on rem sts. These will be the center back 33 sts of the sock.

On calf sts:

- Work rnds 1–8 four times.
- Work rnds 9–14 once.
- Work rnds 15–16 thirteen times.
- Work rnds 17–18 once.
- Work rnds 19–20 until leg measures 13" (33 cm) or desired length to heel—23 sts remain in calf section, 55 sts total.

### Heel

The heel is worked back and forth on 25 sts—the 23 calf sts plus 1 st on each side. Place remaining 30 sts on hold to be worked later.

**Row 1 (RS):** Sl 1 pw, knit.

**Row 2 (WS):** Sl 1 kw, k2, purl to last 3 sts, k3.

Rep these 2 rows until flap measures 2" (5 cm) or desired length.

## Heel Turn

Divide the heel stitches into three sections as follows.

**Next row (WS):** Work 9 sts, place marker, work 7 sts, place marker, work 9 sts.

Continue working garter stitch edges and AT THE SAME TIME, work decreases to turn heel as follows.

**Row 1 (RS):** Work in patt to 2 sts before first marker, k2tog, slip marker, work to second marker, slip marker, ssk, work to end of row.

**Row 2 (WS):** Work in patt to 2 sts before first marker, ssp, slip marker, work to the second marker, slip marker, p2tog, work to end of row.

Rep rows 1 and 2 until 9 sts rem in heel.

## Gusset

Knit across rem heel sts. Pick up sts between garter ridges, one for each ridge, along first side of heel flap; work in Lace Pattern as set across instep sts ; pick up sts between garter ridges, one for each ridge, along second side of heel flap, knit to center of heel for new start of round.

Continue lace patt on instep and St st on foot, and AT THE SAME TIME, dec the outer columns of lace on the instep as on Calf Shaping chart stitches 8–13 and rows 9–12, and work gusset decreases every other rnd until 55 sts rem as follows.

**Dec rnd:** Knit to last 3 sts on sole, k2tog, k1, work instep sts; on sole, k1, ssk, knit to end of rnd.

## Foot

Work even in patterns until foot measures approx 8" (20.5 cm) or 2" (5 cm) shorter than desired foot length.

## Toe

Change to St st and dec 3 sts evenly around before beginning toe shaping—52 sts rem.

Divide sts into 4 equal sections of 13 sts each, separated by markers.

**Left sock:** K2tog at the end of each section every other rnd until 26 sts rem, then every rnd until 8 sts rem.

**Right sock:** SSK at the beg of each section every other rnd until 26 sts rem, then every rnd until 8 sts rem.

Break yarn and thread tail through rem sts and pull gently to fasten off.

## Finishing

Weave in ends, wash and dry flat to block.

# Cuff Chart

| | | | | | | |
|---|---|---|---|---|---|---|
| | | O | ∧ | O | | 2 |
| | | | | | | 1 |

4  2

# Lace Pattern Chart

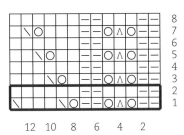

12  10  8  6  4  2

# Calf Shaping Chart

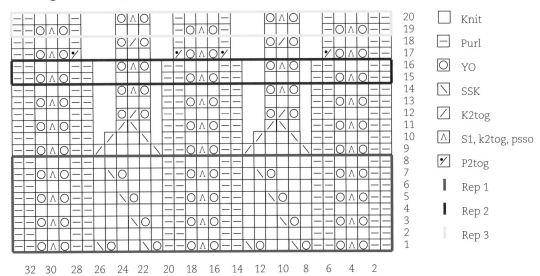

32  30  28  26  24  22  20  18  16  14  12  10  8  6  4  2

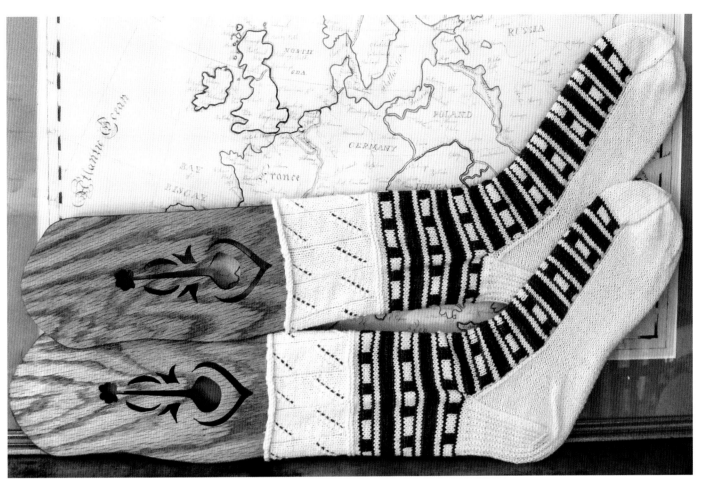

# Žemaitija Striped Resoleable Socks

Žemaitija, or the lowlands, is in the northwestern corner of Lithuania. It is often referred to as *Samogitia* in English-language publications. The landscape consists for the most part of low rolling hills covered with pine forests, meadows, and pastures.

Žemaitijans are known for being hard working, faithful, and stubborn. The area has been traditionally known for dairy farming and a rare breed of horse, and the people have honored handcrafts and folk art. Because the Lithuanians in this part of the country were so loyal to tradition and reluctant to adopt change, this was the last area in all of Europe to convert from paganism to Christianity. Even today, as you drive around the countryside, you can see examples of traditional wooden roadside shrines that feature both Christian and Pagan symbols.

Striped socks were popular for women in Žemaitija, as they were in Aukštaitija, and sometimes the stripes were made more complex with boxes knit inside wider stripes. This style might be made in wool for winter, or in linen for summer. Sometimes the sole of the foot was made solid and knit separately from the top of the foot, so the toe, sole, and heel of the sock could be replaced more easily than with a sock had been knit all in one piece. Lace socks were also made out of linen yarn for summer wear, and I've used one such lace pattern for the cuff on these socks.

## Experience Level

Advanced

## Finished Measurements of Sample

8" (20.5 cm) circumference

6" (15 cm) length cuff to top of heel flap

9" (23 cm) foot length from back of heel to tip of toe, or desired length

For sizing tips, see page 114.

## Materials

Wool or wool and nylon sock yarn, approx 500 yds/457 m

Sample shown in Holiday Yarns Flock Sock (fingering weight, 75% superwash merino, 25% nylon, 400 yds per skein), in Natural and Midnight Blue, 1 skein each

## Needles

US size 0 (2 mm) needles for working in the round: DPNs, 1 long circular or 2 short circulars

US size 1 (2.25 mm) needles for working in the round: DPNs, 1 long circular or 2 short circulars

Tapestry needle

## Gauge

36 sts and 46 rnds = 4"/10 cm over Stripe patt in St st on larger needles

## Special Techniques

Lace Cuff, see page 115.

Easy Lithuanian Heel, see page 116.

Spiral Toe, see page 118.

# Instructions

### Cuff

Using smaller needles and MC, loosely CO 72 sts. Join to knit in the round, being careful not to twist sts.

Work all rounds of Lace Cuff chart once.

(Knit 1 rnd, purl 1 rnd) twice.

### Leg

Change to larger needles. Work all rounds of Žemaitija Stripe chart once.

### Heel

The heel is worked back and forth on 36 sts in MC. Place remaining sts on hold to be worked later.

### Heel Flap

**Row 1 (RS):** (Sl 1, k1) across.

**Row 2:** Sl 1, purl across.

Rep rows 1 and 2 until heel flap measures 2½" (6.5 cm) or desired length. End after working a WS row.

### Heel Turn

The heel turn is worked in heel stitch.

Divide the heel stitches into three sections as follows.

**Next row (WS):** Work 10 sts, place marker, work 16 sts, place marker, work 10 sts.

Continue working garter stitch edges and AT THE SAME TIME, work decreases to turn heel as follows.

**Row 1 (RS):** Work in patt to 2 sts before first marker, k2tog, slip marker, work to second marker, slip marker, ssk, work to end of row.

**Row 2 (WS):** Work in patt to 2 sts before first marker, ssp, slip marker, work to the second marker, slip marker, p2tog, work to end of row.

Rep rows 1 and 2 until 18 sts rem in heel.

## Foot

### Gusset and Sole

The foot of the sock is worked in two separate pieces, flat.

Break yarn. With RS facing and MC, begin at bottom right corner where heel joins foot, with MC and smaller needles and RS facing, pick up 1 st in each slip st along the right side of the heel flap, knit across the rem heel sts, pick up 1 st in each chain along the left side of the heel flap. Turn.

Work back and forth on sole sts creating a slip-stitch chain selvedge as follows.

**Row 1 (WS):** Sl 1, k1, purl to last 2 sts, k1, p1.

**Row 2 (RS):** Sl 1, p1, knit to last 2 sts, p1, k1.

Repeat rows 1 and 2 and AT THE SAME TIME decrease as follows on every RS row: ssk after first purl and k2tog before the last purl until 36 sts rem in sole.

Work even until foot measures approx 7" (18 cm), or 2" (5 cm) shorter than desired length.

### Top of Foot

Working back and forth work in Stripe patt until top of foot measures same as sole, ending after a row of Midnight Blue.

## Toe

Place all sts from sole and top of foot onto needles and divide into 4 equal sections of 15 sts each, separated with markers. Join to work in the round. Work in St st and shape toes as follows.

**Left Sock:** K2tog at the end of each section every other rnd until 32 sts rem, then every rnd until 8 sts rem.

**Right Sock:** SSK at the beg of each section every other rnd until 32 sts rem, then every rnd until 8 sts rem.

Break yarn and thread tail through rem sts and pull gently to fasten off.

### Finishing

Sew instep side seam using mattress stitch. Weave in ends, wash and dry flat to block.

# Lace Cuff Chart

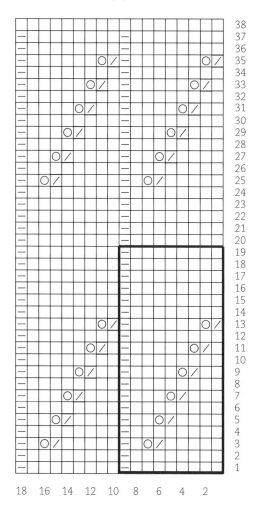

| Knit | ✓ K2tog |
| --- | --- |
| — Purl | ❙ Repeat |
| ⊙ YO | |

# Žemaitija Stripe Chart

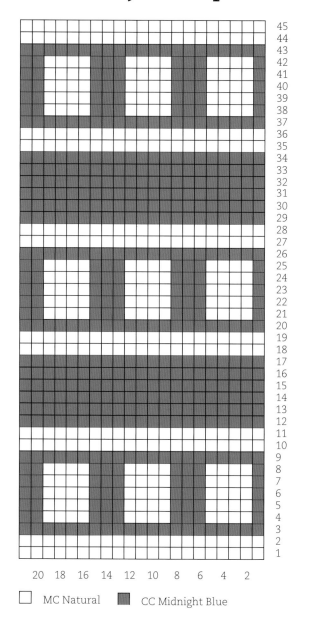

☐ MC Natural    ■ CC Midnight Blue

# Green Bridge Riešinės

The Green Bridge, spanning the Neris River to connect the old and new cities, is the oldest bridge in Vilnius. Originally built in 1536 as a toll bridge, it was built of brick and stone with a wooden cover and a toll-collector's office. The bridge has been rebuilt several times over the centuries, and was first painted green in 1739. The current bridge was built in 1952.

Today the Green Bridge is flanked on all four corners by Soviet-era sculptures. Unlike the busts of Lenin which are languishing under staircases in museums, and eighty-six other Soviet-era statues that are on display at Grūto parkas (Grūtas Park), sometimes called Stalin's World, these four statues celebrate the working people of the USSR—workers, farmers, soldiers, and students— rather than their communist leaders and military officers.

The four statues are:

**Taikos sargyboje (Guardians of Peace)** by Bronius Pundzius

**Žemės ūkis (Agriculture)** by Bernardas Bučas and Petras Vaivada

**Mokslo jaunimas (Youth Education)** by Juozas Mikėnas

**Pramonė ir statyba (Industry and Construction)** by Bronius Vyšniauskas and Napoleonas Petrulis

These gloves are named for the bridge primarily because of the color, and also to remember that the everyday people, the Lithuanian peasants, who wore wristers such as these and were freed in 1961, later became the Soviet citizens who lost their short-term freedom after repeated occupation by Russia, Nazi-Germany, and the USSR.

## Experience Level

All

## Sizes

Beginner (Intermediate, Advanced)

## Finished Measurements of Sample

Approx 4½–5" (11.5–13 cm) long

Approx 5–6" (13–15 cm) circumference

**Note:** These wristers are quite flexible and stretchy. I like them best when they fit very snugly around my wrist, with negative ease, which is the traditional style.

For sizing tips, see page 125.

## Materials

These wristers can be made in very fine, light, or medium-weight yarn. Although the pattern itself is quite easy, beginning knitters may find working with the very small needles and fine yarn to be intimidating or frustrating. Choose the yarn, needles, and beads for your comfort level.

**Beginner:**

Approx 75 yds/68 m of worsted weight wool

Sample shown in: Cascade 220 (100% Peruvian Highland Wool, 220 yds/ 201 m per 100 g ball); 1 ball in: 8267, Forest Green

Approx 200 size 6/0 Czech glass seed beads

**Intermediate:**

Approx 100 yds/91 m of fingering weight wool or sock yarn

Sample shown in: Koigu Premium Merino (100% wool, 175 yd/160 m per 50 g per ball); 1 ball in: 2150, Forest Green

Approx 300 size 8/0 Czech glass seed beads

**Advanced:**

Approx 200 yds/182 m of light fingering or heavy lace-weight yarn

Sample shown in: Estonian Wool (100% wool); 1 ball in: forest green

Approx 250 (320, 400) size 10/0 Czech glass seed beads, additional 300 beads for optional beaded picot trim

## Needles

**Beginner:** US size 5 (3.75 mm) needles

**Intermediate:** US size 2 (2.75 mm) needles

**Advanced:** US size 00 (1.25 mm) needles

**All levels:**

A spare needle of the same size for three-needle bind off

Beading needle, plastic dental floss threader, OR sewing thread, sewing needle with small eye, and quick-drying glue

Tapestry needle

Crochet hook, approx same diameter as knitting needles (optional, for trim)

## Gauge

**Beginner:** 20 sts and 40 rows/20 ridges = 4"/10 cm over garter stitch

**Intermediate:** 35 sts and 70 rows/ 35 ridges = 4"/10 cm over garter stitch

**Advanced:** 40 sts and 80 rows/40 ridges = 4"/10 cm over garter stitch

**Note:** stitches should be dense and tight to hold beads in place and to fit the wrist snugly.

## Special Techniques

Stringing Beads, see page 125.

Knitting with Beads, see page 125.

Crochet Trim, see page 125.

### Stringing Beads

For each wrister, string 125 (160, 200) beads onto the yarn as follows. Thread the tail of the yarn through the beading needle or dental floss threader. Put a bead onto the sewing needle and push it onto the needle and then onto the yarn. Repeat as many times as necessary for the number of beads you want to use. After a little practice you can string more than one bead at a time. You can just scoop the needle into the bowl of beads and several will hop onto the needle at once, or you can individually scoop beads onto the needle and thread, and slide six or eight at a time onto your yarn.

String 50 beads, then keeping those separate from the beads you add next, string on another set of beads the same length as the first 50. This keeps you from having to count so much. String on as many sets of 50 beads as you need for your charted pattern.

Before you begin knitting, gently push each set of 50 beads up onto the yarn, so you have one or two yards of yarn, or more, between each set of beads, and all but the last 50 are pushed 10 or 20 yards up onto the yarn. Push the last 50 beads up about one yard onto the yarn, and spread them out over the yarn so you can pull a few down close to your knitting as you begin each charted row.

## Instructions

Using long-tail CO and 2 needles held together, CO 30 (40, 50) sts very loosely.

Begin following bead chart as follows. (Only WS rows are shown on the chart. RS rows are knit plain.)

**Row 1 (RS):** Knit.

**Row 2 (WS):** Knit 1 for each white square, for each gray square, push one bead up to the work between the needles and then knit 1. After all chart sts have been worked, knit to the end of the row.

**Note:** The bead and the following knit 1 count as 1 stitch. The bead will go to the back of the work, thereby showing on the RS when worn.

Work as set until chart is complete the correct number of times for your yarn:

**Beginner (worsted weight):** 3 times.

**Intermediate (fingering weight):** 4 times.

**Advanced (heavy lace weight):** 5 times.

Knit 1 row.

Do not BO.

### Finishing

Lift each loop of the cast-on edge and place it on a needle. With RS facing, join with three-needle BO, joining the loops from the cast-on edge to the live stitches. Weave in ends, wash and dry flat to block.

### Crochet Trim (optional, shown on Intermediate):

**At wrist edge (edge with beads):** Join yarn and work shells as follows. *Sc in first garter ridge, skip next garter ridge, work 3 dc in next garter ridge; rep from * around. Sl st to join. Fasten off.

### Beaded Crochet Picot Trim (optional, shown on Advanced):

**At wrist edge (edge with beads):** String approx 200 beads for the trim on one wrister, then join yarn with beads and work as follows. Sl st in first garter ridge, *push 9 beads up to the knitting, skip next 2 garter ridges, sl st to next garter ridge, draw up a very large loop and pull the ball of yarn through to secure; rep from * around. Sl st to join. Fasten off.

**Note:** If you prefer, you can use a tapestry needle and knot the yarn after each picot.

Top: Intermediate in fingering weight yarn with crochet trim.
Middle: Beginner in worsted weight yarn with plain edges.
Bottom: Advanced in heavy lace weight yarn with beaded picot trim.

# Beaded Diamonds Chart

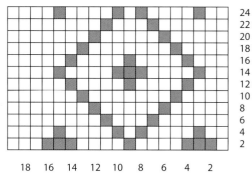

place bead and knit
following stitch

# Blue Skies Over Nida

I've named these wristers for the quiet, relaxing beach town of Nida on the Baltic Sea. Unlike the other two coastal Lithuanian towns—Klaipėda, which is the third largest city in Lithuaina; and Palanga, which is a party resort—Nida is an oasis of peace and quiet.

At the far south end of the 60-mile-long sandbar called the Curonian Spit, which separates the Curonian lagoon from the Baltic Sea, Nida is close enough to the Kaliningrad region of Russia—a tiny piece of land stranded between Lithuania and Poland—to pick up a Russian signal on your cell phone.

With picture-perfect cottages, boating, walking trails in the woods and along the beach near the sand dunes, an annual jazz festival, and little museums and shops scattered around, this is my favorite type of vacation town. Even with its reputation for being a nature resort, Nida is visited by over 300,000 tourists every summer, so for a quiet retreat, it's best to go in late spring or early fall.

Many of the beaded wrist warmers that I saw in museum collections in Lithuania are made with two or more colors of yarn knit in stripes. Sometimes the colors are changed randomly after only two or four rows, and sometimes an even stripe pattern is knit with two, three, or four different colors. In this design, I chose two shades of blue—a color used frequently in Lithuanian national costume recreations by Anastazija Tamošaitienė. I aligned the stripes with the change in direction of the diagonal lines in the bead patterning.

## Experience Level

Intermediate

## Finished Measurements of Sample

5" (12.5 cm) long

6" (15 cm) circumference

**Note:** These wristers are quite flexible and stretchy. I like them best when they fit very snugly around my wrist, with negative ease, which is the traditional style.

For sizing tips, see page 125.

## Materials

Approx 200 yds/182 m of fingering weight wool or sock yarn, 100 yds/91 m in each of 2 colors

Sample shown in Brown Sheep Nature Spun Fingering (100% wool, 310 yd/50 g per ball); 1 ball each in:

  **MC:** N04, Blue Night

  **CC:** 115, Bit of Blue

Approx 800 size 10/0 or 8/0 Czech glass seed beads

## Needles

US size 00 (1.25 mm) needles

A spare needle of the same size for three-needle bind off

Beading needle, plastic dental floss threader, OR sewing thread, sewing needle with small eye, and quick-drying glue

Tapestry needle

Crochet hook, approx same diameter as knitting needles

## Gauge

40 sts and 80 rows/40 ridges = 4"/10 cm over garter stitch

**Note:** Stitches should be dense and tight to hold beads in place and to fit the wrist snugly.

## Special Techniques

Stringing Beads, see page 125.

Knitting with Beads, see page 125.

Crochet Trim, see page 125.

## Instructions

String half of the beads onto each color of yarn.

Using long-tail CO and 2 needles held together, CO 51 sts very loosely.

Begin following Beading chart as follows. (Only WS rows are shown on the chart. RS rows are knit plain in the color of the following WS row.)

**Row 1 (RS):** Knit across in color indicated on chart row 2.

**Row 2 (WS):** With color indicated, knit 1 for each blue square, for each white square, push one bead up to the work between the needles and then knit 1. After all chart sts have been worked, knit to the end of the row.

**Note:** The bead and the following knit 1 count as 1 stitch. The bead will go to the back of the work, thereby showing on the RS when worn.

Work as set until chart is complete.

Knit 1 row.

Do not BO.

### Finishing

Lift each loop of the cast-on edge and place it on a needle. With RS facing, join with three-needle BO, joining the loops from the cast-on edge to the live stitches.

### Crochet Trim

At wrist edge (edge with beads): join CC and work shells as follows. *Sc in first garter ridge, skip next garter ridge, work 3 dc in next garter ridge; rep from * around. Sl st to join. Fasten off.

**At arm edge:** join MC and work sc around opposite edge, making 1 sc in each garter ridge. Join with sl st. Fasten off.

Weave in ends, wash and dry flat to block.

# Beading Chart

63
62
61
60
59
58
57
56
55
54
53
52
51
50
49
48
47
46
45
44
43
42
41
40
39
38
37
36
35
34
33
32
31
30
29
28
27
26
25
24
23
22
21
20
19
18
17
16
15
14
13
12
11
10
9
8
7
6
5
4
3
2
1

50  48  46  44  42  40  38  36  34  32  30  28  26  24  22  20  18  16  14  12  10  8  6  4  2

■ MC: Blue Night

☐ CC: Bit of Blue

☐ Bead stitch

# Songs of Palanga

Everywhere I went in Lithuania, I was amazed by the beautiful and strong voices of everyday people who fearlessly sing at any opportunity. Visiting the Mėguva wool and craft group in Palanga, on the edge of the Baltic Sea; June, Dominic, and I were stuffed full of chocolate, coffee, and brandy as we were serenaded by the group's members, who perform traditional folk songs while dressed in reproductions of national costume ensembles. On the table in front of us, surrounded by coffee cups, was a pile of knitted wrist warmers. Many were made in the traditional holiday style with garter stitch and beads, similar to the Green Bridge Riešinės on page 213, but several others were made with stranded colorwork and would probably have been worn in everyday life during the nineteenth century.

These colorwork wristers are a reproduction of one of the pairs we were shown while visiting the Mėguva group. Knit in the round with an ancient geometric design, these are given a modern touch with the addition of a lace edging.

## Experience Level
Intermediate

## Finished Measurements of Sample
4½" (11.5 cm) long

7" (18 cm) circumference

For sizing tips, see page 125.

## Materials
Approx 100 yds/90 m of sport weight wool yarn, each in MC and CC

Sample shown in Brown Sheep Nature Spun Sport (100% wool, 184 yds/168 m per 50 g ball); 1 ball each of:

**MC:** 135 Hurricane Seas

**CC:** 730 Natural

## Needles
US size 0 (2 mm) needles for working in the round: DPNs, 1 long circular or 2 short circulars

US size 1 (2.25 mm) needles for working in the round: DPNs, 1 long circular or 2 short circulars

Tapestry needle

## Gauge
36 sts and 42 rnds = 4"/10 cm over stranded colorwork stitch with larger needles

# Instructions

Using smaller needles and MC, loosely CO 52 sts. Join to knit in the round, being careful not to twist sts.

Work in K1, P1 ribbing for ½" (1.5 cm).

**Next rnd, increase:** (K4, m1) 12 times, k to end of round—64 sts.

Change to larger needles. K 2 rnds.

Join CC and knit 2 rnds.

Work Colorwork chart around.

Change to smaller needles. With CC, knit 2 rnds. Cut CC.

With MC, knit 2 rnds.

Change to smaller needles.

Work all rnds of Lace Ruffle chart.

**BO loosely as follows:** K1, *k1, insert left ndl into the front of both sts on right ndl and k2tog-tbl; rep from * until 1 stitch remains. Break yarn and pull tail through last st to fasten off.

### Finishing
Weave in ends, wash and dry flat to block.

# Colorwork Chart

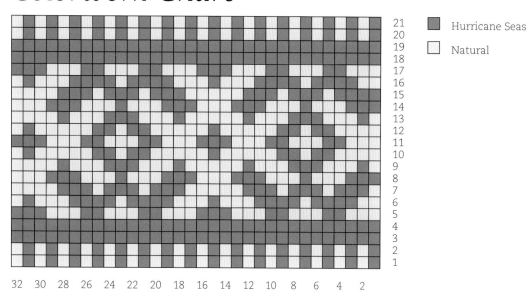

21
20
19
18
17
16
15
14
13
12
11
10
9
8
7
6
5
4
3
2
1

32  30  28  26  24  22  20  18  16  14  12  10  8  6  4  2

■ Hurricane Seas

☐ Natural

# Lace Ruffle Chart

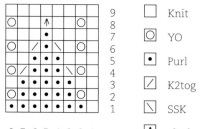

9
8
7
6
5
4
3
2
1

8 7 6 5 4 3 2 1

☐ Knit

⊙ YO

• Purl

⧄ K2tog

⧅ SSK

↑ Sl2, k1, p2sso

# Yarn Resources

A Verb for Keeping Warm Creating
averbforkeepingwarm.com

Brown Sheep Nature Spun Sport &
Fingering brownsheep.com

Cascade 220 Worsted cascadeyarns.com

Colinette Jitterbug colinette.com

Crystal Palace Panda Silk straw.com

Dream in Color Smooshy
dreamincoloryarn.com

Hifa 2 Tykt nordicfiberarts.com

Holiday Yarns Flock Sock holidayyarns.com

Jamieson's Shetland Spindrift
schoolhousepress.com

Kauni Wool 8/2 Effektgarn kauni.com

Knitpicks Stroll knitpicks.com

Koigu Permium Merino koigu.com

Litwool 100% Wool Classic wool.lt

Madelinetosh madelinetosh.com

Rauma Finullgarn nordicfiberarts.com

Shibui Sock shibuiknits.com

Teksrena Wool teksrena.yarns.lt

# Abbreviations

| | |
|---|---|
| 1st | first |
| approx | approximately |
| beg | begin(ning) |
| BO | bind off (cast off) |
| CC | contrasting color |
| CO | cast on |
| dc | double crochet |
| dec | decrease(s)(ing) |
| DPN(s) | double-pointed needle(s) |
| foll | follow(s)(ing) |
| inc | increase(s)(ing) |
| k | knit |
| k2tog | knit 2 together |
| k3tog | knit 3 together |
| m1 | make 1 by lifting the bar between sts with the tip of the left needle and knitting it through the back |
| MC | main color |
| meas | measures |
| ndl(s) | needle(s) |
| p | purl |
| p2tog | purl 2 together |
| patt | pattern(s) |
| pm | place marker |
| pw | purlwise |
| rem | remain(s)(ing) |
| rep | repeat |
| rnd(s) | round(s) |
| RS | right side |
| sc | single crochet |
| sk | skip |
| sl | slip |
| sl st | slip stitch (crochet) |
| sl1, k1, psso | slip 1 st knitwise, knit the next st, pass the slipped st over the one just knit |
| sl1, k2tog, psso | slip 1 st knitwise, knit the next 2 sts together, pass the slipped st over |
| ssk | (slip 1 knitwise) twice, insert the left needle into the fronts of the 2 sts and knit them together |
| ssp | (slip 1 knitwise) twice, put the sts back onto the left needle then insert the right needle into both sts together from left to right in back of the work and purl them together |
| St st | stockinette stitch |
| st(s) | stitch(es) |
| tbl | work through back loop to twist stitch |
| WS | wrong side |
| wyib | with yarn in back |
| wyif | with yarn in front |
| yo | yarn over |

# Index